Living with Hard Times

ECPR Press

ECPR Press is an imprint of the European Consortium for Political Research. It publishes original research from leading political scientists and the best among early career researchers in the discipline. Its scope extends to all fields of political science, international relations and political thought, without restriction in either approach or regional focus. It is also open to interdisciplinary work with a predominant political dimension.

Living with Hard Times

Europeans in the Great Recession

Marco Giugni and Maria Grasso

ecpr PRESS

Published by the European Consortium for Political Research
Harbour House, 6-8 Hythe Quay
Colchester, CO2 8JF, United Kingdom

British Library Cataloguing in Publication Data
A catalogue record for this book is available from the British Library

ISBN: HB 978-1-53815-115-0

Library of Congress Cataloging-in-Publication Data

Names: Giugni, Marco, author. | Grasso, Maria T. (Maria Teresa), 1984- author.
Title: Living with hard times : Europeans in the great recession / Marco Giugni and Maria Grasso.
Description: London : ECPR Press, [2021] | Includes bibliographical references and index. | Summary: "Living with Hard Times provides the first comparative study of the socio-political effects of the Great Recession amongst European citizens. It presents a detailed investigation of heterogeneity in the population within countries with respect to how citizens made sense of the crisis and how this impacted their livelihoods, outlooks and political engagement. It analyses citizens' experiences of the economic crisis, the decline of living standards and deprivation by structural location as well as differences in economic outlooks. It also examines the ways in which citizens from different social groups were able to be resilient to the effects of the economic crisis. Moreover, it shows how social support and social capital emerging from social relations contributed to resilience in the face of the crisis. Furthermore, it explores citizen attitudes to various welfare policies and to immigration, and how support for populist parties is differentiated within the population. Finally, the book looks at the impact of the crisis on different types of political action challenging incumbent governments and protesting against austerity policies"— Provided by publisher.

Identifiers: LCCN 2021014395 (print) | LCCN 2021014396 (ebook) | ISBN 9781538151150 (cloth) | ISBN 9781538151167 (epub)
Subjects: LCSH: Europe—Economic conditions. | Europe—Social conditions. | Financial crises—Europe. | Welfare state—Europe.
Classification: LCC HC240 .G5322 2021 (print) | LCC HC240 (ebook) | DDC 330.94/05611—dc23
LC record available at https://lccn.loc.gov/2021014395
LC ebook record available at https://lccn.loc.gov/2021014396

ecpr.eu/shop

Contents

Acknowledgements

This book presents results obtained from the analysis of data collected within the project 'Living with Hard Times: How Citizens React to Economic Crises and Their Social and Political Consequences' (LIVEWHAT). This project was funded by the European Commission under the Seventh Framework Programme (grant agreement no. 613237). This project was coordinated by Marco Giugni (University of Geneva). Maria Grasso (now at Queen Mary University of London, but based at the University of Sheffield during the course of the grant) provided the scientific supervision for the cross-national survey. We are very grateful to all the LIVEWHAT project researchers and to all those who provided feedback at project presentations and conferences, the ECPR Press Editors, Ian O'Flynn, Laura Sudulich, Andrew Glencross, Liam Weeks, and to Rebecca Anastasi, Brennan Knight, and Dhara Snowden for all their support with getting the manuscript ready for publication, and the anonymous manuscript reviewer for their useful suggestions. All remaining errors are our own and the usual disclaimers apply.

Chapter One

Europeans in the Great Recession

The Great Recession is one of the most significant political and economic events of our time. How did it impact on the lives of Europeans in different countries? More specifically, how did individuals perceive their economic conditions? Did they experience a deterioration in their living standards? How did structural factors such as class produce heterogeneity in the population with respect to these perceptions? How did the differential extent to which the crisis affected European countries lead to differences between individuals across social groups cross-nationally? How were individuals able to be resilient to the effects of the economic crisis? How did social support and social capital emerging from social relations contribute to their resilience in the face of the crisis? Given this wider context, to what extent are Europeans satisfied with government policies such as with respect to welfare and unemployment? How does satisfaction vary by social groups in different countries? And how is support for controls on immigration and populist parties differentiated within national and cross-national populations? What about political activism in times of crisis? How is political action impacted by perceptions of deteriorating living standards and by incumbent parties being blamed for their role in the current crisis? These are the key questions on the experiences of Europeans in the Great Recession tackled in this book.

To answer these questions, this book takes a cross-national perspective by looking at patterns across nine European democracies: France, Germany, Greece, Italy, Poland, Spain, Sweden, Switzerland and the United Kingdom (UK). This allows for a comparative design by examining countries with different welfare arrangements and different levels of experience of the crisis, including, also, a post-Socialist country, Poland, and a country that was not a member of the European Union (EU), Switzerland, at the time of survey. This book provides a detailed analysis of the sociopolitical ramifications of the crisis amongst different groups of Europeans. The data, which has been collected in the same way across these nine countries, allows for direct comparisons. The original survey, conducted in 2015 through YouGov, was developed specifically to include questions designed to allow us to tackle our research questions of interest.

One of the key aims of this book is to examine heterogeneity within the populations of individual countries with respect to experiences of and reactions to the crisis to understand the extent to which these were differentiated by social groups. For example, we examine differences across genders, education levels and occupational class backgrounds among others. This allows the examination of the extent of differences between Europeans in different social groups within and across different countries. This is an important dimension to explore since it allows us to understand whether citizens were more affected based on their social position or on whether they resided in a country that was more deeply affected in the crisis. Moreover, it allows for exploring whether the effect of inequality was more important in those countries with weaker crises resulting in greater differences between middle and lower occupational class members. These aspects are important for understanding the impact of the crisis in terms of deprivation and economic outlooks amongst different sectors of society but also for making sense of which social groups across European countries may have been more resilient to the crisis. It is also important to consider social differentiation to make sense of population differences in attitudes towards welfare policies and immigration as well as differences in support for populist parties and activism in various types of political action. Rather than looking at the impact of the economic crisis from the macro-level and adopting a top-down perspective, we focus on the micro-level and employ a bottom-up perspective exploiting the innovative dataset emerging from our project's original survey in the analyses.

Living with Hard Times: Europeans in the Great Recession provides a comprehensive, comparative study of the sociopolitical effects of the Great Recession in Europe. It analyses Europeans' experiences of the economic crisis, their perceptions of declining living standards and deprivation by structural location, as well as differences in their economic outlooks. It further provides an analysis of Europeans' capacity for resilience in the face of crisis situations based on factors such as social capital as well as a picture of their attitudes towards welfare policies, immigration and populist parties. It also provides an analysis of the impact of the crisis on different types of political action that act to challenge incumbent governments and to protest against austerity policies. Moreover, this study shows how the Great Recession has not just posed constraints and has also opened up opportunities for many Europeans—at least from some groups, both at the personal and political level. While these opportunities may not deterministically lead to given outcomes, profound transformations such as those brought about or accelerated by deep and long-lasting economic downturns like the Great Recession can create 'critical junctures'. The types of outcomes that will flow from these new conditions remain as yet unclear and, as we discuss in our conclusions, will likely depend on various conditions, such as, for example, whether individuals are able to overcome key constraints and seize opportunities that can allow for positive changes out of the experience of the crisis and of hard times.

In terms of the broader context, the economic crisis that spread to Europe in 2008 had been preceded by a financial crisis in 2007, which started off as a credit crunch linked to the so-called housing bubble in the US. A prolonged period of low or negative economic growth, coupled with rising unemployment, led to what has become known as the 'Great Recession', in reference to the other major global economic crisis of the past: the 'Great Depression' of the 1930s. This reference clearly suggests that this was the only other global economic crisis that generated comparable levels of economic hardship in the recent historical past. In this book, we examine how such a significant economic event has impacted the lives of Europeans. We do so by examining experiences of economic hardship as well as resilience, and also attitudes with respect to politicised issues linked to the crisis, such as unemployment, precarity, the welfare state, immigration and support for populist parties. Moreover, we analyse how citizen's perceptions of the crisis and government actions impacted political activism and, therefore, capabilities to influence political life and to develop solutions to current woes.

While the beginning of the Great Recession is generally identified with the collapse of the global financial services firm Lehman Brothers' in September 2008, the end is more of a matter of debate, depending on which operational definition of economic crisis one adopts. For example, according to the National Bureau of Economic Research, the recession in the US started in December 2007 and ended in June 2009 (NBER 2010). For others, however, the crisis lasted much longer, leading some to maintain that the crisis never ended (Cooper 2017). This perspective of no end in sight is all the more widely held when it comes to Europe. While the crisis affected the US, in particular, by leading to increased poverty rates and the shrinking of the middle class (Pew Research Center 2015), Europe has endured the most profound and long-lasting impacts due, in part, to policies implemented to address it, namely austerity (Krugman 2012). Such impacts are documented in a number of studies (see, for example, Giugni and Grasso 2018a). Austerity measures were also encouraged by the so-called Troika of the European Commission, the European Central Bank and the International Monetary Fund in countries hard hit by the crisis, such as Greece, with the aim of lowering deficits and avoiding a debt crisis, in particular, by reducing public expenditures but also by increasing taxation. At the same time, the economic crisis and the falling living standards that often accompanied it across the globe exacerbated the growing social tensions around the political crisis of responsibility and the low economic growth assailing post-industrial democracies which had increasingly embraced neoliberal policies since the 1970s to various degrees (della Porta 2015).

Our investigation in this book is situated in this wider social context and highlights how politics is not simply something that governments do, but rather something that individuals as political agents—joining and forming political organisations and participating in protest mobilisations—can impact on, challenge and contest to shape society. However, we also argue that there are limits to movement mobilisations and important challenges involved in developing a sustained contestation. Democracy allows the people to partake in the running of their political affairs rather than being merely the objects of the whims of various economic forces or governments of different colors. Post-industrial democracies have, for a while now, witnessed a growing crisis of democracy and a declining responsiveness perceived as the inability of governments to listen to their citizenries (Giugni and Grasso 2019c). This has often resulted in abstention and declining political engagement with institutional means. However, on the other side of the coin to this crisis of democracy is vibrant political activism through the contentious sphere of those who are not presently satisfied. In this way, political activism in this new context of crisis-generated opportunities can allow democracy to renew itself and provide avenues towards solutions to the current social, economic and political problems affecting European societies.

To analyse these phenomena, we focus on the individual experiences, attitudes and political actions of Europeans. In this way, we aim to provide a detailed account of their experiences of the crisis, for example in terms of their economic perceptions, as well as of their ability to respond to the negative consequences of the economic crisis and of austerity policies both in terms of social resilience but also with respect to political evaluations and participation.

We pursue three major lines of investigation in this study. In the first part of this book (chapters 2 and 3), we examine how the crisis has impacted different social strata, in terms of perceptions of economic conditions and perceived levels of deprivation, as well as the extent to which Europeans have been able to show resilience and to cope with the negative effects of the crisis. Moreover, we examine the extent to which different social groups have been affected by the economic crisis. While not everyone has the resources to exhibit resilience in the face of crisis, we address these differences to provide an in-depth picture of Europeans' lived experiences. In this way, we document variations in the impact of the crisis on people's perceptions and attitudes as well as on their capacity for resilience.

During times of crisis, certain themes and issues become particularly politicised. In the current crisis, we have seen discussions around unemployment and precarity, as well as immigration and social integration, become central to political debate. As such, in the second part of this book (chapters 4 and 5), we develop our analyses to more specifically look at Europeans' attitudes towards two key political issues: unemployment and immigration. Examining attitudes linked to the themes of unemployment and precarity as well as on immigration and populism allows us to develop novel analyses into how the politicisation of these issues has impinged upon Europeans' understandings of society and the issues it faces in different countries in the aftermath of the economic crisis.

Finally, the third part of this book (chapters 6 and 7) turns to the investigation of the relationship between the Great Recession and civic and political engagement. In this regard, we explore hypotheses which connect individual perceptions and attitudes to the broader context in which they are formed. More specifically, we explore whether the impact of hardship and deprivation on political engagement may be conditional on the potential political opportunities opened up by the crisis.

In the remainder of the current chapter, we discuss the main arguments and key themes of this book. We do so by presenting, in greater detail, the three linked parts of the investigation outlined above. We then turn to the broader economic and institutional context of this study. Finally, we describe the data and methods used in the empirical analyses presented in this book.

WINNERS AND LOSERS OF THE CRISIS

Since 2008 many Europeans have experienced the impact of a severe economic crisis whose negative effects have been said to have been, in many cases, exacerbated by the austerity policies implemented by governments. Unemployment, particularly in some countries, reached very high levels. Salaries stagnated or have been cut, such as, for example, those of public employees in Greece. Access to credit has become more difficult and many Europeans have fallen below the poverty line (Stiglitz 2012). More generally, the risk of poverty and social exclusion increased. This is especially true of the southern European countries such as Greece, Italy and Spain, but also for other countries such as the UK. For example, the number of people in the European Union (twenty-seven countries) who are at risk of poverty or social exclusion has risen from 115,908, in 2008, to 122,230, in 2012.[1] Similarly, the number of severely materially deprived people rose from 41,527, in 2008, to 48,774, in 2012.[2]

Just as countries have been hit by varying degrees by the economic crisis and its negative consequences, different strata of the population have also suffered by varying degrees from its effects, including enacted austerity measures. Just as there are 'winners and losers of globalisation' (Kriesi et al. 2006), there are winners and losers of the Great Recession. The 'winners', in economic terms, are particularly those investors and financial institutions who were able to make financial gains even in the face of economic crisis. There are also 'winners' in political terms. The most visible ones are certainly populist parties—from both the Right and the Left—who have recently made important electoral gains in many European countries, favoured also by the perceived failure by many mainstream traditional parties to propose adequate responses to pressing social problems and concerns amongst the population in the current juncture.

In this book, we are mostly interested in examining those who are the 'losers' of the economic crisis amongst the citizenry, that is, investigating who are those most negative in terms of their economic assessments and outlooks and displaying the lowest capabilities for resilience. In this regard, some have stressed that—especially in the American context but also in Europe—people belonging to the middle class have suffered greatly from the consequences of the crisis, in many cases causing a shift from a comfortable living situation to one of hardship, deprivation and, sometimes, poverty (Whelan, Russell and Maitre 2016). Indeed, this type of shift can be understood as leading to the so-called shrinking of the middle class as many are pushed into lower social strata.

Yet, other social categories and groups may have been the hardest hit by the economic crisis and its related austerity measures. Two social groups are generally seen to be particularly at risk under such conditions: the unemployed, or those in precarious working conditions, and migrants or refugees (Giugni and Grasso 2019d; Giugni and Grasso 2020a). As we discuss in more detail below, we pay special attention to these two groups when examining the experiences and perceptions surrounding economic hardship as well as resilience. We also examine differences by gender, age, nationality and occupation in order to show which social categories and groups have been most impacted by the economic crisis in various respects and how heterogeneity is patterned in the population with respect to attitudes towards welfare policies, immigration, populist parties and activism.

The first substantive chapter of the book, chapter 2, focuses on looking at the effects of the Great Recession on Europeans' perceptions of their economic conditions in the nine countries included in this study. The crisis has worsened the economic conditions for large sections of the population across Europe and has generated feelings of deprivation (Grasso and Giugni 2016b). Such feelings, however, are likely to depend on certain structural factors such as class location (Grasso et al. 2019). In this context, the chapter examines how Europeans have perceived the crisis, to what extent individuals have felt that the crisis has impacted their lives, how they rate their living standards in relation to the past and how hopeful they are that these will improve in the future. As such, the chapter focusses on perceptions of deprivation in order to provide a detailed picture of how the crisis has impacted the ways in which Europeans view their own situations and that of their countries relative to the past and the potential future. We examine the extent to which different social groups have been affected by the economic crisis.

In the second substantive chapter, chapter 3, we then turn to examining Europeans' cabilities for resilience to adversity through various strategies which have allowed them to proactively react to negative external events, and hence to express their agency. Well-anchored in psychology, resilience has become a popular concept in sociology as well as in cognate disciplines including, to some extent, political science. This concept has often been defined as the adaptation to adversity (Luthar et al. 2000; Seery 2011). In the context of our study, it broadly refers to the capacity to resist negative changes in one's life (Batty and Cole 2010; Hall and Lamont 2013). A growing literature in political sociology has started to use the linked concept of alternative forms of resilience—alongside similar notions such as social economy and solidarity (or solidary) economy—to indicate alternative economic practices, located at the crossroad of the political and the social, initiated by citizen groups and networks (Kousis and Paschou 2017). This body of work examines collective efforts by ordinary people to engage in innovative activities and social relations such as solidary bartering, local exchange trading schemes, local and alternative currencies, ethical banks, local market cooperatives, cooperatives for the supply of social services such as health and education, alternative forms of production, critical consumption, spontaneous actions of resistance and reclaimation, and the reproduction of cultural knowledge via oral and artistic expression (Giugni and Grasso 2018b). Following a social movement perspective, this also includes sustainable, community movement organisations (Forno and Graziano 2014), which are new collective initiatives that empower consumer and producer networks on a small scale.

In this respect, in the context of this book, we are particularly interested in the individual capacity to adapt to the negative effects of the economic crisis and austerity, in other words, individuals' resilience. We are, in particular, interested in knowing to what extent individuals in our nine countries feel that they are able to actively and creatively face difficult situations and replace losses they encounter, including those generated by the economic crisis. Chapter 3, thus, examines the ways in which citizens have been able to become resilient to the negative effects of the economic crisis. We argue that such a capacity depends not only on financial means, but also on the availability of social support and, more generally, the level of social capital stemming from the web of social relations. The chapter therefore complements the analysis of the previous chapter by focussing on the ways in which citizens have been able to resist economic crisis in their everyday lives. We also look at how such a capacity for resilience varies across social groups. While not all citizens have the resources to exhibit resilience in the face of crisis, we address these differences to provide an in-depth picture of Europeans' lived experiences of the crisis.

UNEMPLOYMENT AND IMMIGRATION: ATTITUDES IN TWO CONTESTED POLITICAL FIELDS

This book is further interested in examining Europeans' perceptions and attitudes in the context of the Great Recession. Two issue fields, in particular, have been at the centre of political debates in the current juncture: the welfare state and immigration. Unemployment and the welfare state (Giugni 2010) as well as immigration politics (Koopmans et al. 2005) are two key politically contested fields that polarise both political elites and public opinion.

In times of economic crisis, unemployment becomes central in political debates. Rising unemployment is often at the heart of economic crises and characterises them, along with recession. As a result, one can hardly ignore what people think of this key political issue. Moreover, unemployment is more generally related to the welfare state and to attitudes to welfare policies amongst the citizenry.

Within the context of welfare policies and unemployment, debates around precarity have become particularly relevant in the context of the crisis. This is particularly true in some countries such as Italy, where many young people are in precarious situations, but it also applies, for example, to a country like Germany where the Hartz reforms implemented by the Socialist government in the 2000s led to a reduction of unemployment but, at the same time, to an explosion of precarity (Brady and Biegert 2017). Policymakers therefore must increasingly take into account not only what individuals—that is, potential voters—think about unemployment, but also their views about precarity such as who is responsible for it and how should government deal with it.

As such, in chapter 4 we examine attitudes to various welfare policies across Europe and amongst different social groups. The welfare state is a particularly salient and politicised issue field in the context of the crisis. In this chapter, we look specifically at the extent to which citizens are satisfied with government welfare policies on unemployment and precarious employment as well as compare this with policy satisfaction on the economy, more widely, and policies on poverty, education and healthcare. Unemployment, precarious employment, the economy and other types of social spending areas have become a key political field during the crisis, as debate has opened up over whether governments have been doing enough to tackle unemployment along with other economic problems and whether spending cuts were justified.

If unemployment and precarity are often at the centre of political debates and contestation, this is all the more the case for immigration. Immigration has been a key issue in political debates across all European countries in recent years. Views on immigration have been shown to be key for explaining support for extreme-right parties (Ford and Goodwin 2010; Ivarsflaten 2008; Lubbers et al. 2002). Questions about the place of newcomers in host societies, their rights, duties and integration have become a main battleground for these parties and, more generally, the basis for political contention in the public domain, albeit with strong differences in terms of how immigration and diversity are contested in different countries owing to the specific national conceptions of citizenship (Koopmans et al. 2005).

The economic crisis has made immigration an even more central issue in recent national debates and politics. The politicisation of the debate over immigration during the course of the crisis further suggests an increased polarisation both amongst political elites and the citizenry. Two series of events in particular have contributed to such a polarisation on the issue of immigration in the recent context. Firstly, the terrorist attacks by Muslim Jihadists that hit Europe in recent years have directed focus onto the so-called Muslim question, that is, the supposed correlation between the increasing number of Muslims in European countries and those incidents. Secondly, the increasing emergency relating to the inflow of refugees from Sub-Saharan Africa to Europe through various routes—above all, the Mediterranean route—has brought to the fore debates between those supporting solidarity and a welcoming attitude on the one hand and a more closed and intolerant approach on the other hand.

Thus, the economic crisis can be seen to have become intermeshed with a crisis of European cultural identity already underway—leading some to embrace the 'clash of civilisations' thesis (Huntington 1996)—as well as with a 'refugee crisis' that found both the EU and its member states unprepared and incapable of proposing concrete and feasible solutions. In turn, both issues have been exploited by radical right and populist parties for electoral gains. In fact, mobilising and politicising the immigration issue has proven to be crucial for the rise of the radical right and part of a 'winning formula' combining a critique of immigration with an embrace of authoritarianism and market liberalism (Kitschelt 1995). This has allowed such parties to make significant electoral breakthroughs in many European countries.

In this way, the issue of immigration is also central to the rise of various populisms (Ford and Goodwin 2010). Populist parties have benefitted, in particular, from the intermeshing of the economic crisis with the 'Muslim question' and that of the so-called 'refugee crisis'. The 'us the people against them the elites' ideology has been nurtured by the particularly negative effects of the economic crisis for large sectors of the population. Populist parties can thus be seen in many contexts to have scapegoted migrants for wider economic woes. On the other hand, and perhaps also as a reaction to more nativist expressions, a number of people have exhibited solidary attitudes and behaviours towards migrants.

In this context, chapter 5 looks at attitudes to immigration and support for populist parties. This is a key politicised issue field and the subject of fervent debate in the context of the crisis. Migrants have been victimised and scapegoated by various political figures in this period of crisis. Moreover, recent years have witnessed the rise of far-right populist movements and parties focussing on immigration as their main battleground. Our detailed examination of attitudes to immigration and support for populism and how these vary across countries and social groups in Europe allows us to examine how the politicisation of these issues may have impinged upon individuals' understandings of society and the key political issues at stake in the current context.

ECONOMIC CRISIS AND POLITICAL ENGAGEMENT

The Great Recession has arguably had a profound impact on various spheres of the lives of Europeans. It has also impinged on individuals' participation in the political sphere and on their political behaviour, both in the electoral and non-electoral arenas (Giugni and Lorenzini 2020). The most obvious example of this was the thousands of people that marched in protest against the austerity measures implemented by governments and against the growing inequalities they generated across Europe. It is undeniable that the economic crisis has spurred a large number of protests and movements, especially in those countries that were hardest hit by both the effects of the crisis and austerity policies. Another less directly visible sign lies in the emergence of alternative economic practices known as alternative forms of resilience, which multiplied during the crisis and are increasing in political significance in contexts of economic hardship.

The idea that economic hardship impacts political behaviour has a long-standing scholarly history. On the one hand, economic voting theories maintain that voters will punish incumbents in times of economic downturn for their poor economic performance (see Lewis-Beck and Stegmeier 2000 for a review). While not undisputed, this approach has become dominant in the literature on voting behaviour today. The Great Recession has reinvigorated support for such approaches as scholars have examined how the economic crisis has led to a variety of changes in political preferences and voting patterns (Kriesi 2014a). In this regard, some have argued that the effect of economic voting may be stronger in times of crisis (Hernandez and Kriesi 2016). This also relates to the increasing popularity of explanations for voting as well as other forms of political participation stressing the role of blame assignment (Kriesi 2014a; Marsh and Tilley 2010; Wagner 2013; Giugni and Grasso 2017).

On the other hand, social movement scholars are well aware of the so-called breakdown theories of collective action, which were very popular from the 1950s to the 1970s. These kinds of accounts stress the direct impact of grievances on protest behaviour. They assume that social movements form to the extent that people are discontented and are subject to social stress and that those individuals who are most deprived and isolated are more aggrieved and, therefore, more likely to take part in collective behaviour (see Buechler 2004 and Useem 1998 for reviews).

The Great Recession has favoured a further push towards the revival of grievance theories that was already underway (Buechler 2004). A number of works have paid special attention to the role of relative deprivation in the rise of protests within the economic crisis context (Bernburg 2015; Grasso, Karampampas et al. 2017; Rüdig and Karyotis 2014) and have explored the role of grievances in triggering protest (Galais and Lorenzini 2017; Grasso and Giugni 2016a). In this context, grievance theories have led to the expectation of protest to increase in times of crisis and sustained recession, as opposed to in periods of economic growth. Moreover, it would also be expected that individuals who are most affected by the crisis should be more likely to engage in protest activities and social groups who are most affected by the crisis—such as, for example, unemployed and precarious people as well as migrants—should be more likely to form social movements in response to difficult economic conditions (Giugni and Lorenzini 2014).

Grievances, however, can hardly lead to protest in the absence of other conditions that are conducive to translating so-called protest potential into action (Grasso and Giugni 2016a). Studies on Latin America, for example, suggest that collective action in response to neoliberal globalisation results from a combination of factors, including hardship, perceived threats and political alliances (Almeida 2007; Johnston and Almeida 2006). More generally, students of social movements today commonly agree that protest behaviour, in addition to resting upon the capacity of actors to mobilise resources, results from the combination of grievances and a broader context that may provide opportunities for individual grievances to be translated into political action (McAdam et al. 2001). Yet, research most often tends to focus on different explanatory factors separately without engaging, in detail, the ways in which grievances interact with political opportunities to account for protest. Furthermore, in spite of much theorising about the macro-micro linkages in the explanation of protest activities and, more generally, political engagement, studies that effectively test such linkages empirically by combining survey with contextual data are still rare (Grasso and Giugni 2016a; Quaranta 2016).

Focussing in on these important questions for understanding political activism in times of crisis, in chapters 6 and 7, we investigate the interplay of hardship and deprivation, on the one hand, and political opportunities for action, on the other. Chapter 6 looks at the effects of the crisis on political action and, more specifically, how individual-level grievances interact with macro-level factors to spur protest behaviour. In particular, we examine whether deprivation leads to protest and whether this effect is magnified in countries with deeper experiences of the crisis. As such, chapter 6 examines the role of crisis experience at the individual level and of political opportunities at the macro-level for furthering protest activism.

Chapter 7 examines the impact of the crisis on political activism, more generally, and, more specifically, of how individuals' perceptions of the government's role in the economic crisis push them to engage in various contentious political activities. We look at the role of blame assignment and whether blaming the national government for the economic crisis has an impact on participation in different political activities, including voting against incumbents.

THE ECONOMIC AND POLITICAL CONTEXT OF THE CRISIS

A book about how Europeans have perceived and reacted to the economic crisis can hardly avoid presenting a contextualisation of such sociopolitical processes. In this section we therefore provide a discussion aimed at characterising the broader context within which Europeans in the nine countries covered by our study found themselves during the Great Recession. The following contextual aspects are particularly important in this regard: the economic context—providing, in fact, a measure of the extent and severity of the crisis; and the political-institutional context—including the implementation of austerity measures by European governments. We show trends for the period between 2005—that is, a few years before the start of the crisis—and 2014, when most, if not all, countries had at least begun a process of recovery, although not necessarily resulting in recovery from the many deep negative social and political consequences that followed from it, often with a time lag.

We use a variety of economic indicators to characterise the extent and severity of the crisis. Economic growth is one of the most important of these. Rising unemployment levels are another important indicator of recession and economic crisis. As noted earlier, an economic crisis may be defined as a prolonged period of low, or negative, economic growth coupled with rising unemployment. In the next section we thus turn to examining how the nine countries included in our study have fared in some of the key dimensions of crisis.

As we can see in figure 1.1, the development of GDP over time shows a clear interruption in growth in all the countries between 2008 and 2009, with the exception of Poland. This reflects the deepest moment of the economic crisis in macro-economic terms, at least as far as GDP is concerned. After 2009, most countries started to grow again, albeit at a slower pace. Spain and, above all, Greece, are the two exceptions, as these countries had to wait until 2012–2013 to start growing again. As we know, the case of Greece is particularly problematic for a variety of reasons which made front-page news for months, if not years. Not only was the economic recovery very slow but the downturn was particularly marked and had consequences on vast sectors of the population. In contrast, other countries appear to have suffered much less from a macro-economic point of view and to have recovered faster. This is the case, for example, for Germany, Sweden and Switzerland. Furthermore, Poland is still different, insofar as this country does not seem to have been hit at all, in terms of GDP.[3]

That the years between 2007 and 2012 were characterised by a deep economic recession can perhaps be even more clearly seen in figure 1.2, which shows the annual growth rate in the nine countries. Here we can see that the economy has slowed down in all nine countries, including Poland. However, while all of them had to face negative growth rates after 2008, for as long as up to 2013 in the three southern European countries, in most countries the economy started to slowly recover in the last three years of the period under consideration. Once again, the dramatic situation of Greece is clearly visible

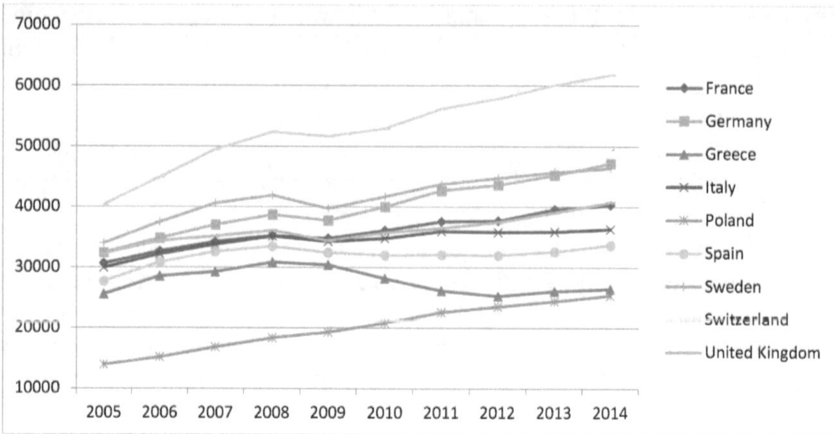

Figure 1.1. GDP by country, 2005-2014 (USD per capita)

here, as is the fact that Poland has been better off as its annual growth rate never fell below zero.

Economic growth—or, conversely, recession—is perhaps the best and most straightforward indicator of the crisis from a purely economic point of view. A rising unemployment rate is another key measure, one that has a clear social component. Figure 1.3 gives us an overview of how unemployment levels have changed during the years of the crisis.[4] The overall picture shows a general decrease in the unemployment rates between 2005 and 2007, followed by an abrupt rise in all nine countries from 2008 onwards, that is, at

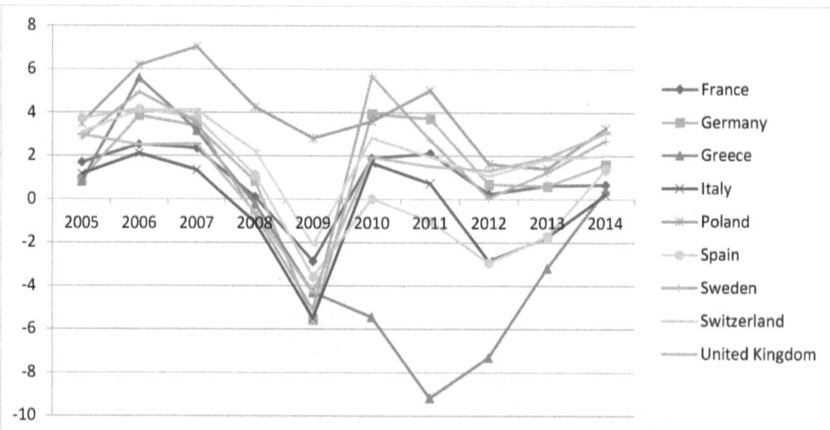

Figure 1.2. Annual growth rate by country, 2005-2014 (percentage)

the start of the crisis. At the same time, however, we also observe differences across countries. The most striking aspect in this regard is the huge rise of unemployment in Spain (from 2008) and Greece (from 2009). The unemployment rate in these two countries went beyond 25 percent in 2013, witnessing all the dramatic consequences of the Great Recession there. In contrast, other countries—most notably, Germany—have even witnessed a decrease in unemployment, perhaps as a result of the so-called Hartz reforms undertaken by the SPD government starting from 2004 that, however, are said to have created more work precarity (Cinalli and Giugni 2013).

The Great Recession was often characterised as a debt crisis (Stiglitz 2012). Therefore, we also examine here how national debt evolved during the years of the crisis. Figure 1.4 shows this side of the story, expressed as percentage of GDP. The general government debt showed a decreasing trend in the years immediately preceding the crisis except, perhaps, in Greece where it was more stable. Then, from 2008 onwards, the debt started to rise in all countries but one. The single exception is Switzerland, whose national debt was not merely stabilised but even reduced through the so-called debt brake. Here we can also see, once again, the particularly difficult situation of the three southern European countries in terms of economic growth, particularly for Greece, after 2011, but also for Italy—with respect to the level of debt both before and after the crisis—and also for Spain—in terms of a rapid increase during the crisis. On the other hand, reflecting what we observed in the unemployment rate, Germany has been largely spared from major issues in this area, as the national debt diminished after 2010.

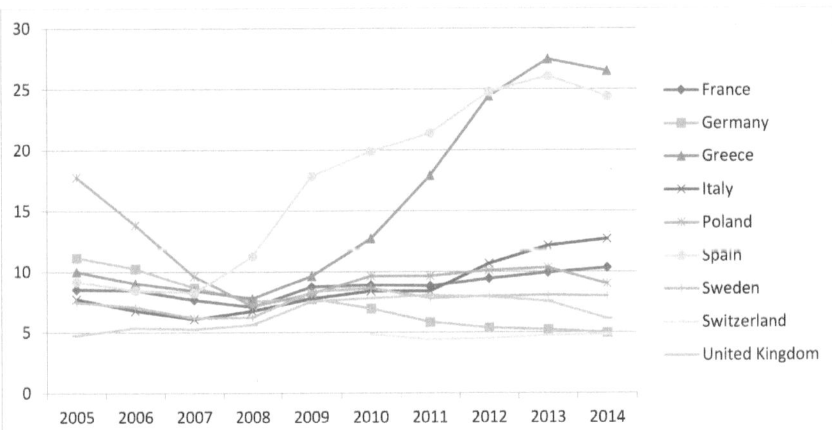

Figure 1.3. Unemployment rate by country, 2005-2014 (percentage of labor force)

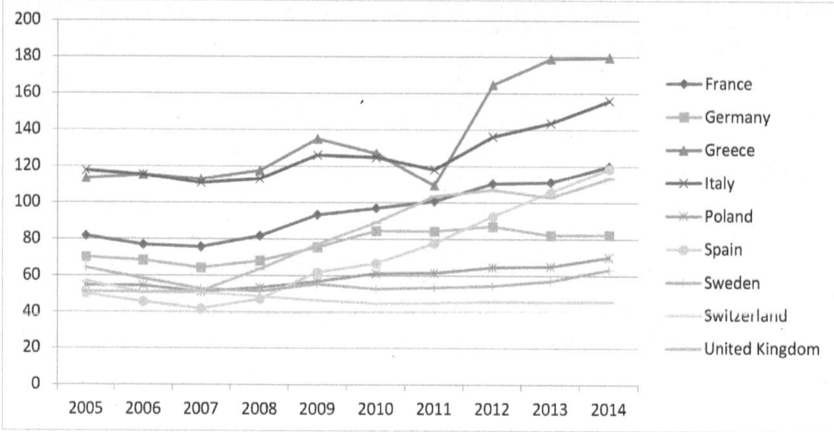

Figure 1.4. General government debt, 2005-2014 (percentage of GDP)

In the eyes of many observers, what caused the greater negative impact of the Great Recession, however, was not so much the severity of the economic crisis as such, but rather more the ways in which European governments tried to address it by implementing austerity policies. Various major economists have argued that austerity measures deepened the negative consequences of the crisis rather than putting an end to them (see, for example, Krugman 2012 and Stiglitz 2012). This has led some to argue that the political reactions to the Great Recession, such as anti-austerity protests, were less related to the economic facts of the crisis itself but, rather, more about government responses (Bermeo and Bartels 2014).

Austerity measures roughly consist of reductions in government spending combined with increases in tax revenues. Thus, to examine the extent to which such measures have been implemented in the nine countries under investigation, we look at trends in spending and taxation. Since austerity measures most often aim to lower government deficits and avoid a debt crisis, we also take these macroeconomic indicators as outputs of austerity policies.[5] While we have already shown the development of national debt, figure 1.5 shows how the general government deficit, expressed as a percentage of GDP, fared during the years of the crisis. Since the two indicators are interdependent, the trends largely reflect those observed for the national debt. The extent of the economic crisis and its effects on government deficit are clearly visible in this graph: all nine countries faced negative deficit at some point during the period under consideration, with the partial exception of Switzerland, which displayed positive figures for most of the time. Yet, even in this country we observe a drop in the early years of the crisis, albeit a much less

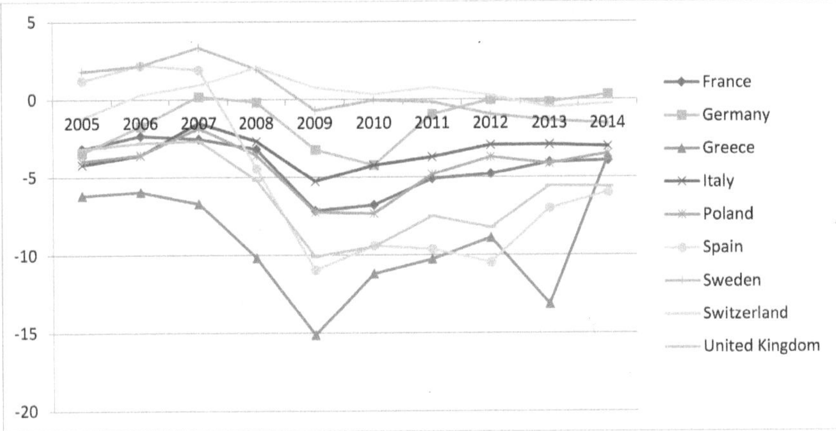

Figure 1.5. General government deficit, 2005-2014 (percentage of GDP)

severe one than in the other countries. Once again, we can see the particularly serious relative situation of certain countries, most notably Greece and Spain but also the UK.

Based on these findings, we can clearly contextualise that in the run-up years preceding the survey upon which this volume is based, which was conducted in 2015, Europe was indeed facing an important economic crisis. In fact, while the economic crisis may have lasted only a couple of years, as we can see in the rise of the economic growth after 2009 (except in Greece), its negative consequences continued to make life particularly difficult for many Europeans, especially so in southern Europe. Europeans, particularly in some countries, also faced the challenge of deep and extensive austerity policies which as we have seen various economists have argued did not help with countering the negative effects of the crisis. Quite on the contrary, they may have rather exacerbated the daily difficulties faced by many individuals, particularly with respect to cuts in welfare spending and other social provisions aimed at aiding the worse-off.

Moreover, it is important to note how the economic crisis was also accompanied by a political crisis in several cases. The most striking example, also due to its international ramifications, was that of Greece. Here, the economic crisis, as well as the poor handling of it by both European and national leaders, brought the country close to collapse. However, the wider political ramifications of the crisis have also been wide-ranging and important among other countries, including Italy and Spain. In some cases, the political crisis preceded the economic crisis as in Poland, where efforts made to avoid the economic crisis led, in fact, to a legitimisation crisis (Theiss and Kurowska

2018). While it is not always easy to disentangle first causes—that is, whether the political crisis was a cause or a consequence of the economic crisis—the important point is that political and economic aspects often intermesh to exacerbate the effects of the economic crisis, making them even more difficult to overcome, for example, where governments lack clear mandates or legitimacy to effect reforms that might improve economies. Moreover, political and economic crises that remain unsolved and ongoing can lead to the development of further social and political problems, thus, further deteriorating social contexts. However, these situations can also offer opportunities for political action and social change, as we will see, in particular, in the final chapters of this book. For now, however, we next turn to looking at the data analysed in this volume the plan of the book, and then to winding to a close this introductory chapter.

THE DATA

The analyses presented in this book are based on original data retrieved in the context of a cross-national research project funded by the European Commission through the Seventh Framework Programme.[6] This project, titled 'Living with Hard Times: How Citizens React to Economic Crises and Their Social and Political Consequences' (LIVEWHAT), spanned three years (December 2013 to December 2016). The project aimed to provide evidence-based knowledge about Europeans' resilience in times of economic crisis. It examined, in particular, the ways in which individuals in nine European countries—France, Germany, Greece, Italy, Poland, Spain, Sweden, Switzerland and the UK–reacted to the crisis that struck Europe since 2008.[7]

The dataset is from a population survey that we employ in the analyses in most chapters. The survey was developed as part of the project with the aim of analysing the individual experiences and responses to the crisis. This project was coordinated by Marco Giugni (University of Geneva). Maria Grasso (now at Queen Mary University of London, but based at the University of Sheffield during the course of the grant) provided the scientific supervision for the cross-national survey. We collected data from across the nine European countries of the project. A specialised polling institute, YouGov, was subcontracted to conduct the survey in each country through the Computer Assisted Web Interviewing (CAWI) method. Each national sample contains about two thousand respondents.[8] Samples were matched to national statistics for gender, age, region and education quotas. Fieldwork started on 26 May 2015 and was completed on 30 July 2015. The survey data form the main empirical basis for chapters 2, 3, 4, 5, 6 and 7. The questionnaire included a wide range of items aimed to capture the effects of the crisis in terms of hardship and deprivation felt by respondents, which are used, above all, in chapter 2 but also in chapter 6. It also included questions on citizens' capacity for resilience, the topic addressed in chapter 3. Finally, it included questions dealing with the attitudes of respondents with respect to unemployment and the welfare state and also immigration and support for radical right parties—the two contested political fields discussed in chapter 4 and chapter 5.

Moreover, some of the analyses also include additional secondary data. This is more specifically the case in chapters 6 and 7, where we show the results of multilevel regression models, combining macro-level variables, with micro-level individual, variables. While the micro indicators originate in our survey data, the macro indicators stem from secondary sources such as the Organisation for Economic Co-operation and Development (OECD) and the World Bank.

PLAN OF THE BOOK

Six chapters form the core of this book in addition to this introduction (chapter 1) and the conclusion (chapter 8) which summarise the main findings of our study and place them in a broader perspective in terms of their significance. Given their content, the chapters in this book can be grouped into three pairs, each group referring to one of the three main lines of investigation outlined earlier.

The first pair deals with the extent of the impact of the economic crisis and how such an impact has been felt differently in the nine European countries analysed and across social strata, also with respect to the capacity that individuals have had to be resilient to the negative effects of the crisis. Thus, chapter 2 looks at the effects of the Great Recession on individual perceptions of economic conditions, with a specific focus on the relationship between deprivation and social structure. On the other hand, chapter 3 examines resilience, looking at the ways in which Europeans have shown capabilities for resilience to the negative effects of the economic crisis and how such a capacity for resilience varies across social groups.

The second pair of chapters examines Europeans' attitudes with respect to unemployment and immigration. Thus, chapter 4 looks at individual attitudes towards welfare policy, unemployment, and precarious employment as well as comparing these with economic policy satisfaction, more widely, and on poverty, education and healthcare. Chapter 5 focusses on Europeans' attitudes towards immigration and levels of support for populist parties. This has become an increasingly politicised area in the current context as migrants have come to be scapegoated by various political figures in these times of economic hardship and recent years have witnessed the rise of populist movements and parties focussing on immigration as their main battleground.

The third pair of chapters look at political activism during the economic crisis. Chapter 6 examines the ways in which individual-level grievances impact protest behaviour, showing the relevance of wider political opportunities. Chapter 7, moreover, looks at how perceptions of the government's role in the economic crisis shape patterns of political action.

Finally, chapter 8 summarises the key findings of this book and draws out the main lessons from our analyses. It reevaluates the issues discussed in the introduction and reassesses them in light of the book's findings. It concludes with a discussion of the economic crisis understood as both constraint and opportunity.

Chapter Two

Deprivation and Social Structure

Even before the Great Recession had struck, inequality had been markedly sharpening across the globe since the 1970s (Piketty 2014). Since 1979, two-thirds of all income gains made by the top tenth of earners were taken by the top 1 percent in the UK (Dorling 2014). In the US, from 1968 to 1990, real income for the bottom 60 percent of families remained the same whereas amongst the top 5 percent it increased by half (Danziger and Gottschalk 1995; Fischer et al. 1996; Massey 1996). As Tilly (1998) notes, at least four major trends contributed to this rising inequality: (1) large moves from relatively well-paid manufacturing employment to lower-paid services employment as the manufacturing base shrunk; (2) deteriorating employment conditions for the poorest sectors of society with the increasing precarisation of labour such as with minimum-wage jobs, sweat-shop conditions and below minimum-wage pay, part-time, temporary and unemployment; (3) rising non-wage income amongst the richest sectors of society, for example, in stocks and returns from investments; (4) and growing disparity in large firm compensations. At the same time, unions were losing political power, and large companies were extending their bureaucracies while shedding lower-level employment, all while business interests were becoming more predominant in government and society at large (Tilly 1998).

The Great Recession hit within this preexistent neoliberal context of growing inequality and deteriorating living conditions for very large sections of the populations of the major democracies worldwide. As Krugman (2012) notes, between 2007 and 2010, both Europe and America fell into deep recession, experiencing a rapid rise in unemployment. However, whereas by 2011–2012 a clear trend in economic improvement had emerged in America, this was not the case in Europe. Krugman (2012) explains this divergence in terms of Europe's political dominance by the 'Austerians' and their embrace of government-imposed spending cuts and tax hikes even with concurrent high unemployment. Moreover, 'savage austerity' (Krugman 2012: xii) was imposed as a condition for financial support to debtor countries. The scale of spending cuts and tax hikes imposed on Greece was enormous and caused suffering in the population, but even the countries that were having no issues with borrowing, such as Germany, imposed modest austerity measures on themselves, in turn leading to a major fiscal contraction in Europe (Krugman 2012); the austerity doctrine suggested that the negative effects of the contraction would be counterbalanced by improving consumer and business confidence, but this did not happen and Europe sunk even deeper into depression. Britain, being outside the Eurozone and enjoying lower borrowing costs, could have employed different policies in order to avoid negative economic consequences but, here too, Cameron's government, coming to power in 2010, also embraced austerity and GDP since the onset of the crisis trailed America, the Euro area and Japan (Krugman 2012). In turn, these political decisions and the negative economic conditions that ensued impacted the living standards of many people, restricting opportunities and choices in their daily lives and leading many to chastise their governments in various elections. Moreover, cuts in public services impacted needy sections of society the most, further exacerbating the negative human impact of the crisis.

By October 2012, the International Monetary Fund (IMF) acknowledged that after 2010 European economies had performed particularly badly. However, the 'Troika' of the IMF, European Central Bank and European Commission continued with imposing austerity in exchange for loans to Greece and Portugal and ask that Spain and Italy do much more in terms of austerity if they wanted to receive debt-management support (Stiglitz 2012). At the same time, concern for inequality was growing around the world as it became increasingly apparent that the economic crisis had further exacerbated these negative trends, particularly for the middle and bottom of income distribution (Stiglitz 2012). In 1980s Britain, inequality was average among advanced industrialised countries, but it had become second only to America while the Libor scandal, amongst other financial upheavals, showed the deep web of hidden connections linking powerful interests together against the backdrop of London as the capital of global financial rent-seeking (Stiglitz 2012). In other parts of Europe, further problems had emerged. As the economic downturn persisted in southern European countries in particular, unemployment continued to rise, and wages, adjusted for inflation, decreased. This, in turn, lead to weakening demand while, at the same time, declining GDPs coupled with rising unemployment rates led tax revenues to fall and social expenses to rise, increasing public deficits (Stiglitz 2012).

Without export growth to compensate for contracting government expenditures, austerity was seen to lead to higher unemployment (Stiglitz 2012). Countries embracing austerity either voluntarily (as with the UK) or involuntarily (most of the Eurozone countries) experienced deteriorating economic conditions. Moreover, the ease with which capital could leave European countries exacerbated the downturn, further eroding confidence in the banking system. Thus, existent problems linked to the economic crisis were further compounded, as illustrated by Spain, wherein the combination of a bursting property bubble and austerity policies lead investors to redirect capital to German banks, leading weakened Spanish banks to restrict loans, thus exacerbating the effects of austerity and the credit squeeze (Stiglitz 2012). In many European countries, rising unemployment had been accompanied by declining wages as well as large cuts in public spending and social services where they were needed most (Stiglitz 2012). Stiglitz (2012) notes, as a critical example, the shortage of life-saving medications in Greece, a problem not usually affecting but the poorest developing nations. While Greece was the worst hit country, the economic situation was also dire in countries like Spain and Italy, and many other European countries suffered at least some negative effects from the depression.

In this way, the depression in Europe was not just the stuff of economic textbooks, but it brought forth real challenges in the daily lives of millions of Europeans. In this context, certain groups are most likely to be affected by economic crisis whereas others are likely to be more insulated from deteriorating economic conditions. Individuals with lower levels of resources or who are more reliant on social services are more likely to be affected, since they will be more likely to lose their jobs, to be squeezed out of the labour market, or to be unable to receive support that previously flowed from higher levels of public spending. On the other hand, those at the top of the income distribution emerge unscathed and the free movement of labour without tax harmonisation meant ongoing competition to the bottom for corporations and high-income individuals through the offer of lower taxes (Stiglitz 2012).

In this context of unequal opportunities, this chapter looks at the effects of the Great Recession on Europeans' experiences of deprivation and their perceptions of their economic conditions. How did the crisis impact these? The crisis has deteriorated the living standards and the economic conditions of many individuals across Europe and has generated feelings of deprivation. How do these vary? Perceptions of economic deprivation are likely to depend on structural position, for example, class belonging and other sociodemographic factors such as gender. To what extent do these vary between the potential winners and losers of the economic crisis? How do individuals perceive the impact of the crisis on their own economic situations and on that of their countries at large? To what extent do individuals feel that the crisis has impacted their lives? How do they rate their living standards in relation to the past? How hopeful are they that these will improve in the future? What is the relationship between deprivation, class and inequality? How has the crisis impacted the ways in which Europeans view their own situations and does this vary based on social position?

The next two sections address these questions from a theoretical point of view, first by discussing the relationship between social structure, economic crisis and deprivation and then by examining how the latter relates to people's evaluations and attitudes about the economy. The following two sections then look at these aspects empirically by analysing survey data to show patterns. In particular, we show how perceptions of economic deprivation vary both across countries and social groups and which factors predict both so-called pocketbook (personal level) retrospective and sociotropic (national level) prospective economic evaluations.

SOCIAL STRUCTURE, ECONOMIC CRISIS AND DEPRIVATION

Intimately related to the debates on rising inequality are debates on the extent of inequalities linked to social position, such as social class and other socioeconomic status (SES) measures, but also others, including gender, age, employment and citizenship status. Moreover, multiple sources of disadvantage can overlap to marginalise deprived groups. In our analysis we will examine differences in experienced deprivation based on important socio-demographic dimensions discussed in the literature such as gender (Skeggs 2004), generation (Chauvel 2006) and education (Vincent et al. 2012).

Amongst the different aspects linked to socio-demographics and social structure which make one more likely to experience deprivation during the crisis is gender. Women tend to be in weaker economic positions than men and to be more reliant on social services and public spending. Women are, on average, more economically vulnerable since they have lower average incomes and also exhibit a higher likelihood to be in unpaid caring roles. Andersen (1999) has argued that women are much more likely to see the effects of social spending; this is because they are more likely to be caring for children or the elderly. As such, given that the recent economic crisis led to restrictions in public spending and austerity across Europe, even amongst those countries that were doing relatively well compared to Spain, Greece or Italy, say, we expect that women would be more likely than men to perceive deprivation. Manza and Brooks (1998) further note how women's greater entry into the workforce has further increased their preference for social spending; this is since working women tend to be employed in the public sector, as well as requiring childcare services. They may also require income maintenance if they are in low paid jobs. Togeby (1994) also points out how women still take on a disproportionate amount of caring and domestic tasks; this thus them to be more supportive of social spending and the provision of state services. This is despite that fact that women have entered new economic roles in the workforce at higher rates which has not been matched by a comparable decrease in home and family responsibilities. Moreover, the literature tends to argue that the austerity spending cuts that the economic crisis brought were most damaging for women again given the fact that they more likely to be in caring roles and thus to use these services (Stacey 1981; Women's Budget Group 2015). All these factors, in turn, lead us to expect that women are thus more likely to have experienced the negative effects of the crisis and austerity measures than men across the countries in our study.

Younger people are understood to be in a particularly vulnerable position in society whereby they are likely to have been negatively impacted by the recent economic crisis and the fallout from the austerity measures implemented by governments across Europe (Bessant et al. 2017). Moreover, the literature emphasises the economic difficulties that young generations are experiencing in relation to their parents (Chauvel 2006). Gardiner (2016: 5) notes how, in contrast to the idea that each younger generation will do better than the one before, 'a typical young person (18–34) earned £8,000 less during their twenties than those in the preceding generation, Generation X'. When asked if they thought the younger generation would be better off than their parents when they reached the same age, only 38 percent of young Brits, 37 percent of young Germans and 15 percent of young French were optimistic (Stokes 2015). In Spain, France, Italy and Greece, there are high levels of youth unemployment which may be linked to these views and protest movements have been stirring in these countries, such as the well-known anti-austerity protest movements but also the 'Nuit Debout' protests against French labour laws. Across European countries, austerity measures are likely to have impacted public services that young people use. Bessant et al. (2017) shows that people under the age of thirty-five in several European countries are facing an increasing economic burden of deprivation, inequality and disadvantage relative to older generations. Dorling (2014) notes how the young are predominantly in low-paid jobs in the UK, and from 1993 to 2013 the proportion of young women employed in low-skilled jobs went up from 7 to 21 percent and from 14 to 25 percent for young men. Given all this, we expect that young people will be more likely than older age groups to experience deprivation across the countries in our study.

Additionally, sociologists would normally expect to see differences in deprivation by socio-economic status (SES). Together with income and occupational class, educational attainment is linked to SES and the literature has shown how it is strongly related to earnings, unemployment and labour-market participation for a variety of reasons including resources, skills and the heuristics used by employers when deciding who to take on for a job (Sparkes and Glennerster 2002). Moreover, higher levels of education are seen as a means to attenuate class differentials in material outcomes (Vincent et al. 2012). Increasingly, qualifications are necessary to access the labour market so that educational cleavages, in terms of who is in a more vulnerable economic position with respect to the effect of the crisis, should be quite visible. Moreover, since people with lower educational attainment are also likely to have lower earnings (Bynner and Parsons 1997) they are more likely to be in vulnerable labour–market positions and therefore more likely to have experienced the negative effects of the crisis and, in particular, the squeeze in social support provided by public spending (which experienced deep cuts in the depression period in many countries). Additionally, low-level education was also linked to other outcomes that make individuals more likely to experience deprivation during the crisis owing to their vulnerable positions, such as low home ownership, low health, and depression (Whitty et al. 1999).

As noted above, linked to educational attainment are earnings and therefore income, also included in the concept of SES. Being at the bottom end of the income distribution is linked to greater odds of experiencing deprivation and even more so in situations of economic crisis bringing declining living standards and contractions in public spending and social services. Poverty is defined as when people's 'resources are so seriously below those commanded by the average individual or family that they are, in effect, excluded from ordinary living patterns, customs and activities' (Townsend 1979: 31). As such, a low—or very low—income contributes to putting people at risk of poverty and therefore of being more likely to experience deprivation in times of crisis where even the middle class experiences the economic squeeze. Poverty has been shown to be associated with a number of negative outcomes from higher morbidity, mortality, lower life expectancy, bad work conditions (Seccombe 2002). Subjective and objective measures of deprivation have furthermore been shown to relate to health inequalities and more negative health outcomes

(Weitz 2001). Poverty is also linked to living alone, to not be married or have children, and less social contact; this is also linked to diminished chances for marriage, and this is because economic insecurity makes marriage less attractive (Wilson 1996). Poverty, unemployment and precarious work further undermine marriages (Conger et al. 1999). Conger et al. (1994) suggested this further links to depression and thus more challenging marital relationships and dissatisfaction.

Different factors might mitigate the risk of deprivation: (1) individual level factors such as those provided by a good education and good mental and physical health, skills, personality and dispositions (Garmezy 1991); (2) family factors e.g. companionship, social contact and support; these shape a family's ability to endure in the face of risk factors and thus allow shielding from the more negative effects of deprivation (Seccombe 2002); and (3) community factors, for example those linked to having wider webs of social contacts (Bowen et al. 2000). In situations of deprivation, social ties can indeed be seen as a form of informal insurance, for example with respect to the provision of financial help and physical assistance (Aldrich 2010). Money-lending, a place to stay, help with looking after children and information are all resources which friends might be able to provide even when it may not be accessible from public or social service organisations and other institutions (Aldrich 2010).

Seminal studies on class have focussed on stratification in society and on social mobility (Erikson et al. 1979). Class has been traditionally understood through occupational status and a worker's position relative to the means of production, and studies have examined the social mobility of the working class (Heath 1981). Individuals in lower social classes, such as those in manual occupations, have generally been considered to be most at risk of deprivation and less likely to be able to move out of poverty. Goldthorpe et al. (1967) argued that despite increased affluence over time, manual workers experience lower mobility relative to middle class individuals. This was found with respect to both lower income and also relative to being more likely to be stuck in repetitive forms of work with little hope for promotion or supervisory roles. Moreover, this was also reflected in manual workers' networks which had remained narrow and limited to family members and a few other working-class contacts. The key conclusions were, thus, that a stratified hierarchy related not only to income or possessions but also to life-chances, experiences, and the nature of relationships with other groups more broadly (Goldthorpe 1967: 27).

Classes are fundamentally distinguished by the nature of people's employment relationships, the nature of the wage contract and also life chances (Goldthorpe 2000). Therefore, class differences with respect to the extent to which classes have had to deal with the negative effects of economic crisis, are central for making sense of relative well-being, life chances, and so forth. While Goldthorpe et al. (1967) largely adopted a neo-Weberian approach to class and stratification, more cultural approaches have increasingly been proposed to study deprivation, and it remains critical, as argued by many (Devine and Savage 2000; Savage and Williams 2008), to examine how class inequalities drive material deprivation in contemporary European societies.

Class is above all is linked to questions of inequality given they are related within a system of hierarchy and stratification, with lower classes most vulnerable to poverty and deprivation. The complexification of the class structure of advanced industrial societies has been moreover linked to nuanced and novel arguments such as that by Crompton (1987) in favour of a Marxist analysis of class for understanding white-collar workers, or the 'property less middle class'. This group was seen as neither proletariat nor bourgeoisie given the expansion of the middle class and the way this challenges traditional distinction between manual and non-manual workers today. Recent work on 'the precariat' has also looked new forms of inequalities beyond the traditional distinctions (Standing 2011). Indeed, the precarity of one's employment status could be a very important indicator for one's vulnerability to deprivation during the crisis. Individuals that are not in full-time employment, are in caring roles, or are unemployed are more likely to depend on the state for social support and, as such, austerity cuts are likely to have impacted them more negatively. Finally, it is likely that migrants and non-citizens, which tend to be more marginalised and have fewer resources would have been more likely to experience deprivation (Morales and Giugni 2011).

DEPRIVATION AND ECONOMIC EVALUATIONS

To measure deprivation, recent scholarship has recommended the use of non-monetary indicators also in order to more fully capture the wider aspects of disadvantage and social exclusion (Nolan and Whelan 2011). Cross-nationally comparative indicators are moreover crucial when performing comparative analyses (Nolan and Whelan 2011), and using non-monetary indicators provides such a clear and comparative measure of deprivation cross-nationally. Indeed, authors like Ringen (1987, 1988) had argued that income did not adequately capture poverty as it was both unreliable and an indirect measure. Moreover, Mack and Lansley (1985) had preferred to employ deprivation indicators to measure social exclusion in Britain; this tradition was then followed by further British 'poverty and social exclusion' studies (Gordon et al. 2000; Pantazis et al. 2006). Other studies identified the 'consistently poor' as those on low income and reporting deprivation (Callan et al. 1993; Nolan and Whelan 1996). This approach also used by the UK which combines low income and material deprivation in a range of indicators to monitor child poverty (DWP 2003). Bradshaw and Finch (2003) also looked at 'core poverty': a very difficult financial situation reported with low income and other types of deprivation. As such, non-monetary indicators as standalone as well as in a variety of combinations have been previously used to measure deprivation in many European nations as well as cross-nationally (Nolan and Whelan 2011). This approach in particular highlights the ways in which poverty and deprivation are 'not just about money'. Social exclusion involves poverty which is not just a financial matter of low resources also other forms of disadvantage including educational opportunities, poor health/access to health services, inadequate housing and exclusion from the labour market to name a few (Burchartdt et al. 2002; Nolan and Whelan 2007, 2011).

Whereas, according to some readings, economic shocks such as economic crises are shared events across the population and thus likely to increase everyone's deprivation in relative terms, for others they are expected to affect diverse groups in the population very differently (Duch and Sagarzazu 2014). Some occupations are seen to be at higher risk than others and therefore making sense of differences in perceived risk associated with one's social position might help to explain differences in deprivation perceptions. In the first case, one would expect similar perceptions reported across social groupings based on, for example, media framing (Duch and Stevenson 2011), whereas in the latter case there should be very large differences between social groups in terms of their perceptions of the recession. Do, for example, rich and poor people say that the crisis affected them differently? Are national economy perceptions different across social groups? Are there large differences between the rich and the poor in terms of how their personal finances were affected? These are some of the questions that we will tackle in the analyses in the following section.

How do economic shocks such as the Great Recession shape economic attitudes? It is presumed that macroeconomic shocks register with all voters in a similar way (Duch and Sagarzazu 2014). On one level, we all watch the same news and therefore experience information on these events together. However, macroeconomic events such as economic crises and policy responses to them, such as austerity measures, have winners and losers and distributional consequences. As a result, those that are most likely to suffer negative consequences may express more negative assessments of macroeconomic performance. In this way, risk exposure should impact one's assessments. For example, it is classically argued that if individuals respond in a self-interested fashion to economic shocks, then the poor would favour redistributive policies tempering the effect of economic shocks on the less lucky, while the rich should be less supportive of them. However, evidence shows that this picture is not supported and institutional factors are normally cited as explanations for this divergence from classical theorising (Pontusson and Lupu 2011; Pontusson and Rueda 2010). Moreover, Duch and Sagarzazu (2014) point out that during crises there tends to be a widespread acceptance of 'no pain no gain' theories of macroeconomy and claims that without radical measures, such as deep austerity cuts (which tend to disproportionately affect the poor), recovery would not be possible. Moreover, poorer sections of society sometimes themselves often favour these policies and provide support for them in their voting choices, such as, for example, policies that make taxes less progressive (Bartels 2005).

In terms of national economic attitudes, the literature tends to assume that voters are attentive to fluctuations in the macroeconomy and that they have an accurate collective sense of such trends (Duch and Sagarzazu 2014). The idea here is that voters are exposed to this information through the media, helping to account for both homogeneity and accuracy in their evaluations (Hetherington 1996). Alternative approaches suggest that the poor are less attentive to the media and this might lead to biased evaluations (Duch et al. 2000). Moreover, while the rich and the poor might have similar assessments of macroeconomic situations, they might have quite different ones of their personal finances; individuals who are more negatively affected tend to register more negative evaluations of the economy (Ansolabehere et al. 2014). However, evidence for the recent crisis suggests that economic perceptions tend to be quite similar for both the rich and the poor (Duch and Sagarzazu 2014). Across Europe, the Great Recession negatively impacted many people and was a prominent feature of the national news across countries for a protracted period of time.

However, it is reasonable to expect that the rich and the poor will have different experiences of deterioration in their personal finances, particularly in times of economic crisis, and evidence from Germany and the UK appears to support this (Duch and Sagarzazu 2014). Respondents in both Germany and the UK were much more positive about their own personal financial situations than the national economy (Duch and Sagarzazu 2014). The difference between the evaluations of the poor and the rich suggests that the disposable income of the rich was more resistant during the crisis—in the UK, for example, the income of the rich increased while the income of the poor remained the same since the 2008 crisis (Duch and Sagarzazu 2014).

DEPRIVATION AND SOCIAL STRUCTURE

Building on the theorising discussed in the previous sections, this chapter addresses two key research questions. The first examines the extent to which Europeans have experienced deprivation during the Great Recession and how this varies across countries in terms of both personal economic, or 'pocketbook', evaluations as well as national level or 'sociotropic' economic evaluations. Moreover, we look at both retrospective and prospective evaluations, including also an intergenerational comparison with one's parents when they were the same age. Our second aim is to investigate the extent to which different social groups have experienced deprivation and the extent to which they have been and expect to continue to be affected by the economic crisis, by examining their economic evaluations and observing how these vary both cross-nationally and amongst different social groups including gender, age, socioeconomic indicators such as income, education and social class, employment status and citizenship status. In this section we address these two questions empirically by examining data from our cross-national survey carried out in 2015. Our survey contained questions asking individuals to rate their economic situation and that of the country relative to the past and relative to the future, as well as to their parents when they were the same age. The questions asked respondents to select points on a 0 to 10 scale, where 0 indicates the feeling that things were, or would be, 'much worse' and 10 indicates the feeling that things were, or would be, 'much better'.

Table 2.1 reports, for each type of economic evaluation, the proportion of individuals in that country saying that they thought things were or would get better (i.e. those selecting points 6 to 10 on the scale above). Let us analyse cross-national differences for each item in turn. These results give us a sense of the extent to which individuals feel that their situation is better than that of the previous generation, the extent to which they experienced household-level deprivation as a result of the crisis and how hopeful they are that things will get better in the future, as well as their assessments about the national economy and how well they think it has been doing and to what extent they are hopeful that it will do better in the future.

To start with, we might expect that the extent to which individuals express that they are worse off than their parents, that they have experienced deprivation and so forth, will be linked to the extent to which their country was hit by the Great Recession and therefore the proportion of individuals experiencing hard times in this context. This should hold particularly true for the household and country-level retrospective items given that these refer to events that have already occurred and do not involve expectations about the future. These might be more positive in countries where the crisis was particularly deep if

Table 2.1. Economic evaluations by country (% better; N = 14,795)

	FR	*DE*	*GR*	*IT*	*PL*	*ES*	*SE*	*CH*	*UK*
Current economic situation of your household compared to how it was 5 yrs. ago	24.5	48.3	7.6	23.8	40.4	25.1	58.5	43.9	42.7
Current economic situation of your household compared to how it was 1 yr. ago	20.3	37.7	12.2	25.1	34.5	27.0	45.9	35.0	33.9
Future economic situation (in the near future) of your household compared to now	24.2	46.4	20.5	33.2	41.4	59.7	48.9	48.0	36.5
Current state of [country]'s economy compared to 1 yr. ago	12.8	43.0	3.9	18.3	30.5	34.3	39.1	25.1	53.6
Future state of [country]'s economy (in 1 yr.) compared to now	16.5	35.5	18.4	28.3	29.2	45.2	36.4	29.2	52.2
Current standard of living compared to your parents when they were your age	39.0	60.8	32.6	40.0	52.7	51.2	68.2	62.8	62.8

Note: % based on respondents selecting points 6–10 on the 0–10 scale; Q: On a scale from 0–10, where 0 means 'much worse' and 10 means 'much better'.

individuals feel that things cannot possibly get worse and hope that some kind of positive change might appear in the horizon. In this way, by examining country levels we are able to analyse the extent to which economic evaluations are linked to the severity of the crisis in the various countries included in our study.

The first two items refer to retrospective household (or pocketbook) economic evaluations. The first asks respondents to compare their current household economic situation with five years ago and the second to compare it to one year ago. If we turn to the five-year retrospective item first, we can see that the Greek respondents stand out as those with, by far, the lowest levels thinking that the current economic situation of their household (in 2015) had improved in the past five years, since 2010. Next is a group of countries that also experienced a deep crisis, Spain and Italy, but also France. Then come Poland, the UK and Switzerland, then Germany and finally Sweden, which stands out as the country where most individuals felt that their household economic situation had improved in the last five years. The second pocketbook retrospective item asks respondents to compare their household economic situation at the time of the survey with a year earlier. Here, once more, the pattern is very similar to that of the five-year retrospective item discussed above. Greece, once more, stands out as the country with the lowest proportion of respondents whose household economic situation improved in the last year, followed by France, Italy and Spain in the next group, and then the UK, Poland, Switzerland and Germany, and once more, with the highest proportion feeling their household economic condition had improved in the last year, we find Sweden.

These figures suggest that, as expected, there is correlation between the intensity of the economic crisis and the levels of deprivation felt by individuals in different countries in terms of their household economic situation during the Great Recession. Greece, the country most hard hit, displays by far the lowest levels of respondents seeing improvements in their household financial situation. Italy and Spain tend to be in the next group, where the crisis was also quite pronounced. France stands out as a country where individuals felt a particular deterioration in their economic household situation, though it is normally classed as having experienced a less marked economic crisis relative to the so called PIIGS countries. At higher levels are Poland and the UK, also seen as countries which experienced a lower level of crisis, and Germany, Switzerland and Sweden as perhaps those where the crisis was the weakest felt of all. However, as discussed, austerity cuts were implemented across the board, even in those countries which could have avoided it given that they did not have such large deficit problems. These cuts, even more than the other indicators of economic crisis are likely to have been felt by Europeans in their 'pocketbook' evaluations.

The third item looks at pocketbook prospective evaluations and asks respondents to compare the current economic situation of their household at the time of the survey with that of a year later. Here we can see that Greece and France have the lowest levels of hopefulness that economic household conditions will improve in the near future. Individuals are a little more hopeful in Italy, the UK and, a bit more still, Poland. At a slightly higher level come Germany, Switzerland, Sweden and finally Spain, where, despite the deep crisis, respondents are very hopeful that things will get better. On the other hand, this compares to France, and even the UK, countries with an arguably much less severe economic crisis than Spain but where respondents are, regardless, relatively pessimistic about the possibility of economic improvement in their household in the near future.

The next two items look at 'sociotropic' evaluations, both retrospective and prospective. The first item asks respondents to compare the current state of the national economy relative to a year earlier, whereas the second asks to compare it to what they expect the situation of the national economy to be one year into the future. As for retrospective evaluations, we would expect, once more, patterns to map neatly along with those regarding the severity of the experiences of the crisis in different countries. Indeed, we find only a minuscule proportion feeling that the Greek economic situation had improved between 2014 and 2015. In the next group, small proportions also felt conditions had improved in France and Italy. As such, France stands out once more as a country where economic evaluations tend to be particularly negative relative to the level of crisis it experienced, suggesting that the Great Recession and the cuts to public services were possibly quite deeply felt across the population. Switzerland, Poland and Spain have higher levels of respondents feeling that the country's economic situation improved since the previous year. At even higher levels are Sweden, Germany and the UK.

With respect to prospective evaluations of the national economy, France stands out as the country with the lowest levels of respondents expecting to see an improvement, closely followed by Greece. Individuals in Italy, Poland and Switzerland were more positive, and those in Germany, Sweden, Spain and the UK, particularly so. French respondents, therefore, once more stand out as quite negative about their national economic situation, particularly when compared to other countries that suffered greater economic slowdowns. The Swiss also stand out as cautious in their optimism for improvement, whereas the Spaniards are particularly hopeful about the future prospects of their national economy.

As we have seen, an important theme in discussions over equity and inequality has been intergenerational fairness and justice, with some claiming that generations coming of age today are increasingly experiencing lower opportunities and prospects than earlier generations that grew up in the postwar boom. In this context, the last item in table 2.1 asks respondents to compare their own standard of living to that of their parents when they were the same age. As we can see, the lowest proportions thinking that their living standards are better than those of their parents were to be found in Greece, France and Italy. Once more, France appears to be more negative than other countries experiencing similar levels of economic slowdown. Next up are Poland and Spain, two countries that experienced dictatorships and totalitarian regimes into the 1970 and 1980s, and next up come Germany (where the East also experienced a regime), Switzerland, the UK, and, finally, Sweden with the highest proportion thinking they were better off.

Our main interest here, however, is not so much how economic evaluations vary across countries but rather to what extent levels of reported deprivation, and related indicators, vary between different social groups within the population of each country. Which groups in society have felt the deepest effects of the crisis? Which are the most hopeful? To answer these questions, we look at the proportion of respondents feeling that the economic situation of their household had improved in the last five years as well as the proportion thinking that economic conditions at the level of the national economy will improve in the next year across gender, age, SES and citizenship status. The two measures of economic evaluations are useful given the first picks up on the personal deprivation experienced by different groups in the period of the crisis, whereas the second one captures hopefulness that country-wide economic conditions will improve going into the future. Tables 2.2 and 2.3 report the proportions expressing positive economic evaluation of, first, pocketbook retrospective and, next, sociotropic prospective, broken down by social group and country. We can read these two tables in two ways: horizontally they tell us to what extent economic evaluations are more or less positive in different countries; vertically, and most interestingly for our present purpose, they show differences in the level of deprivation and economic hopefulness across different social categories and groups. The tables also indicate whether the group differences are statistically significant.

To begin with pocketbook retrospective evaluations (table 2.2), we can see that gender does not appear to be an important discriminating factor for household economic conditions relative to five years ago, as neither men nor women are more likely to have experienced household-level deprivation. On the other hand, belonging to different age groups (18–34, 35–64 and 65+) appears to have a greater discriminating power. The age groups are meant to capture the potential underlying impact of being in the schooling/setting up a family age, in the working or middle age or in retirement or approaching retirement, for experiences of deprivation. We observe significant differences in all nine countries in terms of age groups. Contrary to expectations, in most countries, the youngest age group is more likely than older age groups to claim that their household economic situation has improved in the last five years. In most countries, those least likely to say that conditions improved were those in the retirement age, at 65 and up, but in Greece, Italy and the UK, the middle age respondents were those least likely to say that their household economic conditions had improved between 2010 and 2015. Thus, at least at the level of the household, young people appear to be faring better than tends to be argued by theories on the precarisation of youth and the deteriorating conditions they face as they enter the labour market.

The socioeconomic indicators of education, income and class also show important patterns of cross-national differences in terms of household-level economic conditions. Seven out of nine countries have significant differences in terms of education levels, with those with the lowest educational

Table 2.2. Positive evaluation of household economic conditions relative to 5 years ago, by country and social category (% better)

	FR	*DE*	*GR*	*IT*	*PL*	*ES*	*SE*	*CH*	*UK*
Gender									
Female	23.5	46.1	8.5	23.2	41.2	24.4	57.0	42.2	40.5
Male	25.6	50.3	6.7	24.4	39.4	25.8	60.2	45.5	45.1
Age	***	***	**	*	***	*	**	***	***
18–34	39.1	57.4	10.4	27.9	46.5	29.8	63.9	56.3	56.2
35–64	22.4	46.5	5.9	22.0	37.1	23.8	59.1	39.1	39.1
65+	15.6	35.8	11.5	26.1	34.8	21.6	49.4	37.5	44.2
Education	*		*	***	**	***	***		**
University +	27.4	48.8	9.3	32.6	46.2	30.5	61.7	46.6	46.6
Secondary	25.3	49.7	5.6	22.9	38.9	25.5	59.1	41.7	43.0
< Secondary	19.8	43.1	8.9	19.5	34.9	19.5	53.3	44.5	35.7
Income	***	***	***	***	***	***	***	***	***
Lower (1–5 decile)	20.4	38.9	6.1	19.3	30.4	18.5	41.7	37.8	32.6
Higher (6–10 decile)	29.3	55.7	11.5	32.0	47.3	32.5	66.9	52.5	49.5
Occupation of chief income earner	*	***		***	**	***	***	***	***
Prof. or managerial	28.2	55.6	8.6	34.3	47.3	32.2	67.8	51.0	48.8
Intermediate	25.0	46.7	7.9	22.9	38.4	22.3	57.7	40.1	34.2
Manual	19.6	39.4	6.7	15.4	37.5	20.8	51.7	42.9	38.1
Other	22.1	43.3	5.9	16.4	35.2	22.5	40.6	34.2	39.8
Employment Status	***	***	*	***	***	***	***	***	**
Full-time	31.2	57.2	9.9	29.2	42.7	31.3	68.2	50.6	47.4
Part-time	34.8	40.1	6.6	23.8	43.1	23.0	54.0	38.3	44.1
Education	40.0	57.0	4.0	27.3	47.2	30.2	54.0	51.7	60.0
Unemployed	11.3	9.3	5.2	9.8	26.9	11.2	31.8	27.1	26.1
Retired or disabled	14.5	32.5	9.4	24.0	35.4	22.9	42.9	35.9	39.3
Caregiver	19.7	50.0	3.9	18.6	46.9	17.9	60.7	39.0	32.6
Citizenship Status	**								
Migrant	32.4	50.4	7.2	27.0	35.6	28.5	54.7	44.5	46.4
Native	22.8	47.9	7.6	23.6	40.6	24.8	59.6	43.5	42.1

Note: % based on respondents selecting points 6–10 on the 0–10 scale; Q: On a scale from 0–10, where 0 means 'much worse' and 10 means 'much better'; $N = 14,795$.
* $p < 0.05$ ** $p < 0.01$ *** $p < 0.001$

qualifications least likely to have experienced economic improvements at the household level, with the exception of Greece. Income differences are also particularly marked across the nine countries, with those showing lower incomes much less likely to have experienced an improvement in household financial situations in the previous five years. Patterns by class are also significant in eight out of nine countries, with those in manual occupations much less likely to have experienced improvements in their household economic situation than those in the intermediate or professional classes.

There are also important differences cross-nationally by employment status, following our expectations, with those in full-time employment most likely to say that their household economic situation had improved. Those in education and those in part-time employment are next likely to say that their household economic conditions had improved, followed by those in caring and retired or disabled groups. On the other hand, across countries, the unemployed are those least likely to say that their household conditions had improved. Finally, there are no significant differences based on citizenship status. Migrants were not less likely to have experienced improvement in household economic conditions.

Moving on to group differences in prospective sociotropic economic evaluations (table 2.3), we can see that here gender is a significant predictor of differences. With the exception of Greece and Sweden, women are less likely to be optimistic about the prospects for future improvement in the national economy. On the other hand, age group differences are only significant in four of the nine countries, and young people, once more, tend to be more positive than older generations, with the exception of the UK, where retirees are most positive about the future state of the national economy. On the other hand, France shows an almost opposite pattern, with particularly low levels of hopefulness for the future of the national economy amongst those in retirement, similarly to Sweden. In Switzerland, on the other hand, the lowest levels of optimism for the improvement of the country's economy are to be found amongst those in their middle age.

As far as the SES indicators are concerned, group differences appear less marked here than for household level evaluations, which follows the idea that these types of evaluations are influenced by the media and shared by people living within the same country and consuming the same modes of information. However, there are still quite important differences between people in different social groups, particularly by income and class, which suggests that individuals, at least in part, consider their own personal conditions when forming their expectations about the national economy and its prospects for future improvement. While differences by education group are less marked, being significant in only three countries (France, Italy and Spain), the lowest education group is the one that is the least hopeful about economic recovery looking into the future. On the other hand, income differences were significant in five of the nine countries, with those with lower incomes much less likely to express hopefulness about future economic recovery in Germany, Italy, Poland, Spain and the UK. This could be suggesting that despite inhabiting the same national contexts, individuals' social position impacts also on sociotropic evaluations. Income differences were significant in a mix of countries between those hard hit and those less hard hit by the crisis,

Table 2.3. Positive evaluation of country-wide economy in a year compared to now, by country and social category (% better)

	FR	*DE*	*GR*	*IT*	*PL*	*ES*	*SE*	*CH*	*UK*
Gender	***	***	*	***	*	***	***	*	*
Female	13.6	31.2	20.2	22.8	25.9	39.8	40.5	26.4	49.1
Male	19.8	39.2	16.3	33.7	33.0	50.1	32.1	31.9	55.6
Age	*						***	***	*
18–34	20.8	39.7	20.9	27.4	30.9	40.6	44.6	36.1	51.5
35–64	16.2	33.8	16.9	27.5	27.5	46.6	36.7	25.6	50.2
65+	12.4	34.7	23.1	36.6	37.1	47.7	24.7	31.8	58.7
Education	**			**		***			
University+	21.1	35.6	16.6	35.1	31.0	53.1	36.7	30.6	50.8
Secondary	14.5	37.0	19.4	27.3	28.5	45.9	38.8	27.4	54.9
< Secondary	13.8	30.4	20.4	25.5	28.5	36.9	32.8	31.4	50.6
Income		*		***	**	***			***
Low (1–5 decile)	15.0	32.6	19.3	25.6	25.5	37.8	33.5	28.3	46.3
High (6–10 decile)	18.1	37.8	16.0	33.3	31.7	53.3	37.9	30.5	56.2
Occup. of Chief Income Earner	*	*		***	*	***			**
Prof. | Mngr.	18.0	39.7	18.4	38.1	32.6	54.7	37.7	31.0	56.7
Intermediate	18.4	35.2	20.2	26.1	30.4	38.8	37.5	27.7	49.0
Manual	12.4	28.5	17.8	21.1	27.6	42.6	34.8	27.1	45.7
Other	12.9	33.7	16.4	25.5	20.7	44.4	31.3	36.0	48.2
Employment Stat.	*			***	**	***	***	*	
Full-time	17.6	37.5	17.6	31.2	29.5	50.7	39.5	31.5	53.2
Part-time	22.3	35.0	18.9	27.2	37.7	46.5	42.9	24.8	55.1
Education	23.3	37.8	20.0	30.9	41.7	39.7	44.0	37.1	55.0
Unemployed	12.1	25.9	17.8	16.8	21.3	34.8	34.9	28.0	43.5
Retired | Disabled	13.7	31.0	20.3	37.1	28.8	41.7	24.9	29.4	52.6
Caring	14.8	34.4	22.1	19.5	21.4	34.7	42.9	20.0	39.5
Citizenship Stat.	**							*	
Migrant	22.5	34.8	15.4	24.7	28.7	46.5	35.0	32.5	53.6
Native	15.2	35.7	18.8	28.5	29.2	45.1	36.8	27.0	51.9

Note: % based on respondents selecting points 6–10 on the 0–10 scale; Q: On a scale from 0–10, where 0 means 'much worse' and 10 means 'much better'; N = 14,795.
* $p < 0.05$ ** $p < 0.01$ *** $p < 0.001$

suggesting that inequalities play similar roles in evaluations across different crisis contexts. Moreover, class differences were also significant across six of the nine countries (France, Germany, Italy, Poland, Spain and the UK), with those in the manual classes much less likely to express hopeful attitudes about national economic improvement in the future and those in the professional or managerial classes the most optimistic.

We also see significant differences by employment status in six of the nine countries (France, Italy, Poland, Spain, Sweden and Switzerland), where those in full-time employment, part-time employment and in education tend to be more optimistic, with those who are unemployed in particular, but also those in caring and retired/disabled groups less likely to be optimistic. Finally, migrants are more likely to be positive about the national economic situation looking into the future in France and Switzerland.

In sum, this descriptive analysis provides a number of important insights in terms of how Europeans have experienced their household economic conditions during the crisis as well as the extent to which they are hopeful that these might improve and so forth. Firstly, we saw that there was a close link between economic evaluations and the severity of crisis experiences at the national level with countries like Greece that were particularly hard hit consistently scoring the lowest in terms of experiencing or expecting to experience improvement in their household or country-wide economic conditions. On the other hand, countries like Sweden, Germany, and Switzerland, that suffered only a very weak crisis, showed higher levels expecting improvements or expressing positive outlooks. However, respondents in some countries, such as France, were particularly negative relative to the severity of the crisis compared to other countries, whereas others, such as respondents in Spain, were particularly hopeful for the future, relative to how deep their experience of the crisis had been. Moreover, in the UK, respondents were on the whole much more positive about their national economy than their household level experiences, suggesting a disjoint between the criteria applied for evaluations of the two in the minds of respondents. Furthermore, we found that SES and employment status differences were particularly marked for household-level experiences in the past five years, whereas, while still present in many countries, they were less marked for prospective outlooks. On the other hand, gender differences appeared more relevant for looking into the future with women generally more negative about the chances for improvement of the national economy.

CORRELATES OF ECONOMIC EVALUATIONS

In the previous section we examined descriptive patterns. However, in order to assess which variables are most important for predicting whether someone will have experienced an improvement in living standards or not during the economic crisis we need to include the different variables into models which control for the other variables at the same time. We conduct step-wide models by introducing different types of factors in turn: first we include gender, then age, then the SES variables (education, income and occupational class); next we include employment status, then citizenship status, the extent to which the respondent had to reduce their consumption of staple goods as a result of the crisis, the extent to which the crisis impacted on their work situation; and, finally, three social capital measures (social trust, how often the respondent met with friends and their associational membership) given what we said earlier about these being understood as relevant predictors for being better able to cope with difficult situations.

In the regression models, we take into account country differences by estimating multilevel regression models that treat country variation as random effects. The results of this analysis are shown in tables 2.4 and 2.5, respectively for household retrospective evaluations relative to five years ago and country-wide prospective economic evaluations in the next year. We ran eight models, each including, in turn, the variables or groups of variables discussed above. All the models have been set at the same number of cases so as to makes statistical tests comparable across models.

First, we look at household level retrospective evaluations in the five-year framework (table 2.4), starting with model 1, which looks at gender effects. The results show that women are less likely than men to say that their household economic situation has improved between 2010 and 2015, reflecting arguments in the literature that women have been particularly hard hit by the Great Recession. Model 2 introduces age and shows that the middle age and older age groups are less likely, relative to the youngest age group, to say that their household economic conditions had improved in the last five years. It also shows that the effect of gender increases when age is included in the model, suggesting that it is in particular middle age and retired women that have suffered deprivation during the 2010 to 2015 period. This is consistent with discussions of how the cuts in particular are likely to have impacted women who are more likely to be in caring roles and to be reliant on public services for support.

Model 3 introduces the SES variables. Results show that when we control for all the relevant variables, there remain independent effects of income and class, whereas education is not significant. Individuals with lower incomes are less likely to have experienced an improvement in their household economic situations than those with a higher income, and individuals in the manual, intermediate and other (mainly, farming) classes are less likely to have experienced an improvement in their household conditions. Including the SES variables in the model leaves the effects of gender and age in place, suggesting that they are independent. In model 4 we include employment status and we find that individuals that are employed part time, are in education, are unemployed, are retired or disabled or are in caring roles are all less likely than those in professional roles to have experienced improvements in their household living conditions. Introducing employment status removes the effect of gender, suggesting that women's employment status underlies why they are less likely than men to have experienced an improvement in their conditions, for example, due to their greater representation amongst caring roles or more precarious employment arrangements. All the other effects of age and the SES variables remained when employment status was included, suggesting that they operate in their own right.

Turning to model 5, which includes citizenship status, there is no effect of being a migrant on one's household-level evaluations. However, including the objective grievance variable for reduced consumption in model 6 shows that the effect of being a migrant becomes significant and suggests that amongst those migrants that had to reduce consumption they were less likely to express that their household conditions had improved. Individuals who had to reduce consumption were less likely to say their household conditions had improved. The other variables' effects remain as those from the previous models. The same is true in model 7, which includes a variable measuring whether individuals experienced negative impacts on their work conditions as a result of the crisis which also has a negative effect, as might be expected, on whether someone experienced an improvement in their household conditions. Finally, model 8 includes the three social capital variables: social trust, whether someone met friends at least once a week and associational membership. All three factors are linked to a higher likelihood of having experienced an improvement in household economic conditions, while the effects of the other variables in the model remain as previously discussed. The inclusion of the social capital variables reduces the effects of social class, suggesting that such effects depend in part on having higher stocks of social capital.

Moving to prospective country-level economic evaluations (Table 2.5), model 1 includes gender and shows that women are less likely than men to expect economic improvement at the national level in the next year. Model 2 includes age and shows that the middle- and retired-age groups are less likely to expect improvements than young people, with a slight increase in the effect of gender with its inclusion, suggesting, as was found before, that it is particularly middle-age and retired women with the more negative expectations. These findings thus support the literature in its theorising that women are in particularly vulnerable economic positions and likely to have suffered in the Great Recession.

Model 3 includes the socioeconomic variables and shows that while income and class have an effect, education does not. Individuals with lower incomes and those in intermediate, manual and other (mainly, farming) classes are much less likely than those in professional occupations to have positive expectations for the future of the country's economy. Moreover, model 4 includes employment status and shows that there are smaller differences on

Table 2.4. Multilevel regression models on positive household economic evaluations retrospective to 5 years ago

Model	*(1)*	*(2)*	*(3)*	*(4)*	*(5)*	*(6)*	*(7)*	*(8)*
Sociodemographic characteristics								
Gender (female)	–0.09*	–0.13***	–0.10*	–0.05	–0.05	–0.02	–0.02	–0.01
	(0.04)	(0.04)	(0.04)	(0.04)	(0.04)	(0.04)	(0.04)	(0.04)
Age groups (ref.: 18–34)								
35–64	–	–0.49***	–0.55***	–0.55***	–0.55***	–0.59***	–0.59***	–0.61***
	–	(0.04)	(0.04)	(0.05)	(0.05)	(0.05)	(0.05)	(0.05)
65+	–	–0.64***	–0.71***	–0.46***	–0.45***	–0.65***	–0.68***	–0.74***
	–	(0.07)	(0.07)	(0.09)	(0.09)	(0.09)	(0.09)	(0.09)
Education group (ref.: university +)								
Secondary	–	–	–0.03	–0.00	0.00	0.03	0.02	0.05
	–	–	(0.05)	(0.05)	(0.05)	(0.05)	(0.05)	(0.05)
< secondary	–	–	–0.08	–0.03	–0.03	0.03	0.00	0.07
	–	–	(0.05)	(0.06)	(0.06)	(0.06)	(0.06)	(0.06)
Income (low; 1–5 decile)	–	–	–0.65***	–0.57***	–0.57***	–0.34***	–0.34***	–0.35***
	–	–	(0.04)	(0.04)	(0.04)	(0.04)	(0.04)	(0.04)
Occup. of chief income earner (ref. prof. | mngr.)								
Intermediate	–	–	–0.27***	–0.27***	–0.27***	–0.25***	–0.26***	–0.24***
	–	–	(0.05)	(0.05)	(0.05)	(0.05)	(0.05)	(0.05)
Manual	–	–	–0.37***	–0.33***	–0.33***	–0.28***	–0.28***	–0.24***
	–	–	(0.06)	(0.06)	(0.06)	(0.06)	(0.06)	(0.06)
Other	–	–	–0.51***	–0.43***	–0.43***	–0.40***	–0.41***	–0.38***
	–	–	(0.08)	(0.08)	(0.08)	(0.08)	(0.08)	(0.08)
Employment status (ref. full–time)								
Part–time	–	–	–	–0.26***	–0.26***	–0.19**	–0.18**	–0.20***
	–	–	–	(0.06)	(0.06)	(0.06)	(0.06)	(0.06)
In education	–	–	–	–0.23*	–0.23*	–0.23*	–0.25*	–0.27**
	–	–	–	(0.10)	(0.10)	(0.10)	(0.10)	(0.10)

Unemployed	–	–	–	−0.99***	−0.99***	−0.82***	−0.81***	−0.81***
	–	–	–	(0.08)	(0.08)	(0.09)	(0.09)	(0.09)
Retired | Disabled	–	–	–	−0.47***	−0.47***	−0.46***	−0.50***	−0.50***
	–	–	–	(0.07)	(0.07)	(0.07)	(0.07)	(0.07)
Caring	–	–	–	−0.31***	−0.31***	−0.32***	−0.37***	−0.35***
	–	–	–	(0.09)	(0.09)	(0.09)	(0.10)	(0.10)
Citizenship status (migrant)	–	–	–	–	0.06	0.11*	0.11*	0.11*
	–	–	–	–	(0.05)	(0.05)	(0.05)	(0.05)
Objective grievances								
Reduced consumption	–	–	–	–	–	−2.11***	−1.92***	−1.89***
	–	–	–	–	–	(0.09)	(0.09)	(0.09)
Crisis impacted work situation	–	–	–	–	–	–	−0.48***	−0.49***
	–	–	–	–	–	–	(0.09)	(0.09)
Social capital								
Social trust	–	–	–	–	–	–	–	0.74***
	–	–	–	–	–	–	–	(0.08)
Met friends at least 1x per wk.	–	–	–	–	–	–	–	0.11**
	–	–	–	–	–	–	–	(0.04)
Associational membership	–	–	–	–	–	–	–	0.12**
	–	–	–	–	–	–	–	(0.04)
Constant	−0.68*	−0.28	0.30	0.40	0.39	0.81***	0.94***	0.47*
	(0.27)	(0.28)	(0.26)	(0.25)	(0.25)	(0.20)	(0.19)	(0.19)
Log likelihood	−8,802.76	−8,725.23	−8,489.29	−8,393.93	−8,393.31	−8,054.84	−8,040.61	−7,981.75
AIC	17,611.51	17,460.46	17,000.59	16,819.86	16,820.61	16,145.68	16,119.21	16,007.49
BIC	17,634.32	17,498.47	17,084.21	16,941.49	16,949.85	16,282.52	16,263.65	16,174.74
Sigma u	0.80	0.82	0.77	0.74	0.73	0.56	0.55	0.53
Rho	0.16	0.17	0.15	0.14	0.14	0.09	0.08	0.08

Standard errors in parentheses; *N*=14,795
* $p < 0.05$ ** $p < 0.01$ *** $p < 0.001$

Table 2.5. Multilevel regression models on positive country-wide economic evaluations prospective to a year from now

Model	*(1)*	*(2)*	*(3)*	*(4)*	*(5)*	*(6)*	*(7)*	*(8)*
Sociodemographic characteristics								
Gender (female)	−0.23***	−0.25***	−0.23***	−0.22***	−0.22***	−0.21***	−0.22***	−0.20***
	(0.04)	(0.04)	(0.04)	(0.04)	(0.04)	(0.04)	(0.04)	(0.04)
Age groups (ref. 18–34)								
35–64	–	−0.20***	−0.21***	−0.19***	−0.19***	−0.19***	−0.20***	−0.23***
	–	(0.04)	(0.04)	(0.05)	(0.05)	(0.05)	(0.05)	(0.05)
65+	–	−0.14*	−0.17*	−0.06	−0.06	−0.14	−0.16	−0.25**
	–	(0.07)	(0.07)	(0.09)	(0.09)	(0.09)	(0.09)	(0.09)
Education group (ref. university +)								
Secondary	–	–	0.02	0.03	0.03	0.04	0.03	0.08
	–	–	(0.04)	(0.04)	(0.04)	(0.04)	(0.04)	(0.05)
< secondary	–	–	−0.09	−0.06	−0.06	−0.03	−0.06	0.02
	–	–	(0.05)	(0.05)	(0.05)	(0.05)	(0.05)	(0.06)
Income (low; 1–5 decile)	–	–	−0.22***	−0.20***	−0.20***	−0.08*	−0.08*	−0.09*
	–	–	(0.04)	(0.04)	(0.04)	(0.04)	(0.04)	(0.04)
Occup. of chief income earner (ref. prof. | mngr.)								
Intermediate	–	–	−0.16***	−0.16***	−0.16***	−0.15**	−0.15**	−0.13**
	–	–	(0.05)	(0.05)	(0.05)	(0.05)	(0.05)	(0.05)
Manual	–	–	−0.27***	−0.25***	−0.26***	−0.23***	−0.23***	−0.18**
	–	–	(0.06)	(0.06)	(0.06)	(0.06)	(0.06)	(0.06)
Other	–	–	−0.27***	−0.24***	−0.24***	−0.23**	−0.24**	−0.18*
	–	–	(0.07)	(0.07)	(0.07)	(0.07)	(0.07)	(0.07)
Employment status (ref. full-time)								
Part-time	–	–	–	0.06	0.05	0.09	0.10	0.08
	–	–	–	(0.06)	(0.06)	(0.06)	(0.06)	(0.06)
In education	–	–	–	0.03	0.03	0.04	0.02	−0.00
	–	–	–	(0.10)	(0.10)	(0.10)	(0.10)	(0.10)

Unemployed	–	–	–	−0.31***	−0.31***	−0.22**	−0.21**	−0.20**
	–	–	–	(0.07)	(0.07)	(0.07)	(0.07)	(0.07)
Retired | Disabled	–	–	–	−0.16*	−0.16*	−0.15*	−0.19**	−0.18**
	–	–	–	(0.07)	(0.07)	(0.07)	(0.07)	(0.07)
Caring	–	–	–	−0.24**	−0.25**	−0.25**	−0.29**	−0.28**
	–	–	–	(0.09)	(0.09)	(0.09)	(0.09)	(0.10)
Citizenship status (migrant)	–	–	–	–	0.07	0.09	0.09	0.08
	–	–	–	–	(0.05)	(0.05)	(0.05)	(0.05)
Objective grievances								
Reduced consumption	–	–	–	–	–	−0.92***	−0.75***	−0.69***
	–	–	–	–	–	(0.08)	(0.08)	(0.09)
Crisis impacted work situation	–	–	–	–	–	–	−0.44***	−0.44***
	–	–	–	–	–	–	(0.08)	(0.09)
Social capital								
Social trust	–	–	–	–	–	–	–	1.08***
	–	–	–	–	–	–	–	(0.08)
Met friends at least 1x per wk.	–	–	–	–	–	–	–	0.08*
	–	–	–	–	–	–	–	(0.04)
Associational membership	–	–	–	–	–	–	–	0.07
	–	–	–	–	–	–	–	(0.04)
Constant	−0.67***	−0.52**	−0.26	−0.26	−0.27	−0.10	0.02	−0.58***
	(0.17)	(0.18)	(0.18)	(0.18)	(0.18)	(0.16)	(0.17)	(0.16)
Log likelihood	−8,913.15	−8,902.59	−8,852.00	−8,834.68	−8,833.79	−8,760.48	−8,746.72	−8,630.89
AIC	17,832.30	17,815.17	17,725.99	17,701.36	17,701.58	17,556.97	17,531.43	17,305.77
BIC	17,855.11	17,853.18	17,809.62	17,822.99	17,830.81	17,693.80	17,675.87	17,473.02
Sigma u	0.52	0.52	0.50	0.50	0.50	0.46	0.47	0.43
Rho	0.08	0.08	0.07	0.07	0.07	0.06	0.06	0.05

Standard errors in parentheses; $N = 14,795$.
* $p < 0.05$ ** $p < 0.01$ *** $p < 0.001$

this basis relative to those for household retrospective evaluations. The key difference here is between the unemployed, retired/disabled and those in caring roles and full-time employees, whereas those in part-time employment or those in education are not less positive than full-time workers. Moreover, the effect of being in the older age group is gone, suggesting that it is particularly people in retirement or caring roles that are more pessimistic about the future of the economy amongst those in the oldest age group.

Moving on to model 5, which also includes citizenship status, we can see that there are no significant effects in this respect. Thus, nationals and migrants do not have substantially distinct evaluations about how the economy would fare one year into the future. On the other hand, model 6, which includes the variable for reduced consumption, shows that individuals experiencing this were more negative about the changes for improvement in the national economy's future. The inclusion of this variable particularly erodes the effect of unemployment, suggesting that those unemployed people who had to make reductions in consumption were particularly likely to say that they did not expect things to improve in the future of the national economy. As such, it seems that some types of personal experiences of the crisis do end up having an impact on wider, sociotropic evaluations as well. Similarly, those who experienced a deterioration of their work conditions due to the crisis were also less likely to expect improvement in the national economy in the following year, once more underscoring the idea that personal experience impacts economic evaluations also at the national level, at least amongst certain groups. Finally, the inclusion of the social capital variables in model 8 shows that this kind of resource is related to more positive prospective sociotropic evaluations but not associational membership, and that it has a large influence on whether older people are more or less positive about the national economy. There is also a relatively large erosion in the effect of class, showing that part of this effect passes through social capital.

Thus far we have examined the results of regression analyses to understand the predictors of pocketbook and sociotropic economic evaluations in times of crisis. Before discussing the implications of our findings in the concluding section, we examine how certain social categories and groups are predicted to evaluate their households' economic conditions retrospectively and countries' economic conditions prospectively based on various characteristics. While we have examined, so far, the effect of each variable in turn, here we examine how individuals with different combinations of belonging to social groups might score. Tables 2.6 and 2.7 show the combination of gender, class, age and education effects on both household retrospectives and country-level prospective evaluations. Results show there are important cumulative effects. While 46 percent of younger men in professional occupations with a

Table 2.6. Predicted probabilities of positive household evaluations relative to 5 years ago depending on gender, age, education and occupation (% better)

		Male		Female	
Occupation	*Education*	*18–34*	*65+*	*18–34*	*65+*
Professional or managerial	University +	46.4	22.7	45.2	21.9
	< Secondary	47.1	23.2	45.9	22.4
Manual	University +	40.4	18.7	39.3	18.0
	< Secondary	41.1	19.2	39.9	18.4

Note: Based on estimates from a multilevel logistic regression with all the predictors as in model of table 2.4 (except that employment status was replaced by just a dummy for unemployed); N = 14,795.

Table 2.7. Predicted probabilities of positive country-wide evaluations in a year relative to now depending on gender, age, education and occupation (% better)

		Male		Female	
Occupation	*Education*	*18–34*	*65+*	*18–34*	*65+*
Professional or managerial	University +	39.1	30.2	34.3	26.0
	< Secondary	39.1	30.3	34.3	26.1
Manual	University +	34.9	26.5	30.3	22.7
	< Secondary	34.9	26.6	30.4	22.7

Note: Based on estimates from a multilevel logistic regression with all the predictors as in model of table 2.5 (except that employment status was replaced by just a dummy for unemployed); N = 14,795.

university or higher education hold positive retrospective household-level evaluations, only about 18 percent of older females in the manual class and with lower education do (table 2.6). For prospective country-level evaluations, differences are not as large but we can see that while about 39 percent of younger men in professional occupations and with a university or higher education hold positive retrospective household level evaluations, only about 23 percent of older females in the manual class and with lower education do (table 2.7).

As for the combination of belonging to the two specific groups of the unemployed and migrants, which are potentially more vulnerable to the negative effects of the economic crisis and related austerity measures, tables 2.8 and 2.9 show that the major differences are between those in employment and those outside of employment with differences between migrants and non-migrants being minimal. Moreover, being a migrant is associated with more positive economic evaluations. About 34 percent of employed migrants have positive retrospective household evaluations (table 2.8), whereas 19 percent of unemployed natives do (table 2.9). About 32 percent of employed migrants

Table 2.8. Predicted probabilities of positive household evaluations relative to 5 years ago depending on employment and citizenship status (% better)

	Employed	*Unemployed*
Native	31.4	18.9
Migrant	33.6	20.5

Note: Based on estimates from a multilevel logistic regression with all the predictors as in model of table 2.4 (except that employment status was replaced by just a dummy for unemployed); $N = 14{,}795$.

Table 2.9. Predicted probabilities of positive country-wide evaluations in a year relative to now depending on employment and citizenship status (% better)

	Employed	*Unemployed*
Native	30.6	27.0
Migrant	32.4	28.6

Note: Based on estimates from a multilevel logistic regression with all the predictors as in model of table 2.5 (except that employment status was replaced by just a dummy for unemployed); $N = 14{,}795$.

have positive prospective country-wide evaluations (table 2.8), but only about 27 percent of native unemployed do (table 2.9).

CONCLUSION

In this chapter we analysed the effects of the Great Recession on citizen experiences of deprivation and their perceptions of economic conditions. The crisis has deteriorated living standards and economic conditions of many individuals across Europe and has generated feelings of deprivation. It has also increasingly led to an increased focus on issues of inequity and inequality. Such perceptions of economic deprivation, however, are likely to depend on individuals' structural positions, for example, class belonging and other sociodemographic factors such as gender. We examined how Europeans perceived the impact of the crisis on their own economic situations and on that of their countries at large, to what extent individuals felt that the crisis had impacted on their lives, how they rated their living standards in relation to the past, as well as how hopeful they were that these, as well as their country's economy, would improve in the future. In brief, we addressed the relationship between deprivation, class and inequality in order to show how the crisis has impacted the ways in which Europeans view their own situations and how this varies based on their social positions in society.

We focussed on two types of economic evaluations in particular: retrospective household-level (pocketbook) and prospective country-level (sociotropic). While the former is closely linked to individuals' experiences of the crisis in their personal lives and in the contraction of living standards, the latter also introduces a wider look and an element of hope for the future. The results of this chapter showed that both types of evaluations are linked to the severity of the crisis in different national contexts to some extent. In those countries hardest hit by the crisis, perceptions tended to be less positive. However, there were also some exceptions to this simple linear pattern between severity of the crisis and perceptions of individuals. For example, in countries such as France, which did not do too poorly in relative terms during the crisis, evaluations were more negative than would have been expected. This suggests that the ways in which austerity cuts are felt at the level of the population might vary with respect to the intensity of the crisis at the national level in terms of macroeconomic indicators. Moreover, sharp changes such as neoliberal reforms in contexts such as France, that have resisted these moves for a long time, might have resulted in more marked negative effects at the level of the population and in the daily lived experiences of individuals, as well as for their sense of hope that things might go better in the future.

Individuals across Europe did not see their living standards improve much during the 2010 to 2015 period and they are not particularly hopeful that the national economies might fare better in the future. Moreover, there are important group-based differences in both retrospective pocketbook and prospective sociotropic evaluations. In particular, women, individuals in lower social classes and with lower incomes, as well as those in more precarious employment situations were less likely to have experienced improvement in living standards or to say that they expected the national economy to get better. We also saw that the impact of factors is cumulative, with younger and better-off men more positive than older, working-class women.

Thus, our results indicate that, as expected, individuals in less vulnerable positions and with more resources were much better able to weather the crisis, to experience better living standards, and to be optimistic about future improvement in national economy. On the other hand, the opposite was true for those occupying higher risk positions in the social structure. Finally, we also examined the role of another kind of resource, namely social capital. We found both a direct and an indirect effect—through social class—in terms of social trust, the frequency of meeting with friends and membership in voluntary associations. This kind of resource, as we shall see in the next chapter, is particularly important once we consider the extent to which individuals can be resilient to the negative effects of the economic crisis.

Chapter Three

Crisis and Resilience

In the previous chapter, we examined the extent to which the economic crisis and austerity measures impacted divergently on different social categories and groups, how they related to the feelings of deprivation amongst the population and how such feelings might be linked depend to certain structural factors such as class position. Individuals, however, are not simply passive recipients of whatever happens to them. Generally, they react to challenging external occurrences such as accidents, serious illnesses or other events that upsets one's own life. This also applies to deep economic losses and other related negative effects of economic downturns. Individuals are often resilient to these kinds of negative external events. Such a capacity for resilience, of course, is not distributed equally amongst people, as some are more resilient than others. The capacity for resilience depends on the possession of certain individual resources, such as psychological strength and determination, as well as relational resources.

This chapter deals with the relationship between deprivation, social capital and resilience. It looks at the ways in which individuals have been able to become resilient to the negative effects of the economic crisis and addresses two main research questions: (1) To what extent does the capacity of resilience of individuals vary across countries and, above all, across social categories and groups?; and (2) How does resilience link to factors such as the social characteristics of people, their perceptions of the state of the economy, the ways in which governments are dealing with the economic crisis—so-called sociotropic evaluations—feelings of relative deprivation and the perceptions of the crisis on one's personal situation—so-called egotropic or pocketbook evaluations—and to the broader social networks at one's disposal and the social capital they may generate? Concerning the latter aspect, in particular, we argue that the capacity for resilience depends not only on individuals' financial means but also on the availability of social support and, more generally, the level of social capital stemming from their web of social relations and their respective capacities for resilience. This chapter therefore complements the previous chapter's analysis of the individual perceptions of the negative effects of the crisis by focussing on the ways in which individuals have been able to pose resistance to these in their everyday lives. We also look at how such a capacity for resilience varies across social groups to investigate if we find patterns of inequality as we did for the negative perceptions of the effects of the crisis also in this respect.

The next section discusses, from a theoretical point of view, the linkages between economic crises, individual hardship and resilience. In this regard, we distinguish between two broad forms of resilience: *proactive* and *community-based* resilience. We then address, again theoretically, how social support and social capital, more generally, might mitigate the negative effects of the crisis. The following two sections are then devoted to an empirical assessment of Europeans' capacity for resilience. Firstly, we examine how such a capacity varies both across the nine countries included in our study as well as across social groups as we did also in the previous chapter. Secondly, we adopt a more explanatory approach to investigate the correlates of resilience, that is, which macro-level and micro-level factors are associated with the capacity for resilience displayed by individuals.

ECONOMIC CRISIS, HARDSHIP, AND RESILIENCE

This chapter focusses on the capacity for resilience that individuals in the nine countries covered by our study have or have not been able to show during the Great Recession. However, the question arises: What do we mean by resilience? This is a tricky and perhaps abused—sometimes even misused—concept. It is employed in a variety of disciplines and subdisciplines but, for what interests us here, primarily in sociology and psychology. Resilience can be generally defined as 'the capability of a strained body to recover its size and shape after deformation caused especially by compressive stress', or 'an ability to recover from or adjust easily to misfortune or change'.[1] Our usage of the concept comes closer to the way in which it is generally defined in psychology:

> resilience is the process of adapting well in the face of adversity, trauma, tragedy, threats or significant sources of stress—such as family and relationship problems, serious health problems or workplace and financial stressors. It means 'bouncing back' from difficult experiences.[2]

Thus, we mainly refer to the capacity of individuals to resist the negative consequences of the economic crisis and the austerity policies enacted by governments in response to it. This, however, only covers one side of what we would like to capture. It is an individualistic definition referring to how one reacts and resists, as an individual, to potentially negative external events and situations.

A number of works have recently used the notion of resilience with reference to collective initiatives to cope with the effects of the economic crisis. This body of literature focusses on what has been referred to by some as 'social resilience' (Batty and Cole 2010; Hall and Lamont 2013), by others as 'alternative forms of resilience' and by others still as 'social economy' (Laville 2010), 'solidarity (or solidary) economy', and the like. These notions, however, stretch beyond the more specific focus on resilience to the economic crisis—hence stressing the collective dimension of the efforts made to deal with hard times. They refer to alternative economic practices, located at the crossroads of the political and the social and initiated by citizen groups and networks (Kousis and Paschou 2017). They include a wide variety of innovative activities and social relations such as solidary bartering, local-exchange trading schemes, local and alternative currencies, ethical banks, local market cooperatives, cooperatives for the supply of social services such as in health and education, alternative forms of production, critical consumption, spontaneous actions of resistance and reclamation, and the reproduction of cultural knowledge via oral and artistic expression (Giugni and Grasso 2019a). They also include, following a social movement perspective, sustainable community movement organisations (Forno and Graziano 2014), that is, new collective initiatives which empower consumer and producer networks on a smaller scale.

While we do not deal directly with such actions and initiatives here, the related literature directs our attention to the collective dimension of resilience and more specifically to its community dimension. Accordingly, in the analyses below, in addition to the individual-based form of resilience to the economic crisis and related austerity policies, which we call proactive resilience, we also examine what we term community-based resilience. This refers broadly to the relationship that individuals have with the communities in which they live and, more specifically, with feelings of attachment to those communities. The rationale behind this form of resilience is that a strong attachment to the community is both a component of how one reacts to negative external events and situations such as, for example, the hardship generated by an economic crisis, as well as something that helps them react positively to such events and situations.

Both forms of resilience become important on certain occasions. The hardship caused by a deep and long-lasting economic recession such as the one that we are dealing with in this book is certainly one example. In times of increased social vulnerability, there is a growing emphasis on the individual's resilience and responsibility to bounce back and stand against economic hardship and a decreasing emphasis on social solidarity as an institution (Clegg and Clasen 2011; Hemerijck 2012). In times of crisis, there is an increased risk of diminishing solidarity associated with the emergence of new divides between weak and strong social groups, as well as broader adverse social situations. At the same time, the distance between the winners and the losers of the global economy becomes greater, and conventional wisdom about when and why economic growth fails to trickle down as well as assistance for the most vulnerable is challenged (Kenworthy 2011).

Given the profound impact that the Great Recession and austerity measures have had on the citizenry, especially in some countries, we have to ask: To what extent are individuals able to become resilient to the negative effects of these events? Do people passively suffer from whatever happens to them or, as it is more likely, are they able to proactively adapt to new situations and conditions? In other words, are they passive objects of external events or do they show agency in facing such events? Work in sociology, psychology and social psychology shows how individuals find ways to pull themselves out of adversity as well as out of difficult times and situations—including financial hardship—often in quite creative and unusual fashions. The psychological literature, in particular, commonly uses concepts of coping and coping strategies to refer to the responses to adversity and the distress that results from it (Carver and Connor-Smith 2010; Folkman and Moscowitz 2004). Similarly, the sociological literature refers to survival or coping strategies, often in relation to marginal groups such as ethnic minorities or the poor (Wallace 1993). Whether one uses the notion of coping—especially in terms of coping strategies—the underlying idea is that of an agentic individual able not only to adapt to adversity but also to move beyond it. This applies, in our case, to the extent to which individuals have been able to proactively react to the negative consequences of the economic crisis and its related austerity policies.

Not everybody, however, has the same ability to respond to external events and situations. Thus, the question is also: Who is more endowed to be resilient to the negative effects of the economic crisis and related austerity measures? In this regard, one may expect particularly vulnerable people to be less resourceful and therefore to have a lower capacity to be resilient to adversity. This could be the case, for example, for migrants and the unemployed, which have been shown to lack resources (Morales and Giugni 2011). Not only does the specific status of these two groups often create the preconditions for social vulnerability and feelings of deprivation leading to greater psychological weakness, but their attachment to the broader community in which they live may also be lower and therefore meaning they have lower levels of social support in adversity more generally. On the other hand, one could also argue that it is precisely because of vulnerability and deprivation that an individual must becomes more resilient and strengthens what we call proactive resilience. This has been shown, for example, by research on people experiencing job loss, unemployment—especially long-term unemployment (Beck et al. 2005), social-assistance recipients (Marttila et al. 2010), immigrants (Aysa-Lastra and Cachón 2015) and still other social categories and groups. Furthermore, people belonging to these social groups might well have weaker ties with their broader communities and populations, but at the same time they might also show stronger attachments to narrower communities or groups to which they belong, which might in turn favour what we call community-based resilience. The important point here is that the capacity for resilience might vary depending on the social status of individuals, but also on the extent to which they are able to activate certain resources that might make them more likely to become resilient to adversity. This leads us to move on to discussing next these other resources and, more generally, the factors that may be associated to resilience.

WHERE DOES RESILIENCE COME FROM? THE ROLE OF HUMAN AND SOCIAL CAPITAL

While resilience is, at least following our approach in this chapter, an individual resource, whereby some people have more of it than others, such a resource does not come from nowhere. As we said earlier, some individuals are more likely than others to be resilient to the economic crisis and its negative effects. This depends, at least in part, on whether they possess other resources that might help them become more resilient. Two such resources have been shown to play a key role in this respect: human capital and social capital.

The concept of human capital has important roots in certain strands of economics (Becker 1993; Mincer 1958; Schultz 1961) and has been used extensively in a variety of subdisciplines such as, for example, organisational studies (Burton-Jones and Spender 2011). It may be defined broadly as knowledge and skills with education being a key component—or a determinant—of human capital (Becker 1993). Moreover, it has also been found to be a strong determinant of involvement in politics (Berinsky and Lenz 2011)—an aspect to which we pay special attention to in this book—as it tends to be associated with higher resources and skills for making sense of information spurring political action (Grasso 2013). Thus, human capital—and, more specifically, education—may be expected to play an important role in increasing the ability of individuals to be resilient to economic hardship: the more human capital and education one has, the more resilient one should be. In our analysis of the correlates of resilience below, we will therefore include education as a major source of the capacity for resilience to the economic crisis.

Of course, the capacity for resilience may be associated with individual characteristics other than skills and knowledge, that is, human capital and, more specifically, education. For example, people's financial and economic endowment should make them more resilient or, obviously, at least less vulnerable to the negative effects of the crisis. Similarly, and relatedly, occupation might play a role as well. This is a more structural aspect that does not directly pertain to human capital. Yet, it is part of a broader notion of social class which might also be related to the capacity for resilience. In brief, we may expect richer individuals and individuals from upper social classes to be more endowed with human capital and, therefore, to display a stronger capacity for resilience, with particular reference to the ability to cope with the economic crisis.

Human capital subsumes a number of individual characteristics that may or may not lead to greater resilience in adversity. Another set of factors pertains to what is often referred to as social capital. This is a broad notion that has become popular in political science especially since seminal works by Putnam (1993, 2000), but other key contributions have been made both before and after, especially in sociology (Bourdieu 1985; Coleman 1988, 1990; Lin 2001; see Stolle 2007 for a review). This literature points to two approaches to social capital: a group-level approach (Putnam 9993, 2000) that stresses the collective goods and sees social capital as 'features of social organisations, such as networks, norms, and trust, that facilitate action and cooperation for mutual benefit' (Putnam 1993: 36), on the one hand, and an individual level approach (Coleman 1988, 1990) that focusses on individual resources and according to which 'social capital stands for the ability of actors to secure benefits by virtue of membership in social networks or other social structures' (Portes 1998: 6), on the other. In both cases, social capital can be seen as a specific kind of resource linked to the structure of relations amongst groups or individuals (Giugni and Lorenzini 2017).

We believe that the ability to secure benefits mentioned by Portes (1998) as well as the networks, norms and trust which Putnam (1993) alludes to—in brief, the resources that can be acquired through investment in social networks and ties—can have a positive impact on the individuals' capacity for becoming resilient to economic hardship and, more specifically, the negative effects of the crisis and austerity policies. One hypothesis in this regard could be that the more social capital one has, the stronger one's capacity for resilience. We will explore this hypothesis empirically in our analysis below by including relational variables.

Social relations, however, can impinge upon resilience not only by virtue of the social capital that they are able to generate but also by providing more tangible resources, for example, in the form of social support. Research has shown that the resources provided by the social support individuals receive from various relational circles—partners, parents, friends, and so forth—can alleviate or compensate for the potential negative consequences of unemployment or, at least, reduce them (Broman et al. 2001; Gore 1978; Huffman et al. 2015; Kieselbach 2003; Lorenzini and Giugni 2011; Thoits 1995). Thus, social relations may not only be a potential source of social capital but can also provide the emotional, financial and material resources needed to cope with hardship and difficult times, such as a situation of enduring unemployment. While our analysis does not allow us to distinguish, in a clear-cut fashion, whether a hypothetical impact on resilience stems from social capital or other resources provided by the support received from various social relations, by including social trust along with two relational variables in our analyses—namely, frequency of meeting with friends and associational involvement—we can aim to address the mechanisms at work. More generally, however, we wish to examine whether resilience is associated with relational resources, in addition to those discussed earlier with reference to human capital.

In addition to examining the direct effect of social relations on the capacity of proactive and community-based resilience, we will also consider their indirect effect. More specifically, we would like to inquire into the potential moderating effect of social relations on the two forms of resilience, i.e. proactive and community-based. The capacity for resilience may be enhanced by the resources such relations provide, but the latter might also alter the effect of some other variables, such as those pertaining to human capital. We shall consider such an indirect impact in our analysis below.

Finally, when confronting resilience theory with our survey data below, we will also consider other potential correlates of the two forms of resilience we have distinguished. In particular, we pay attention to those aspects most closely related to the economic crisis and austerity policies, such as perceptions of the severity of the crisis, feelings of relative deprivation and perceptions about the impact of the crisis on one's own life. We will take into account the extent to which such views, feelings and perceptions impinge upon individuals' capacities for resilience but also whether and how their impact depends on social capital and support resulting from a dense web of social relations.

WHO IS MOST RESILIENT?

At the start of this chapter, we outlined two main research questions. The first asks to what extent Europeans have proved resilient to the Great Recession as well as its negative consequences and how their capacity for resilience varies across countries, as well as across social categories and groups. In this section, we address this question from an empirical point of view. Our survey contained a question aimed at capturing the capacity for resilience of respondents as well as their sense of belonging to the community in which they live. The question read as follows: 'Please rate each of the following items on a scale from 0 to 10 where 0 means 'Completely unlike me' and 10 means 'Just like me'. Six response items were then offered: 'I look for creative ways to alter difficult situations'; 'I actively look for ways to replace the losses I encounter in life'; 'I have a hard time making it through stressful events'; 'I keep myself active in the community where I live'; 'I feel that I do not have much in common with the larger community in which I live'; 'No one in the community where I live seems to care much about me'. The latter two items refer to the sentiment of not being considered or 'accepted' in some way by one's community.

Let us first take a look at each of these items in turn with respect to cross-national patterns. Table 3.1 shows the means of each of the six items in the nine countries covered by our study. This gives us a rough sense of 'how resilient' people in different countries are on average. We theorise that the capacity for resilience as aggregated at the country level is likely to depend on how hard a given country was hit by the economic crisis and, therefore, on how many people have gone through particularly hard times in economic or financial terms. This holds especially for the first three items, which explicitly refer to difficult situations, losses or stressful events. So, by looking at the overall means in each country we are able to ascertain the extent to which the capacity for resilience is associated with the severity and depth of the economic crisis, at the aggregate level.

The first two items are the most strongly correlated among all six aspects considered here (Pearson's $r = 0.52$), as they tap on to a similar underlying dimension, namely the ability to do something to actively face hard times. As a result, they point to similar, although not identical, directions. In terms of looking for creative ways to alter difficult situations (first item), Greeks seem the most resilient among the respondents of all nine countries, followed by the Italians, Swiss, Germans and Poles more or less on the same level, and finally by the Swedes, Brits and French, again about at the same level. In terms of actively looking for ways to replace the losses encountered

Table 3.1. Resilience items by country (means)

	FR	*DE*	*GR*	*IT*	*PL*	*ES*	*SE*	*CH*	*UK*
I look for creative ways to alter difficult situations	6.01	6.50	7.09	6.60	6.47	6.45	6.06	6.60	6.05
I actively look for ways to replace the losses I encounter in life	5.93	5.87	6.85	6.82	5.75	6.49	4.07	5.89	5.73
I have a hard time making it through stressful events	5.54	4.33	4.64	4.67	4.52	6.02	4.46	4.33	4.38
I keep myself active in the community where I live	5.78	4.57	4.76	5.05	5.18	4.88	3.78	5.27	4.49
I feel I don't have much in common with the larger community in which I live	4.99	3.93	4.83	4.70	4.73	5.18	4.67	3.83	4.75
No one in the community where I live seems to care much about me	4.99	2.96	5.27	4.54	5.16	5.14	4.13	3.26	4.45

Note: 0–10 scales, from 'completely unlike me' to 'just like me'.

in life (second item), Greeks are again the most resilient, this time along with the Italians, followed by the French, Swiss, Germans, Poles and Brits more or less on the same level, then by the Spanish, and finally by the Swedes at a much lower level. These figures suggest that there is, at best, only a weak correlation between the intensity of the economic crisis and the capacity for resilience at the country level. Greece—the country that was arguably hardest hit by the crisis and austerity measures—on the one hand, displays the highest average scores on both counts along with the other two southern European countries, while we also observe high scores in countries, like Germany and Switzerland, that have been largely spared from the hardest negative effects of the economic crisis. The intensity of the crisis, therefore, does not seem to impact patterns of resilience in this respect. However, this does not mean that resilience does not matter. Quite on the contrary, it can be a powerful resource for those individuals in countries hardest hit by the crisis.

The third item tackles resilience from a slightly different angle, focussing specifically on stressful events. To read it in terms of the capacity for resilience, furthermore, we need to interpret the distributions in a reversed fashion as compared to the previous ones: the lower the score, the higher the level of resilience. So, in this regard, Germany and Switzerland, but also the UK and Sweden and, to a lesser extent, Greece and Italy, all show quite similar levels of resilience, whereas a higher share of people in France and, above all, Spain say that they have a hard time making it though stressful events.

The last three items are linked through an explicit reference to the communities in which respondents live. As such, they refer to a collective and relational component of resilience. The latter two in particular show a fairly strong correlation (Pearson's $r = 0.45$), whereas the former has a slightly different meaning due to the reference to keeping active in the community. This can also be seen in the fact that the latter two items follow a rather similar distribution across countries while the former one behaves a bit differently. Once again, we need to reverse the direction of the latter two items to have them matching the scales of the other ones, whereby 0 means 'weak resilience' and 10 'strong resilience'. The French stand out in this type of resilience, keeping active in the community in which one lives, followed at some distance by the Swiss, Polish and Italians, then by the Spanish and Greeks, followed by the Germans and Brits and finally by the Swedes. When it comes to the sense of belonging to the community—the last two response items—finally, Germans and Swiss clearly show a stronger sense of belonging. These two countries stand out for the lower share of both people who feel that they do not have much in common with the larger community in which they live and people who believe that no one in the community where they live cares much about them. On the opposite side, Spanish respondents have, on average, the weakest sense of community belonging, especially in terms of not feeling much in common with it, while the Greeks are particularly skeptical about the extent to which others care about them. Polish and, to a lesser extent, French respondents also show a low sense of belonging, but the other countries are not far from the same levels.

Our main interest in this chapter, however, is not so much in how the capacity for resilience of Europeans varies across countries but, rather, in how, within each country, it varies across social categories and groups. In other words, we ask: Which sectors of society prove to be more resilient to the economic crisis and its negative effects? To answer this question, we compare two measures of resilience across a number of social characteristics: gender, age group, education level, income level, occupation, employment status and citizenship status. The two measures of resilience reflect our conceptual distinction between two forms of resilience: proactive and community-based. We conducted a (confirmatory) factor analysis on the six items of resilience.[3] The following two items are linked to the first factor: 'I look for creative ways to alter difficult situations' and 'I actively look for ways to replace the losses I encounter in life'. The following two items are linked to the second factor: 'I feel that I do not have much in common with the larger community in which I live' and 'No one in the community where I live seems to care much about me'. Given the content of these items, we can say that the first factor taps onto what we called proactive resilience, while the second one taps into what we called community-based resilience. So, from now on we only consider these items grouped, as explained, into the two forms of resilience.[4] Tables 3.2 and 3.3 show the means of the two measures of resilience broken down by social group and by country. These two tables can be read in two ways: horizontally they tell us to what extent the capacity for resilience of a given social category or group is stronger or weaker in certain countries; vertically they show differences in the level of resilience across social categories and groups. The tables also indicate whether the group differences are statistically significant.

The overall indicator of proactive resilience suggests that there is at least some correlation between the severity with which a country was hit by the economic crisis and the related austerity measures and the capacity of people to be resilient to them (table 3.2). Indeed, the three countries hardest hit—Greece, Italy and Spain—are also those who display the highest aggregate levels of resilience. It may be thus that this is related to the idea, indtroduced earlier, that by definition, in order to become resilient, one must encounter difficulties such as those brought about by the crisis or equally other events. Supporting this line of reasoning is the fact that, one of the countries that has largely been spared by the Great Recession—Sweden—displays the lower levels of resilience. At the same time, however, France and Switzerland, two countries that have not been so hard hit—especially the latter—also show rather high scores on the resilience scale. This means that overall there is no simple linear relationship between the intensity of the economic crisis across countries and the overall level of resilience reported by the people living in them.

Now we turn to our main interest and focus: group differences. As we can see in the first row, which shows the presence of statistically significant differences, gender does not seem to be much of a discriminating factor in this first, descriptive analysis, except in the UK and, to some extent, also in Italy, where women show a stronger capacity for proactive resilience than men. Age has more discriminating power then gender. We observe significant differences in five countries in terms of age groups. These include both countries severely hit by the economic crisis, such as Greece and Italy, but also countries which have largely been spared from it, as well as a country like France that would be placed somewhere in between deep and weaker effects of the crisis. However, there is no consistent pattern across these countries: in some

Table 3.2. Proactive resilience by country and social category (means)

	FR	*DE*	*GR*	*IT*	*PL*	*ES*	*SE*	*CH*	*UK*
Gender				*					***
Female	5.90	5.66	6.19	6.23	5.84	5.90	4.61	5.94	5.52
Male	5.87	5.61	6.28	6.06	5.75	5.94	4.63	5.87	5.20
Age	*	*	***	*				***	***
18–34	5.83	5.47	6.02	6.05	5.67	5.81	4.59	5.62	5.11
35–64	5.97	5.72	6.38	6.23	5.90	5.96	4.65	6.03	5.20
65+	5.62	5.62	5.76	5.93	5.64	5.97	4.53	6.10	6.02
Education		***	**			**	***	**	***
University+	6.05	5.79	6.40	6.27	5.83	6.08	5.09	6.09	5.59
Secondary	5.81	5.68	6.10	6.15	5.72	5.94	4.57	5.85	5.43
< Secondary	5.80	5.22	6.20	6.07	6.05	5.75	4.06	5.74	4.94
Income		*							
Low (1–5 decile)	5.87	5.50	6.25	6.16	5.78	5.92	4.50	5.92	5.33
High (6–10 decile)	5.91	5.73	6.20	6.13	5.82	5.92	4.67	5.90	5.39
Occup. of Chief Income Earner		**				**	***	***	***
Prof. | Mngr.	5.87	5.54	6.24	6.20	5.76	5.87	4.57	5.88	5.18
Intermediate	5.70	5.42	6.11	6.06	5.88	5.86	4.34	5.64	4.87
Manual	5.87	5.65	6.16	6.01	5.70	5.61	4.27	5.85	5.50
Other	5.87	5.54	6.24	6.20	5.76	5.87	4.57	5.88	5.18
Employment Stat.		*							
Unemployed	5.67	5.17	6.24	6.19	5.74	5.76	4.91	5.90	5.03
Other	5.91	5.65	6.23	6.14	5.81	5.96	4.60	5.91	5.38
Citizenship status			*						*
Migrant	5.83	5.60	5.99	5.96	5.87	5.80	4.60	5.89	5.61
Native	5.90	5.64	6.27	6.16	5.80	5.94	4.62	5.92	5.32
Full sample	5.89	5.63	6.24	6.15	5.80	5.92	4.62	5.91	5.37

Note: 0–10 scales, from lowest to highest resilience.
* $p < 0.05$ ** $p < 0.01$ *** $p < 0.001$

cases (Switzerland and the UK) the older groups are more resilient, while in others (France, Greece and Italy), those who are in the middle age group are. Yet, in all five countries—and also in others—the youngest age group proves to be the least resilient.

Education, income and social class are shown to be intimately related and tend to be grouped by sociologists within the notion of socioeconomic status (Brady et al. 1995). Does proactive resilience vary depending on these factors? The answer is a qualified yes. Education clearly has an important impact, as six out of the nine countries display significant differences. In all six cases, those who have a university degree are more resilient than those who have a lower-level degree, although the difference is larger in some countries than others. Social class seems to matter, too. This variable is significant in five countries (Germany, Spain, Sweden, Switzerland and the UK). The more resilient category, however, differs from one country to the next. While in Germany, the UK and Switzerland, to some extent, the manual classes are the most resilient—or amongst the most resilient, in the Swiss' case—in Spain and Sweden they show the weakest capacity for resilience while professionals and managers are the most resilient or, in Spain's case, amongst the most resilient classes. Income, in contrast, has little to no discriminating power, as we observe a single significant difference in Germany, where people with higher incomes are somewhat more resilient than those with lower incomes.

Finally, we can take a look at the two specific groups of the unemployed and migrants. These two groups have lower resources and therefore should be more vulnerable to the negative effects of the economic crisis and its related austerity measures, and we may expect this to have an impact on their capacity for resilience, although it is hard to say in which direction. Our data provides little support for this hypothesis, as occupational status (unemployed versus employed) is significant in only one country, while citizenship status (migrant versus native) is significant in only two of the nine countries. Again, the inconsistent patterns make it difficult to provide a straightforward interpretation of the results that hold across countries. Specifically, unemployed people tend to have a lower capacity for resilience in Germany, while migrants are more resilient in Greece, but less so in the UK.

Moving to our second dimension of resilience—community-based resilience—we observe both similarities and differences with proactive resilience (table 3.3). At the most general level, we observe something similar to what we saw for the other dimension, namely that two countries that have not been hard hit by the economic crisis—Germany and Switzerland—have the highest overall level of community-based resilience, followed by Sweden. Thus, the three countries that have largely been spared the negative effects of the crisis and austerity measures are also the ones that display the strongest overall sense of community-based resilience. In contrast, two of the countries hardest hit—Greece and Italy—display the lowest aggregate levels of community-based resilience.

What about the group differences on this dimension of resilience? Gender seems to play a stronger role for community-based resilience, as compared to proactive resilience. In four countries (Germany, Italy, Switzerland and the UK) women are consistently more resilient than men in this respect. Age matters in six out of the nine countries (France, Germany, Greece, Italy, Sweden and the UK) in a similarly clear-cut fashion: the youngest age group is consistently less resilient than the older ones.

Table 3.3. Community-based resilience by country and social category (means)

	FR	*DE*	*GR*	*IT*	*PL*	*ES*	*SE*	*CH*	*UK*
Gender		**		*				***	*
Female	5.02	6.72	4.92	5.50	5.02	4.90	5.59	6.69	5.50
Male	4.98	6.39	4.97	5.24	5.10	4.80	5.52	6.17	5.24
Age	*	***	*	*			***		***
18–34	4.82	6.31	4.75	5.13	5.00	4.86	5.19	6.55	4.73
35–64	5.01	6.58	5.06	5.47	5.09	4.84	5.60	6.40	5.29
65+	5.26	7.11	5.13	5.59	5.12	4.91	5.96	6.36	6.12
Education			*		*	**			
University+	5.06	6.73	5.02	5.43	5.12	5.01	5.71	6.52	5.45
Secondary	5.06	6.47	4.98	5.32	5.12	4.82	5.41	6.47	5.26
< Secondary	4.86	6.51	4.60	5.45	4.71	4.70	5.57	6.24	5.44
Income	***	***	***	***	**	**	***	***	**
Low (1–5 decile)	4.78	6.30	4.83	5.24	4.88	4.73	5.19	6.28	5.15
High (6–10 decile)	5.28	6.75	5.27	5.63	5.18	4.98	5.75	6.67	5.53
Occup. of Chief Income Earner	*	***			**	*	***	***	***
Prof. | Mngr.	5.21	6.86	5.04	5.38	5.22	5.06	5.76	6.61	5.70
Intermediate	4.90	6.49	4.95	5.40	5.13	4.74	5.52	6.45	5.04
Manual	4.86	6.27	4.89	5.29	4.72	4.78	5.20	6.41	5.12
Other	5.16	6.10	4.82	5.49	5.26	4.71	5.91	5.72	4.80
Employment Stat.	**	***	***	***	*			**	
Unemployed	4.50	5.18	4.56	4.92	4.70	4.78	5.20	5.92	4.89
Other	5.06	6.60	5.09	5.47	5.10	4.86	5.58	6.48	5.40
Citizenship Stat.		**						***	
Migrant	4.89	6.18	4.67	5.63	5.45	4.87	5.38	6.22	5.33
Native	5.03	6.63	4.99	5.36	5.04	4.85	5.61	6.59	5.39
Full sample	5.00	6.55	4.95	5.38	5.06	4.85	5.56	6.44	5.38

Note: 0–10 scales, from lowest to highest resilience.
* $p < 0.05$ ** $p < 0.01$ *** $p < 0.001$

As far as education, income and social class are concerned, we observe somewhat different results than in the case of proactive resilience. Specifically, higher education is positively associated with community-based resilience, but only in Greece, Poland and Spain, while there is no significant correlation in the other six countries. Social class is also associated with this form of resilience in of all the countries except two (Greece and Italy), just like with the other form. In this case, however, professionals and managers are consistently more resilient than other classes. Yet, the most important difference lies in the role of income. While income has little, if any, discriminatory power for proactive resilience, respondents with higher incomes display a stronger sense of community-based resilience in all nine countries, suggesting that this is a key resource in this respect.

Employment status also has a different role for this form of resilience—a stronger one. While it does not discriminate between groups with regard to proactive resilience, unemployed people show a lower degree of community-based resilience in six of the nine countries (France, Germany, Greece, Italy, Poland and Switzerland). Thus, it appears that in both countries hardest hit by the economic crisis and in countries that were largely spared, jobless individuals tend to have a weaker sense of resilience linked to the communities in which they live. This is consistent with studies that have shown the social isolation of the unemployed, especially when they get caught up in cycles of long-term unemployment (Jahoda et al. 1971), which may lead to a diminished sense of social integration. Finally, similar to what we saw for proactive resilience, citizenship status does not seem to be so relevant for community-based resilience, although migrants are less resilient than natives in Germany and Switzerland—two countries largely spared from the most negative effects of the economic crisis.

In sum, this descriptive analysis yields a number of insights about how the two forms of resilience vary across countries, as well as across social categories and groups. Firstly, at the country level, proactive resilience—the capability to actively react to adversity—is more common in countries hardest hit by the economic crisis and the related austerity measures, whereas community-based resilience—the sense of belonging to a community—tends to be stronger in countries that have largely been spared from negative effects. Secondly, gender and age play some role (especially age), but not everywhere. Where they do matter, women tend to be more resilient than men, while the pattern for age is more wavering, but the younger age group is less resilient than older ones, in general. Thirdly, cultural and economic resources seem to matter, too, albeit in different ways: education is important for both forms of resilience but especially so for its community-based form; income is important, but only for community-based resilience; and social class—as measured through the occupation of the main income earner—is a discriminating factor for both forms of resilience in most countries, whereby professionals and managers tend to be more resilient than other classes, especially when it comes to community-based resilience. Fourthly, apart from a few exceptions, employment status and citizenship status play a relevant role only in one instance: unemployed people show less community-based resilience than employed people. In a few countries, however, migrants are also less resilient—in both forms—than non-migrants.

These results, however, should not be overemphasised as they are based on simple bivariate cross-tabulations. To get a better and more accurate grasp on how the two forms of resilience might depend on certain social characteristics we need to provide a stronger test by means of multivariate analyses.

We do so next section, where we also examine the role of perceptions of the economic crisis and its effect on one's personal life as well as social networks and capital.

CORRELATES OF RESILIENCE

Our second main research question in this chapter deals with the factors that are potentially associated with resilience. This is the object of the present section. We resort to regression analysis to show how different factors correlate with the two forms of resilience we have been focussing upon. These factors form five clusters, as discussed earlier: the sociodemographic characteristics considered in the above descriptive analyses (gender, age, education, income, occupation, employment status and citizenship status), the respondents' perceptions of the economic crisis and how the government has dealt with it, their feelings of relative deprivation, their perceptions of how the crisis has impacted on their personal lives and their amount of social capital.

In this analysis we do not focus on cross-national differences in the capacity for resilience, which we explored earlier. We take into account country differences by estimating multilevel regression models that treat country variation as random effects. The results of this analysis are shown in tables 3.4 and 3.5, respectively, for proactive resilience and community-based resilience. We ran six models, each including one of the five groups of variables mentioned above and the last one being the full model that also includes the control for the other dimension of resilience. All of the independent variables have been standardised and are either dummies or 0 to 1 scales, except for the measures of resilience included in the final models. Moreover, all the models have been set at the same number of cases so as to makes statistical tests comparable across models.

Starting with proactive resilience, model 1 looks at the effects of the seven sociodemographic variables examined earlier (table 3.4). As such, it largely reflects the previous descriptive analyses, although here we control the other variables in the model. In brief, we can see that women are more resilient than men, the younger (the category of reference for age groups) are less resilient than older age groups, more educated people (the category of reference for education) are more resilient than people with a lower education and professionals and managers (the reference category for occupation) are more resilient than other social classes. In contrast, neither the income level nor being unemployed or of migrant origin matters.

Including the respondents' views about the severity of the economic crisis, their perceptions of the present state of the economy as compared to one year

Table 3.4. Multi-level regression models on proactive resilience (fixed part only)

Model	*(1)*	*(2)*	*(3)*	*(4)*	*(5)*	*(6)*
Gender (female)	0.12***	0.12***	0.11***	0.12***	0.16***	0.17***
	(0.03)	(0.03)	(0.03)	(0.03)	(0.03)	(0.03)
Age groups (ref.: 18–34) 35–64	0.20***	0.19***	0.23***	0.27***	0.29***	0.31***
	(0.04)	(0.04)	(0.04)	(0.04)	(0.04)	(0.04)
65+	0.23***	0.21***	0.29***	0.47***	0.44***	0.47***
	(0.06)	(0.06)	(0.06)	(0.06)	(0.06)	(0.06)
Education group (Ref.: University and above)						
Secondary	−0.16***	−0.15***	−0.17***	−0.16***	−0.11**	−0.11**
	(0.04)	(0.04)	(0.04)	(0.04)	(0.04)	(0.04)
< secondary	−0.32***	−0.31***	−0.32***	−0.30***	−0.22***	−0.22***
	(0.05)	(0.05)	(0.05)	(0.05)	(0.05)	(0.05)
Income (low, 1st to 5th decile)	0.03	0.03	0.02	−0.06	−0.06	−0.07*
	(0.03)	(0.03)	(0.04)	(0.04)	(0.03)	(0.03)
Occupation of chief wage earner (Ref.: Professional or managerial)						
Intermediate occupation	−0.19***	−0.19***	−0.18***	−0.18***	−0.14***	−0.15***
	(0.04)	(0.04)	(0.04)	(0.04)	(0.04)	(0.04)
Manual occupation	−0.23***	−0.23***	−0.22***	−0.22***	−0.16***	−0.17***
	(0.05)	(0.05)	(0.05)	(0.05)	(0.05)	(0.05)
Other occupation	−0.28***	−0.27***	−0.26***	−0.24***	−0.21***	−0.21***
	(0.06)	(0.06)	(0.06)	(0.06)	(0.06)	(0.06)
Unemployed	0.01	0.01	−0.02	−0.09	−0.05	−0.06
	(0.05)	(0.05)	(0.05)	(0.05)	(0.05)	(0.05)
Citizenship status (migrant)	−0.01	−0.01	−0.02	−0.04	−0.04	−0.05
	(0.05)	(0.05)	(0.05)	(0.05)	(0.04)	(0.04)

Serious crisis	–	0.17***	0.17***	0.12**	0.14***	0.15***
	–	(0.04)	(0.04)	(0.04)	(0.04)	(0.04)
Sociotropic evals. past yr.	–	–0.26**	–0.47***	–0.45***	–0.50***	–0.51***
	–	(0.09)	(0.10)	(0.10)	(0.10)	(0.10)
Satisfaction with government	–	0.41***	0.37***	0.41***	0.34***	0.33***
	–	(0.07)	(0.07)	(0.07)	(0.07)	(0.07)
Pocketbook retrospective evals.	–	–	–0.48***	–0.19*	–0.25**	–0.26**
5 yrs.	–	–	(0.08)	(0.08)	(0.08)	(0.08)
Pocketbook prospective evals.	–	–	1.06***	1.09***	0.97***	1.02***
1 yr.	–	–	(0.09)	(0.09)	(0.09)	(0.09)
Reduced consumption	–	–	–	0.60***	0.60***	0.53***
	–	–	–	(0.07)	(0.07)	(0.07)
Impact of crisis on working	–	–	–	0.65***	0.56***	0.52***
situation	–	–	–	(0.07)	(0.07)	(0.07)
Social trust	–	–	–	–	0.51***	0.57***
	–	–	–	–	(0.06)	(0.06)
Meets friends at least every wk.	–	–	–	–	0.48***	0.52***
	–	–	–	–	(0.03)	(0.03)
Associational membership	–	–	–	–	0.41***	0.41***
	–	–	–	–	(0.03)	(0.03)
Community–based resilience	–	–	–	–	–	–0.07***
	–	–	–	–	–	(0.01)
Constant	5.83***	5.70***	5.47***	4.92***	4.38***	4.72***
	(0.16)	(0.16)	(0.15)	(0.15)	(0.16)	(0.17)
Log likelihood	–30,981.610	–30,961.063	–30,886.334	–30,768.928	–30,531.285	–30,478.558

Note: Standard errors in parentheses; $N = 14,795$.
* $p < 0.05$ ** $p < 0.01$ *** $p < 0.001$

earlier and their degree of satisfaction with the way in which the government is dealing with the economy in model 2, does not fundamentally alter the effects of the sociodemographic variables. The impact of the latter therefore hold, once controlling for these additional variables. These variables have a statistically significant effect as well. Specifically, believing that one's own country was suffering a very serious crisis is associated with a higher level of proactive resilience; believing that the state of the economy over the past year has deteriorated is associated with a lower level of resilience; and being satisfied with the way the government is dealing with the economy is associated with a higher level of resilience.[5]

Model 3 adds two variables capturing the respondents' feelings of relative deprivation. The first refers to the past, asking whether the economic situation of the household was better or worse than it was five years earlier, while the second is prospective insofar as it asks whether the respondents expected their household financial situation in the near future to be better or worse than it was at the time of the survey. Both are indicators of so-called egotropic, or pocketbook evaluations, as opposed to sociotropic evaluations most often related to the state of the national economy (Kinder and Kiewiet 1981). As we can see, these kinds of feelings of deprivation are significantly associated with proactive resilience, both in their retrospective and prospective forms. The direction of the relationship, however, is different: while retrospective deprivation is negatively associated with the capacity for resilience, prospective deprivation shows a positive sign. This suggests, on the one hand, that the capability to proactively react to the negative effects of the economic crisis—or to any kind of adversity, for that matter—is linked to the extent to which one believes that their situation has deteriorated. More specifically, the more one believes that their situation has deteriorated, the less resilient they report themselves to be. On the other hand, those who believe that their situation will improve tend to be more resilient. Again, we can only speculate on the direction of the relationship here. One could argue that people with strong resilience are optimists and, conversely, that people who have a lower level of proactive resilience tend to have a more pessimistic view. Moreover, the inclusion of retrospective and prospective egotropic deprivation keeps all previously statistically significant effects intact, but alters the size of some of the effects, in particular, those of age and evaluations of the state of the economy. The effect on proactive resilience of belonging to the older age groups becomes somewhat stronger. More importantly, the effect of sociotropic deprivation is considerably strengthened.[6]

The concrete impact of the economic crisis on one's living conditions on consumption patterns and working conditions, in particular, also seems to matter. As shown in model 4, both variables are positively associated with proactive resilience: those who say they had to face restrictions for financial or economic reasons during the five years prior to the survey and those who say that negative things occurred in the workplace during the same period of time tend to be more resilient. Thus, taking into account the aspects introduced in models 2 to 4, resilience seems related to the way people assess the overall state of the economy—that is, by their sociotropic evaluations—to how they assess their own personal economic situations—that is, their pocketbook evaluations—at least in prospective terms, and to the 'objective' negative impact of the economic crisis on their living conditions. Once again, the inclusion of additional variables pertaining to the deterioration of living conditions leaves all other effects unchanged in terms of statistical significance—that is, in terms of their existence—but modifies the size of some of the effects. Here we observe an increase in the effect of belonging to the older age groups but this time, to some extent, to the erosion of the effect of the belief that there is a serious crisis, meaning that the latter is partly explained by the fact that people feel that the crisis has had a strong negative impact on their everyday lives.

Model 5 refers to the role of social capital for resilience. To investigate this role empirically, we included three variables that are traditionally associated with higher levels of social capital as discussed earlier: a 0 to 1 scale measuring generalised social trust,[7] a dummy coded 1 when respondents said they had met with friends at least every week during the past month and a dummy coded 1 when respondents are members of at least one voluntary association. All three variables are significantly and positively correlated to proactive resilience. Firstly, the more one trusts other people, the more resilient one is likely to be. Secondly, those who meet frequently with friends are more resilient than those who do so more sporadically. Thirdly, members of voluntary associations are more resilient than non-members. Thus, we can say that the capacity of people to cope with the negative effects of the economic crisis is enhanced by the amount of social capital that they have at their disposal.

The social capital variables do not only have a direct impact on proactive resilience but also an indirect one. This can be seen in the fact that, once included in the model, a number of the other variables increase their effects, albeit not dramatically so. We see, for example, that the effect of having secondary education or less is eroded when including the social capital variables in the model, suggesting that part of that effect is explained by the greater social capital of the respondent. We observe a similar phenomenon with social class. Again, the inclusion of the social capital variables produces a partial reduction of the effects of the three occupational categories other than professionals and managers, a sign that such effects depend, in part, on having higher stocks of social capital at one's disposal. Further, some of the effects of the attitudinal variables are also related to social capital. This is, for example, the case for satisfaction with the way government is dealing with the crisis, of expectations for the future of the economy and of the assessment of the impact of the economic crisis on one's working conditions. All three aspects are partly explained by the amount of individual social capital.

In the final model (6), we have included community-based resilience amongst the predictors, as we saw that the two dimensions of resilience capture different sides of the phenomenon. Apart from showing that these two dimensions are orthogonal and therefore largely uncorrelated, this last model suggests that the sense of belonging to the community in which one lives does not play an important role when it comes to predicting proactive resilience. Much more relevant here are actual social relations and the level of trust, as we have previously seen. The inclusion of this variable also changes the role of some of the other variables but only to a limited extent, most notably by increasing the effects of prospective feelings of relative deprivation, social trust and meeting with friends, while reducing those of perceptions that the economic crisis has impacted on one's consumption patterns and the assessment of the impact of the economic crisis on one's working conditions.

Moving to community-based resilience, model 1 once again simply reflects the descriptive analyses, showing the impact of gender, age, income, social class, employment status and citizenship status, but not of education, on the community-based resilience (table 3.5). The remaining models follow the same stepwise approach adopted for the analysis of proactive resilience, whereby each subsequent model aims to show the direct and indirect effects of the variables added to the model.

Just like for proactive resilience, the perceptions of the state of the economy as well as the degree of satisfaction with the way the government is dealing with it are associated with greater community-based resilience, as we can see from the their statistically significant and positive effects. In this case, furthermore, including these two variables in model 2 leads to few changes in the effects of some of the other variables. Specifically, we observe a small reduction in the effects of income, belonging to manual classes and unemployed status, suggesting that part of the effect of these three variables is related on sociotropic evaluations of the economy. Such a reduction, however, remains of a limited magnitude.

As we can see in model 3, retrospective and prospective egotropic relative deprivation are significantly and positively associated with community-based resilience. Also, the effects of income, of belonging to manual classes and unemployed status are further eroded once we include them in the model.

Table 3.5. Multilevel regression models on community-based resilience (fixed part only)

Model	*(1)*	*(2)*	*(3)*	*(4)*	*(5)*	*(6)*
Gender (female)	0.22***	0.25***	0.24***	0.24***	0.26***	0.28***
	(0.04)	(0.04)	(0.04)	(0.04)	(0.04)	(0.04)
Age groups (ref.: 18–34) 35–64	0.16***	0.19***	0.27***	0.22***	0.25***	0.28***
	(0.05)	(0.05)	(0.05)	(0.05)	(0.05)	(0.05)
65+	0.51***	0.52***	0.65***	0.45***	0.42***	0.46***
	(0.07)	(0.07)	(0.07)	(0.07)	(0.07)	(0.07)
Education group (Ref.: University and above)						
Secondary	0.00	0.01	–0.00	–0.00	0.03	0.02
	(0.05)	(0.05)	(0.05)	(0.05)	(0.05)	(0.05)
< secondary	–0.04	–0.03	–0.03	–0.03	0.03	0.01
	(0.06)	(0.06)	(0.06)	(0.06)	(0.06)	(0.06)
Income (low, 1st to 5th decile)	–0.36***	–0.33***	–0.29***	–0.17***	–0.18***	–0.18***
	(0.04)	(0.04)	(0.04)	(0.04)	(0.04)	(0.04)
Occupation of chief wage earner (Ref.: Professional or managerial)						
Intermediate occupation	–0.15**	–0.14**	–0.12*	–0.12*	–0.09	–0.10*
	(0.05)	(0.05)	(0.05)	(0.05)	(0.05)	(0.05)
Manual occupation	–0.21***	–0.18**	–0.15*	–0.14*	–0.09	–0.10
	(0.06)	(0.06)	(0.06)	(0.06)	(0.06)	(0.06)
Other occupation	–0.11	–0.09	–0.05	–0.07	–0.04	–0.07
	(0.07)	(0.07)	(0.07)	(0.07)	(0.07)	(0.07)
Unemployed	–0.27***	–0.23***	–0.19**	–0.11	–0.11	–0.11
	(0.07)	(0.07)	(0.07)	(0.07)	(0.06)	(0.06)
Citizenship status (migrant)	–0.16**	–0.17**	–0.18**	–0.14**	–0.13*	–0.14*
	(0.05)	(0.05)	(0.05)	(0.05)	(0.05)	(0.05)

(continued)

Table 3.5. *(continued)*

Model	*(1)*	*(2)*	*(3)*	*(4)*	*(5)*	*(6)*
Serious crisis	–	–0.07	–0.04	0.01	0.03	0.05
	–	(0.05)	(0.05)	(0.05)	(0.05)	(0.05)
Sociotropic evaluations past yr.	–	0.57***	0.08	0.06	–0.02	–0.07
	–	(0.11)	(0.12)	(0.12)	(0.12)	(0.12)
Satisfaction with govt.	–	0.23**	0.14	0.09	–0.02	0.02
	–	(0.09)	(0.09)	(0.09)	(0.09)	(0.09)
Pocketbook retrospective evals.	–	–	0.29**	–0.11	–0.14	–0.17
5 yrs.	–	–	(0.10)	(0.10)	(0.10)	(0.10)
Pocketbook prospective evals.	–	–	0.97***	0.93***	0.79***	0.89***
1 yr.	–	–	(0.10)	(0.10)	(0.10)	(0.10)
Reduced consumption	–	–	–	–1.02***	–0.94***	–0.88***
	–	–	–	(0.09)	(0.09)	(0.09)
Impact of crisis on working	–	–	–	–0.48***	–0.50***	–0.45***
situation	–	–	–	(0.08)	(0.08)	(0.08)
Social trust	–	–	–	–	0.77***	0.83***
	–	–	–	–	(0.08)	(0.08)
Meets friends at least every wk.	–	–	–	–	0.55***	0.60***
	–	–	–	–	(0.04)	(0.04)
Associational membership	–	–	–	–	0.02	0.06
	–	–	–	–	(0.04)	(0.04)
Proactive resilience	–	–	–	–	–	–0.10***
	–	–	–	–	–	(0.01)
Constant	5.58***	5.22***	4.74***	5.38***	4.85***	5.30***
	(0.21)	(0.20)	(0.20)	(0.20)	(0.20)	(0.21)
Log likelihood	–33,615.709	–33,577.988	–33,511.712	–33,388.980	–33,232.863	–33,180.125

Note: Standard errors in parentheses; N = 14,795.
* $p < 0.05$ ** $p < 0.01$ *** $p < 0.001$

Additionally, when including these variables, the effect of age group is also reduced to some extent. Yet, the most dramatic reductions are observed in the respondents' perceptions of the economic crisis and how the government has dealt with it. In this case the effects of these two variables disappear altogether as they are no longer statistically significant, unveiling spurious relationships in the previous model. When it comes to community-based resilience, therefore, egotropic feelings of relative deprivation capture the relationship between evaluations of the economic crisis and related austerity policies—or, more accurately, of the government's handling of the economy—on the one hand, and this form of resilience, on the other. To put it more simply, what seems to matter for people feeling close to the communities in which they live is not so much what they think about the state of the economy and the actions of their government, but the extent to which their own financial and economic situation was affected by these developments.

While the perceptions of how the crisis has impacted the personal life were seen to be positively associated with proactive resilience, they show in model 4 a negative correlation with community-based resilience. Those who say that they had to face restrictions for financial or economic reasons and that negative things occurred in the workplace also tend to be less resilient in this respect, that is, they are characterised by a weaker community-based resilience. In this model, we also see a number of sociodemographic variables whose effects become smaller as compared to the previous model. These are age group, income and migrant status. This suggests, once again, that how the crisis has impacted the personal life explains part of the effect of these sociodemographic characteristics on resilience. Furthermore, we can see that adding the respondents' perceptions of how the crisis has impacted on their personal life results in the effect of retrospective relative deprivation disappearing, suggesting that behind the effect of feelings of relative deprivation, hides the awareness that the economic crisis has had a tangible impact on living conditions.

Models 5 includes the variables pertaining to social capital. Compared to what we observed in the case of proactive resilience, there seems to be less going on here. To begin with, not all social capital variables are statistically significant. While the degree of social trust and the frequency of meeting with friends are both positively associated with community-based resilience, associational membership—which has often been considered as a key 'provider' of social capital (Putnam 1993, 2000)—is not. Furthermore, a more limited number of other effects are modified by the inclusion of these variables than for the dimension of proactive resilience. This is the namely the case for prospective feelings of relative deprivation and perceptions that the economic crisis has impacted one's consumption patterns. Both effects are slightly reduced by the inclusion of the social capital variables, suggesting that part of their effects is explained by the latter.

Finally, model 6 simply adds the other form of resilience as a control. This produces a few changes in the role of other variables in a similar fashion to what we observed for proactive resilience, most notably by increasing the effect of prospective feelings of relative deprivation, social trust and meeting with friends, while reducing those of perceptions that the economic crisis has impacted on one's consumption patterns and the assessment of the impact of the economic crisis on one's working conditions.

We have spent some time discussing, in some detail, the results of our regression analyses as they are important to understand the impact on the two forms of resilience of social characteristics and attitudes towards the economic crisis as well as its effects on personal life and how they interact with social capital. We discuss the implications of these as well as the previous findings in the concluding section. Before we do so, however, we would like to take an extra step and show how certain social categories and groups may be predicted to be resilient to the economic crisis, in both of the dimensions we have distinguished. So far, we considered the effect of each category separately, but often social characteristics and group affiliations have a cumulative effect, in this case on the capacity for resilience. For example, social class might combine with age group and education to lead to either more or less resilience. Tables 3.6 and 3.7 show exactly this combination of factors for the two forms of resilience, focussing on the extreme categories of each variable. As we can see, there is indeed a cumulative effect: while 75 percent of older women with a professional or managerial occupation and high levels of education display a strong capacity for resilience, the percentage falls to less than 50 percent for younger men who have a manual occupations and lower levels of education (table 3.6). The difference is somewhat narrower but still sizeable when it comes to community-based resilience: 57 percent for older women from higher classes and with higher education versus 40 percent for younger men from lower classes and with lower education (table 3.7).

Finally, it is worth taking a look also at the combination of belonging to the two specific groups of the unemployed and migrants, which are potentially more vulnerable to the negative effects of the economic crisis and related austerity measures, and which we expected to be less resilient, although our results point in a different direction. Tables 3.8 and 3.9 show this for the two forms of resilience. In line with such results, combining an unfavourable employment and citizenship status does not seem to make a big difference. Yet, the share of unemployed migrants that display a strong capacity for proactive resilience is somewhat lower than that of natives who have a job. Similarly,

Table 3.6. Predicted probabilities of strong proactive resilience depending on gender, age, education and occupation (%)

		Male		*Female*	
Occupation	*Education*	*18–34*	*65+*	*18–34*	*65+*
Professional or managerial	University +	59.8	71.1	64.4	75.1
	< Secondary	52.0	64.4	56.9	68.7
Manual	University +	56.4	68.3	61.1	72.4
	< Secondary	48.6	61.1	53.5	65.7

Note: Based on estimates from a multilevel logistic regression with all the predictors as in model of table 3.4. The resilience scale has been dichotomized around the median.

Table 3.7. Predicted probabilities of strong community-based resilience depending on gender, age, education and occupation (%)

		Male		*Female*	
Occupation	*Education*	*18–34*	*65+*	*18–34*	*65+*
Professional or managerial	University +	44.7	51.8	50.2	57.3
	< Secondary	41.9	49.0	47.3	54.5
Manual	University +	43.1	50.3	48.6	55.8
	< Secondary	40.3	47.4	45.8	52.9

Note: Based on estimates from a multilevel logistic regression with all the predictors as in model of table 3.5. The resilience scale has been dichotomized around the median.

Table 3.8. Predicted probabilities of strong proactive resilience depending on employment status and citizenship status (%)

	Employed	*Unemployed*
Native	63.3	60.3
Migrant	62.8	59.9

Note: Based on estimates from a multilevel logistic regression with all the predictors as in model of table 3.4. The resilience scale has been dichotomized around the median.

Table 3.9. Predicted probabilities of strong community-based resilience depending on employment status and citizenship status (%)

	Employed	*Unemployed*
Native	50.0	48.3
Migrant	46.9	45.3

Note: Based on estimates from a multilevel logistic regression with all the predictors as in model of table 3.5. The resilience scale has been dichotomized around the median.

the former are also less likely than the latter to have a higher score concerning community-based resilience.

CONCLUSION

In this chapter we have investigated the capacity for resilience shown by Europeans in the nine countries covered by our study and how this is in turn associated with their levels of social capital. Our analysis was guided by two main research questions: (1) To what extent does the capacity for resilience of individuals vary across countries and, above all, across different social categories and groups?; and (2) How does resilience link up to other factors such social characteristics, perceptions of the state of the economy and the ways in which governments are dealing with the economic crisis, feelings of relative deprivation and perceptions of the crisis in personal situations, broader social networks and related social capital?

We have distinguished between two main forms of resilience: a proactive form consisting in individuals proactively and often creatively doing something to adapt, cope and possibly overcome adversity, hence showing a capacity for agency, and a community-based form of resilience relating to the feeling of attachment to community. While the former clearly reflects common definitions of resilience, the latter is closer to an idea of group belonging as a way to cope with negative external events and situations. Our analysis has shown that both forms of resilience are important for Europeans in dealing with the negative effects of the Great Recession, as well as the austerity policies implemented by governments during the economic crisis.

Overall, the key message of this chapter is thus that Europeans have been shown to be resilient, to an important extent, to the deprivation and hardship generated by the economic crisis and related austerity measures, both in terms of being able to proactively face adversity and in terms of the communities in which they live. At the same time, however, both forms of resilience vary both across countries and across social categories and groups. In terms of countries, while proactive resilience is more common in those that have been hardest hit by the economic crisis and the related austerity measures, community-based resilience tends to be stronger amongst those that have been less strongly hit. Most importantly, our analysis shows that, net of country variations certain social categories and groups are more resilient than others. In particular, women, older people and upper social classes have a stronger capacity for proactive resilience. Additionally, poorer individuals, the unemployed and migrants are also more likely to have a strong capacity for community-based resilience. We also saw that the impact of these factors is cumulative: older women who have professional or managerial occupations and a higher level of education are more resilient than younger men who have manual occupations and a lower level of education. Such a cumulative effect, however, is much less important for employment status and citizenship status, as combining an unfavourable employment and citizenship status does not seem to make a big difference for resilience.

These findings suggest that certain resources, some of which can be subsumed under the label of human capital, are of key importance for people to be able to overcome the deprivation and hardship emerging from a deep and long-lasting economic crisis such as the one that Europe has witnessed since 2008. Furthermore, we have also examined the role of another kind of resource, namely social capital. Here we found both a direct and an indirect impact of social capital, as measured through the level of social trust, the frequency of meeting with friends and membership in voluntary associations. The impact of these variables, however, is more pronounced for proactive resilience than for community-based resilience.

Finally, individuals' capacity for resilience is also related to their perceptions of the economic crisis and how the government has dealt with it, their feelings of relative deprivation and their perceptions of how the crisis has impacted their personal lives. The effect of these variables, however, is not homogeneous across the two forms of resilience.

Our discussion and analyses so far have dealt with the role of the economic crisis in general—including the impact of austerity policies—meaning that we considered the role of perceptions of deprivation and hardship (chapter 2) as well as the capacity for resilience (chapter 3) of citizens in the nine countries covered by our study. The next two chapters zoom in on two more specific issues: unemployment—along with precarity and the welfare state (chapter 4)—and immigration (chapter 5). These are two key issues that have been at the centre of national and international political debates during the Great Recession.

Chapter Four

Unemployment and the Welfare State

This chapter looks at the effects of the Great Recession in the field of unemployment politics. We look specifically at the extent to which Europeans are satisfied with government policy on unemployment and precarious employment as well as comparing these with satisfaction with economic policy, more widely, and policies on poverty, education and healthcare. Unemployment, precarious employment, the economy and other types of social spending areas became a key politicised field during the crisis, as debate opened about whether governments were doing enough to tackle unemployment and whether spending cuts were justified. While governments implemented austerity policies, many were left wondering whether a spending injection—such as that applied in America, lifting the country out of recession—should not also be the chosen policy in Europe. Moreover, anti-austerity movements developed across the continent, generating large protests against austerity cuts to public services. In a situation of economic crisis, where the poor are particularly vulnerable to exacerbated economic conditions, cuts to public spending further deteriorated the living standards of those at the bottom and most reliant on such spending. In this way, social policy became one of the main battlegrounds in the context of the crisis, where both old and new actors from inside and outside the political institution opposed each other.

Other than being a critical battleground of politics during the Great Recession, popular attitudes towards welfare state policies are also important, since they comprise a large share of public spending and, further, because those attitudes tell us something quite important about individuals' preferences for different sorts of democracy (Kumlin 2007). Research on the welfare state and support for it has been a growing field in the last few decades. One of its pioneers, Coughlin (1980), noted how mass publics of different countries differed with respect to more generalised ideological welfare state support from those in low-spending countries being less supportive, but attitudes towards specific programmes were generally positive in most countries. This is linked to the fact that attitudes towards the welfare state are, at the most general level, closely linked to left–right values due to the state's intervention in the economy being one of its key dimensions (Kumlin 2007). In general, those who support social equality, the public sector and redistribution are more likely to see themselves on the left. However, more specific policy preferences, while generally correlated with the higher-level ideological dimension (Kaase and Newton 1995), tend to be more complex. There is also considerable variation between particular policies, with social protection for old people, sick and disabled people mostly favoured, while support for families with children in need, unemployed people and, finally, social assistance are less favoured (van Oorschot 2006). In this regard, extant research suggests that there are differences in support for various policies due to self-interest, social justice perceptions and feedback effects of policy design (Kumlin 2007).

Whereas general welfare support and specific policy preferences are the subject of many studies and surveys, perceptions and evaluations of welfare state performance are not as widely researched (Kumlin 2007). Yet, performance dissatisfaction is becoming increasingly salient in European politics and the policy choice of 'permanent austerity' espoused by many governments makes it increasingly difficult to finance traditional welfare programmes (Pierson 2001a). Performance dissatisfaction has been found to be linked with support for higher spending in those areas. Edlund (2006) and Huseby (2000) show how performance evaluations in three policy areas—the economy, basic social welfare and the environment—were linked to trust in the political system. Kumlin (2007) further shows that dissatisfaction with public health services and education is negatively associated with political trust in fifteen western European democracies, while unrelated to more general welfare state support. The dissatisfaction in this respect is also directed at the European Union (Kumlin 2004a). Moreover, whereas the economic voting literature argues that sociotropic perceptions resulting from political elites, experts and the media play a more important role than personal experiences in the construction of political conclusions, research shows that more personal perceptions and experiences might be linked to welfare performance evaluations (Kumlin 2004b; Kumlin and Rothstein 2005).

While many post-industrial democracies experienced dips in welfare state support during the 1970s and 1980s, support recovered or strengthened quickly in response to spending and benefit cuts and to increasing levels of inequality (Allberg 2003; Shapiro and Young 1989). And while there were dips in generalised welfare state support, that for specific policies remained stable over time (Svallfors 1996; Taylor-Gooby 1985). Moreover, research has found that welfare state attitudes become more supportive in times of unemployment and recession, and hardship could be seen to fuel demands for more welfare since more people feel at risk of becoming unemployed, social needs taking centre stage and unemployment becoming more clearly visible as a broader social and political problem rather than one merely linked to specific individuals (Blekesaune and Quadagno 2003). Furthermore, the strength of trade unions has historically been an important factor in the support of welfare policies, particularly amongst the working class (Korpi 1983).

In terms of individual support for various welfare policies, socioeconomic status variables such as education, income and class have generally been central (Borre and Scarbrough 1995). Unskilled workers tend to be the most supportive and those in professional occupations the least (Svallfors 2006), but class effects vary in strength across countries, being stronger in Sweden than Germany and the UK. Scholarship has examined whether the link between class and welfare support is based on differences in risks, interests, resources and education levels, but empirical studies show that these types of proxy variables cannot capture the full effect, suggesting that group-level processes such as interests and solidarity, or elite discourse politicising welfare topics, might be at play (Kumlin 2007). Moreover, Dunleavy (1979) noted that there was a sectoral cleavage within the middle classes between those employed in the public sector and those that were not. However, by and large, evidence shows that self-interest does not play a large role in welfare state attitudes (Kumlin 2007).

Further research has examined how conceptions of social justice impact welfare attitudes as well as policy feedback effects in terms of how welfare state policies impact attitudes themselves (Kumlin 2007). Some studies have looked at how different welfare regimes, following Esping-Andersen's (1990) classical typology, differ in individuals' attitudes towards them. For example, whether individuals in 'liberal' type regimes are less supportive than those in 'social democratic' ones, whether class is more important for explaining support in liberal regimes, relative to social democratic ones, given the differences between more universal and more targeted public policies, or whether gender is more relevant in social democratic regimes and insider-outsider dimensions more salient in conservative types. In this chapter we look at both sociodemographic differences in support of various welfare policies as well as cross-national differences. What are the effects of the Great Recession on these patterns? To what extent do Europeans feel satisfied with government policy on unemployment and precarious employment? What about on the economy, more generally, or poverty, healthcare and education? Moreover, which groups were particularly dissatisfied with government action in these areas in the aftermath of the economic crisis? Do we see major differences between the winners and losers of the crisis? These are important areas of investigation as they will allow us to identify those groups that are particularly dissatisfied with the activities of mainstream political parties and, potentially, which pools of citizens could form the basis of support for new challenger, or populist, parties.

The next three sections discuss, theoretically, the social bases of support for welfare policies in the context of the economic crisis, the role of opportunities for the politicisation of unemployment and welfare issues, and how public attitudes in these areas are linked to the decline of state capacity and the fiscal crisis of the state. The following two sections, then, move to the analysis of our survey data, first descriptively and then with a more explanatory approach.

THE SOCIAL BASES OF SUPPORT FOR WELFARE POLICIES

Standing (2011) has argued that class structure has become more complex and has distinguished seven groups: (1) an elite of the super-rich, (2) the salariat in full and stable employment, (3) professional technicians that are not in standard employment, (4) a shrinking core of manual employees, (5) a growing precariat, (6) the unemployed and, finally, (7) an underclass. The emerging precariat is defined as 'people who have minimal trust relationships with capital or the state', which sets them apart from the salariat as well as the proletariat, enjoying none of its social contract of labour security for contingent loyalty in the historic compromise underpinning the welfare state settlement (Standing 2011: 14). In Italy, the term *precariato* implies a more generalised state of precarious existence (Grimm and Robbeberger 2007). As such, the main way to understand the precariat is as lacking in seven-forms of labour security which social democrats, workers' parties and trade unions struggled for and won in the postwar period for the industrial proletariat: (1) labour-market security (e.g. adequate income-earning opportunities and government commitment to full employment); (2) employment security (e.g. protection against arbitrary dismissal, hiring and firing regulations); (3) job security (e.g. ability to retain employment, opportunities for social mobility); (4) work security (e.g. protection from accidents and illness, limits on working hours, etc.); (5) skill reproduction security (e.g. opportunity to develop skills, training and make use of one's talents) (6) income security (e.g. stable income, minimum wage, wage indexation, progressive taxation, social security); (7) representation security (e.g. a collective voice in the labour market with independent trade unions and the right to strike) (Standing 2011: 17).

While employment insecurity such as the lack of long-term contracts and protection from loss of employment tends to be the focus in discussions on the emerging precariat, job security is also a very important feature that needs to be taken into account, and being moved around between jobs is also likely to be very personally disruptive, as the tragic example of France Telecom's 'Time to Move' scheme showed (Standing 2011). The precariat's income insecurity is also particularly problematic given that it can make people more vulnerable than many on lower incomes but who can still rely on traditional forms of support, while also being more vulnerable than salaried employees who have similar incomes but can access state and enterprise benefits (Standing 2011). As such, the amount of income is less relevant in a sense, relative to the absence of alternative sources of support in times of crisis and rapid economic upheaval, and this in turn leaves the precariat particularly vulnerable. The precariat can also be seen to lack a sense of work-based identity as individuals tend to be employed in jobs without a career, without professional ethos or community practices and norms of behaviour, including feelings of community and solidarity. This, in turn, is linked to alienation and instrumentality, including opportunism, given that there appear to be no future possible repercussions given one could be 'out' tomorrow (Standing 2011).

Standing (2011) further identifies the members of the precariat as 'denizens', that is, those enjoying a more limited range of rights than full citizens whether civil (equality in law and protection from harm), cultural (ability to participate in cultural life of the community), social (social protection and other welfare support), economic (entitlement to labour-market activity) or political (the right to vote, run and engage in politics). Migrants and criminalised or convicted groups—often linked to petty crimes and 'antisocial behaviors'—clearly stand out as two examples of denizens that are deprived of various key rights. Moreover, given the way labour statistics tend to be set up, it becomes increasingly hard to estimate the number of people that fit into the ranks of the precariat today (Standing 2011). However, one can analyse the main groups that form part of the precariat: those who find themselves in temporary jobs which have been growing sharply in the past three decades, those in part-time employment (i.e. less than thirty hours per week) which has helped to conceal the extent of unemployment and underemployment, dependent contractors which have little control over the tasks they are allocated to by others, and the army of the call centres, interns and other forms of insecure labour that are unlikely to assist individuals in building desirable identities or careers (Standing 2011).

Globalisation has helped the growth of the precariat through the commitment to market principles and flexible labour practices, reducing high, direct taxes now recast as disincentives to labour while, at the same time, restricting social protection to dealing only with means-tested poor and even workfare schemes (Standing 2011). Unemployment, in particular, is a key component of the existence of the precariat and, in neoliberal frameworks, it comes to be increasingly seen as the responsibility of the individual, leading to the demonisation of the unemployed (Standing 2011). With the backdrop of these more long-term changes, the Great Recession put more pressure on firms to cut labour costs which meant that employees in precarious conditions, such as temporary contracts, were those first to be made redundant. As firms cut jobs, regrowth of employment focussed on temporary labour (Simonian 2010). At the same time, the economic crisis was also used as a means to cut public sector job security, for example, by declaring public pensions unaffordable or too risky, and public deficits were also used as reasons for budget cuts. In Greece, Italy, Spain, Ireland and Portugal, as well as in many other countries across the European continent including the UK, pressure on public services was further exacerbated during the crisis, meaning that even a once-secure sector, dominated by the salariat, is now increasingly under attack with attempts to 'precarise' it.

Given all these developments, when we think of the social bases of satisfaction with various economic and welfare government policy performance, we would expect that those sectors of society that are most vulnerable and most likely to enter the ranks of the precariat, will be the most likely to be dissatisfied. This is since they are most likely to experience the negative effects of the economic situation, unemployment, precarious employment and the inadequacies of healthcare and education, including cuts in this respect. As we have seen in chapter 2, young people are the most likely to experience the negative effects of the crisis, though perhaps older people are more likely to experience problems with healthcare and middle-age people with child care and education. Youth are also quite likely to be in more precarious situations (Bessant et al. 2017). Moreover, women, due to their caring roles, are also likely to experience dissatisfaction given that they are the users of, or close to the users of, social services. They have also taken on a growing share of precarious jobs since they are more likely to have short-term or no contracts (Standing 2011). People with lower socioeconomic status (SES), including lower educational attainment and class are, by the same logic, also more likely to be dissatisfied. Moreover, individuals in unemployed and precarious work situations are also less likely to be satisfied with government performance at least in these areas. Finally, because migrants tend to have lower resources and to be in more precarious conditions, the same may be expected for this group in terms of lower satisfaction relative to non-migrants.

OPPORTUNITIES FOR THE POLITICISATION OF UNEMPLOYMENT AND WELFARE ISSUES

The concept of political opportunities has been used to explain the impact of the political-institutional context on collective action in general (Eisinger 1973; Kitschelt 1986; Kriesi et al. 1995; McAdam 1982; Tarrow 1989; Tilly 1978). However, more recent work has noted how the structure of opportunities varies across issue fields (Chabanet and Giugni 2008; Koopmans et al. 2005). In this context, a full analysis of the unemployment field must also take into account welfare state approaches to unemployment and the labour market (Berclaz and Giugni 2005; Berclaz et al. 2004; Giugni et al. 2009). These works have considered the literature on welfare regimes and the distinctions characterising the liberal, continental and universal Scandinavian models. While Esping-Andersen (1990) also examines welfare state regimes, he focussed on stable institutional arrangements between market, state and private spheres beyond state intervention. The argument of scholars examining the welfare approaches to unemployment and the labour market to make sense of the politicisation of unemployment in diverse contexts (Cinalli and Giugni 2010, 2013) follow seminal scholarship on social exclusion, such as Gallie and Paugam (2000) who focussed on the role of 'unemployment-providence' regimes including the degree of coverage, the level of financial compensation and the importance of active measures for employment. At the same time, labour market regulations are key to the welfare state (Esping-Andersen 1990, 1996) and are closely linked to employment policies (Bonoli 2003). Moreover, flexibility tends to vary quite a bit cross-nationally. The UK and Switzerland, for example, tend to have a more flexible labour market, combining low levels of unemployment with high levels of wage inequality, whereas France, Germany and Italy are more rigid, privileging insiders versus outsiders, and Sweden represents an intermediate case where flexibility is combined with higher chances that the unemployed will enter the labour market (Giugni et al. 2009).

Cinalli and Giugni (2010) developed a measure of unemployment and labour market regulations by translating them into indicators from -1 to +1 (see also Cinalli and Giugni 2013). In the first dimension of unemployment regulations with +1 being inclusion and -1 exclusion from conditions of access to rights and welfare provisions for the unemployed, as well as the obligations attached to full enjoyment of rights and provisions including formal prerequisites for obtaining social provision, level and extension of coverage, social aid, the role of public and private employment agencies, sanctions for unemployment system abuse, and the number of people receiving unemployment benefits. The second dimension looked at the continuum from −1 to

+1, meaning, respectively, rigidity and flexibilityin terms of labour market regulations and took into account the extent of a clear distinction between protected workers, precarious workers and the unemployed as a consequence of the type of labour market flexibility, including regulations for dismissals, temporary work, unions' protection of workers, measures tackling recruitment discrimination of ethnic and geographical forms, externalisation of childcare and the amount of flexible workers. Based on this scheme, Cinalli and Giugni (2010) have shown that there is a large amount of variation between different European countries. They have found large differences between countries that exclude the unemployed, such as Germany and Italy, and countries that are highly inclusive, such as France and Sweden. Variations in the labour market regulations dimension were less marked but showed that Italy stood out for its rigidity, and France was not particularly flexible either, followed by Germany, Switzerland and the UK, with Sweden as the most flexible.

Unemployment has been a critical political issue across Europe for some time and, as we have seen, different countries have offered different policy answers in terms of unemployment and labour market regulations. Unemployment has been politicised to different degrees in different countries. In this respect, the level of politicisation of the unemployment issue can be reflected in different action repertoires of collective action (Tilly et al. 1975; Tilly 1978; Traugott 1995). In Cinalli and Giugni's 2010 study, France stands out as the country where unemployment is the most politicised, based on the highest levels of contentiousness in this field. On the other hand, the UK stands out as a pacified country, where there is not much contention in the area of unemployment, the unemployed are weak as a collective group and cannot access public space, with Germany and Sweden exhibiting a similar picture but here this is more likely linked to their within-institutions role in decision-making, whereas Switzerland comes closer to the contentious model of France, and Italy stands in the middle between these two groups. More rigidity in the labour market was found to be linked to more opportunities for politicisation, suggesting that this, as opposed to flexibility, aids the cause of the unemployed. Flexibility, on the other hand, it is argued, reinforces precariousness. Overall, findings show that the national contexts differ widely and also with respect to the politicisation of unemployment and welfare issues.

THE DECLINE OF STATE CAPACITY AND THE FISCAL CRISIS OF THE STATE

Other than different welfare regimes and employment and labour market regulations, satisfaction with government policy in these areas is also related to individuals' ability to influence decisions-making. As Schäfer and Streeck (2013) note, for democracy to have any meaning it must depend on the people's ability to influence government through elections and other modes of political engagement. However, today it seems that post-industrial democracies are increasingly in situations wherein governments cannot practice different policies, so that there appears to be little choice left to individuals in terms of political alternatives (Schäfer and Streeck 2013). This, in turn, is linked to the deficits that OECD (Organisation for Co-operation and Development) countries have been running for nearly three decades, while rising interest payments and welfare-state maturation have meant that smaller and smaller proportions of contemporary government revenue can be earmarked for social investment and discretionary spending (Schäfer and Streeck 2013). Within this wider context, the financial and fiscal crisis of 2008 has acted as an accelerator of the shrinkage of government wriggle-room in the budget all along, while Europeans can be seen to have lost belief in the possibility of real policy change, particularly so in those countries hardest hit by the 'Second Great Contraction' (Reinhart and Rogoff 2009), namely Ireland, Italy, Portugal, Spain and Greece.

Pierson (2001b, 2001c), in fact, predicted this regime of 'permanent austerity' in the face of the limited ability to generate revenues and the rising spending needs resulting from diminished growth, welfare-state maturation and ageing populations. Indeed, as growth slowed down in the 1970s, revenues grew more slowly and public expenditure exceeded government receipts almost everywhere (Streeck and Mertens 2013). While this could have been counteracted through higher taxes, international tax competition meant that this was not practicable in most cases (Genschel and Schwarz 2013). Moreover, given that wages had grown more slowly, taxing ordinary citizens more heavily had also become more costly in political terms (Pierson 2001b). In all OECD countries except Norway, Sweden and Switzerland, the need to save banks was linked to sharp rises in public debt, with that debt more than doubling since the start of the crisis, exceeding 100 percent GDP in eight countries in 2012 (Obinger 2012). This was particularly problematic given that the budget would be taking up expenditure commitments (Schäfer and Streeck 2013). Moreover, it meant that governments needing to make unpopular and fiscally prudent choices did not match individuals' needs and demands, in turn making governments less responsive (Mair 2013).

The rise of public debts was a universal phenomenon since the 1970s, affecting liberal market economies such as the UK and social democratic countries like Sweden alike, as well as coordinated systems like Germany and Italy, and all a manner of different political arrangements from proportional to first-past-the-post (Schäfer and Streeck 2013). The high inflation of the 1970s in the capitalist countries helped to devalue national debts for a while, like growth had in earlier times. However, when the US Federal Reserve ended inflation in the 1980s, structural unemployment translated into a rising demand on the welfare state, the end of the 'bracket creep' under progressive taxation brought tax resistance, and lower nominal growth on top of the preexisting low real growth meant that past debts could no longer be devalued with time (Schäfer and Streeck 2013). Moreover, the lower interest rates following the end of inflation encouraged governments to borrow, and the deregulation of the financial industry in the US allowed them to absorb foreign capital from surplus countries in the Middle East and Asia, looking for safe havens for their earnings. However, this very same deregulation was the main underlying reason for the 2008 crash, which resulted in a huge rise in public debt that lead to fiscal crises across most advanced industrialised countries (Schäfer and Streeck 2013). The 1990s had seen the Clinton-led OECD-wide attempt to consolidate debt through various types of privatisation and spending cuts, but this process did not seem to have much of an impact, with the exception of Sweden undergoing a dramatic financial and fiscal crisis in the mid-1990s (Steinmo 2013) and the US running a budget surplus by the 2000s (Schäfer and Streeck 2013). However, the large rise in public debt caused by the financial and fiscal crisis of 2008 wiped out any gains from the consolidation period, which had been very costly for many governments across Europe in political terms.

As Schäfer and Streeck (2013) note, concerns over a 'fiscal crisis of the state' had already emerged in the 1970s (Bell 1976; O'Connor 1973**[AU]**). However, the deficit growth was not paralleled by a growth in participation or contention that challenged governments and markets and, rather, turnout started to decline, particularly amongst those groups presumably most in need of welfare while, at the same time, trade unions were considerably weakened (Visser 2006). Collective bargaining and wages at the lower end of the labour market fell, while the earnings of managers and shareholders improved dramatically, leading to a sustained and sharp rise in inequality (Salverda and Mayhew 2009; OECD 2011; Schäfer 2013). Globalisation was repeatedly invoked to justify neoliberal restructuring—the end of guaranteed full employment—leading to the growth of precariousness, the privatisation of the public service and the recommodification of social policy (Schäfer and Streeck 2013). In this way, during a period of declining political engagement and the decline of organised labour movements, public debt mounted while economic liberalisation was enacted and further undermined previous commitments to welfare that had been extracted from the capitalist state in the postwar settlement (Schäfer and Streeck 2013).

In this context, spending cuts and decreased public spending are likely to lead to higher proportions of mandatory spending at the expense of 'social investment' (Morel et al. 2011), leaving less money to support those who most depend on public assistance as well as those working in the public sector, as wages will fall, leading to greater inequalities in society (Schäfer and Streeck 2013). These trends are likely to lead to a growing 'post-democracy' (Crouch 2004), as governments further withdraw from correcting markets. Moreover, the growth of privatisation is likely to lead to the growth of tax resistance by those at the top end of the income distribution who resent paying twice for services (privately for those they use and publicly for those they do not use) and who, thus, 'exit' from the community and no longer need to 'voice' their discontent (Hirschman 1970). At the same time, those at the bottom lose hope that public services can get better given ceilings on spending (Schäfer and Streeck 2013). The need for credit on the part of states also means that, increasingly, in the contemporary austerity state that has taken hold of democratic capitalism, the needs of people are being set against those of markets as rival constituencies, which often exert more significant pressures than citizens in policy-making (Schäfer and Streeck 2013). In this sense, democratic capitalist governments today are facing a crisis of both 'input legitimacy', or the capacity to be responsive to the evolving demands of citizens, as well as 'output legitimacy', the question of whether governments are able to perform public functions on behalf of their citizens (Scharpf 1970, 2000).

Streeck and Mertens (2013) note the tendency of public finance shares, available for discretionary spending, to shrink, which in turn raises fundamental questions about future-oriented public investment into the support of such social elements as education, research and development, family support and active labour market policy. These types of government spending develop human capital and industrial innovation and provide the basis for economic growth and the opportunity for greater social equality, as well as the integration of minorities, gender equality, equality of opportunity for children from poor and rich homes, the employability of the unemployed, and so forth (Schäfer and Streeck 2013). By examining data, from 1981 to 2007, for Germany, Sweden and the US regarding public investment relative to GPD or the share in a country's yearly economic output, Streeck and Mertens (2013) show how public expenditure in education, research and development, family support and active labour market policy generally shows a declining trend across all three nations. This supports their argument that it tends to be the most important forms of social investment that suffer when cuts in spending are practiced. This further suggests that Europeans' satisfaction with government policy is likely to be low and declining in the period of the crisis and moving forward. As such, declining government capability suggests citizen dissatisfaction with government policies.

SATISFACTION WITH GOVERNMENT POLICIES IN THE WAKE OF THE GREAT RECESSION

This chapter addresses two key research questions. The first examines the extent to which Europeans express satisfaction with government policies on unemployment and precarious employment, the economy, in general, and poverty, education and healthcare, as well as how this varies by country. Our second aim is to investigate the extent to which different social groups express satisfaction with government action in these policy areas and how these vary both cross-nationally and amongst different social groups, including differences between gender, age, SES indicators such as income, education and social class, employment status, and citizenship status. In this section we address these two questions empirically, by examining data from our cross-national survey carried out in 2015.

The survey contained questions asking individuals to rate their satisfaction with the way in which their country's government was dealing with various policy areas on a scale from 0, if they were 'extremely dissatisfied', to 10, if they were 'extremely satisfied'. Table 4.1 reports, for each policy area, the proportion of respondents in each country expressing satisfaction with their government's action in that area (i.e. those selecting points 6 through 10 on the above scale). Let us first turn to analysing cross-national differences for each item in turn. These results give us a sense of the extent to which Europeans are satisfied with government action in tackling some of the most pernicious negative effects of the Great Recession: the rise in unemployment and precarious forms of employment, as well as negative economic conditions, more generally, rising poverty, and cuts to public spending in education and healthcare amongst other things.

In this context, we would thus expect that the extent to which Europeans express that they are satisfied with government action on unemployment, precarious employment, the economy, poverty, education and healthcare should be linked to the extent to which their country was hit by the Great Recession and, therefore, the proportion of individuals experiencing hard times. This should hold particularly true for unemployment and precarious employment given they were perhaps the most obvious negative repercussions of the Great Recession in many countries. By examining country levels, we are thus able to analyse the extent to which welfare policy satisfaction is linked to the severity of the crisis in the various countries included in our study.

Looking at unemployment first, we can see that the Greek respondents stand out as those by far the least satisfied with their government's action on unemployment. Next is France, followed by Poland and the two other southern European countries that also experienced a deep crisis, Italy and Spain.

Table 4.1. Satisfaction with government in welfare policy areas (% satisfied)

	FR	*DE*	*GR*	*IT*	*PL*	*ES*	*SE*	*CH*	*UK*
Unemployment	11.3	33.3	7.2	13.0	12.5	12.9	18.8	44.5	36.5
Precarious employment	15.8	22.9	9.0	15.8	10.7	11.4	24.8	38.9	23.9
The economy	16.7	53.7	10.9	16.1	25.5	20.0	32.1	60.4	47.6
Poverty	13.8	21.9	10.2	13.3	10.0	10.3	21.4	34.1	23.2
Education	27.2	35.4	10.5	22.1	29.3	17.7	34.8	65.2	37.6
Healthcare	37.5	39.3	11.7	27.8	11.7	26.1	29.6	54.6	34.1

Note: % based on respondents selecting points 6–10 on the 0–10 scale. Q: How satisfied are you with the way in which your country's government is dealing with the following on a scale from 0–10, where 0 means 'extremely dissatisfied' and 10 means 'extremely satisfied'?; *N* = 14,795.

Swedish respondents are also not very satisfied with government action on unemployment, particularly considering that the crisis was not too deep there. In Germany, the UK and, particularly, Switzerland, respondents were more satisfied with government action in this area. The patterns for satisfaction with government action on precarious employment are similar, with Greece once more standing out as having the lowest levels, followed by Poland, Spain and then France and Italy. On the other hand, Germany, Sweden and the UK have higher levels of satisfaction, with these being even higher in Switzerland.

These patterns suggest quite a strong correlation between satisfaction with government action on unemployment and precarious employment, on the one hand, and the intensity of the economic crisis, on the other, albeit with some exceptions. While Greece, the country hardest hit displays the lowest levels of satisfaction with government action on both unemployment and precarious employment, and Italy and Spain tend to be in the lower group, where the crisis was also quite pronounced, France and especially Poland stand out as countries where the crisis was not as bad as in the PIIGS countries but where respondents were particularly unsatisfied with government policies in these areas, at the same low levels as in those countries most hard hit. This reflects patterns uncovered earlier in chapter 2 for France, which also stood out in terms of economic evaluations being quite negative and pessimistic relative to the depth of the crisis there. With respect to unemployment and precarious employment policy satisfaction, Sweden also stands out as a country where respondents are particularly unsatisfied given also that the crisis was very weak there. It appears that the liberal reforms of the 1990s and the ensuing economic crisis might have left Swedish citizens unhappy with the break-down of the welfare state and its security nets for employment. Moreover, Germany's Hartz reforms also appear to have had an impact in dampening satisfaction levels in these two areas, despite the economy performing well in the context of the crisis, similarly to Switzerland, which however shows higher satisfaction levels. Moreover, as discussed earlier, austerity cuts were implemented across the board, even in those countries which could have avoided it given that they did not have such large deficit problems or ties to the Euro, such as the UK. These cuts are likely to have been felt by individuals and particularly by those in precarious employment conditions, linking back to dissatisfaction levels with government policy in these areas.

Government action in dealing with the economy in general shows, once more, the lowest satisfaction levels in Greece, followed by Italy and France and, at a slightly higher level, Spain and Poland, once more revealing France and Poland as countries with particularly negative policy evaluations given their relatively weak depth of crisis experience. Moreover, Sweden also has relatively low levels of satisfaction with government action on the economy, particularly relative to what would have been expected given its weaker experience of crisis. Levels of satisfaction were higher in the UK, Germany and Switzerland, in particular.

Concerning government action on poverty, Greece, Spain and Poland stand out as having the lowest levels of satisfaction, followed by Italy and France. Sweden, Germany and the UK have slightly higher levels, and Switzerland the highest. Again, the data confirm the pattern that the southern European countries, where the crisis hit the hardest, tend to be those where satisfaction with policy areas is also the lowest, though Poland and France also show low levels of satisfaction despite low levels of crisis impact. Sweden has particularly low levels of satisfaction given that the crisis was not very serious there at all. Despite experiencing a relatively strong crisis and deep budget cuts as a result of austerity policies, satisfaction levels with government action on poverty are relatively high in the UK. They are also quite high in Germany and, in particular, Switzerland, countries that, like Sweden, also experienced a weaker economic crisis.

The last two items look at satisfaction with welfare policies on education and healthcare. With respect to the first, we can see that satisfaction is lowest in Greece, with Spain next up. Satisfaction levels with education are slightly higher in Italy, France and Poland, followed by Sweden, Germany and the UK, with the highest levels found, once more, in Switzerland. Finally, the healthcare levels show, once more, the lowest satisfaction levels in Greece and Poland, but they are higher in Spain, Italy and Sweden and higher still in the UK, France, Germany and Switzerland. As such, Sweden appears to be doing slightly worse in education and healthcare policy satisfaction than one would expect, and France does particularly well in healthcare, particularly compared to its lower levels of satisfaction with all the other policy areas, also with respect to the extent of the crisis felt by the country. On the other hand, it might be that austerity cuts have not affected healthcare in France or education in the UK, say, as much as they have in other countries such as Greece, which experienced a much deeper economic crisis, so that respondents did not feel these effects as much.

Just as we did for economic evaluations in chapter 2 and for resilience in chapter 3, however, our key aim here is to move beyond the analysis of cross-national variation in policy satisfaction and to examine the way in which policy satisfaction in different areas varies between social groups with the populations of each country. Which groups in society are the most dissatisfied with government action on unemployment and precarious employment? To answer this question, we look at the proportion of respondents that said they were satisfied with government action on unemployment and precarious employment, in turn, across gender, age groups, socioeconomic status, employment status and citizenship status. We focus on unemployment and precarious employment since they reflect the clearest negative repercussions of the economic crisis. Tables 4.2 and 4.3 show the percentages of respondents saying that they were satisfied with government action on unemployment and precarious employment policies. Horizontally, the tables tell us whether satisfaction is higher or lower in different countries within each category, whereas vertically, they give us group-based differences. They also show if these group differences are statistically significant.

Gender differences in satisfaction with government policies on unemployment are significant in six of the nine countries, with women less likely to be satisfied across all six (table 4.2). On the other hand, belonging to different age groups only leads to significant differences in France, Switzerland and the UK, with younger age groups more satisfied in the former two, whereas the oldest are more satisfied in the latter. While the literature tends to speak of a precarisation of youth and their difficulties in finding employment, this does not appear to be reflected in the patterns shown for satisfaction with government policy on unemployment or, at least, not to be translated by youth into policy dissatisfaction.

As for the SES indicators, education, income and class show significant differences in Germany, Poland and Switzerland, education and class in Italy and Sweden, education and income in Spain, and income and class in the UK. Six of the nine countries have significant differences in terms of education levels, with those with the lowest educational qualifications least likely to to be satisfied with government action on unemployment. Income differences are also particularly marked across five of the nine countries, with those with lower income much less likely to be satisfied. Patterns by class are also significant in six of the nine countries, with those in manual occupations

Table 4.2. Satisfaction with government action on unemployment, by country and social category (% better)

	FR	*DE*	*GR*	*IT*	*PL*	*ES*	*SE*	*CH*	*UK*
Gender	**	***		**	***			***	***
Female	9.2	27.9	7.8	10.8	8.9	11.5	18.7	40.6	30.8
Male	13.7	37.9	6.6	15.1	16.4	14.2	18.9	48.4	42.7
Age	*							**	*
18–34	15.0	36.0	7.0	15.5	14.2	14.6	20.2	52.0	34.0
35–64	11.0	31.9	7.3	11.9	11.8	12.3	17.9	41.2	34.9
65+	7.8	34.7	7.7	14.1	9.0	13.6	19.8	43.2	42.7
Education		*		**	*	*	**	***	
University+	12.1	34.5	7.6	17.7	15.4	15.5	23.0	50.8	36.7
Secondary	10.6	34.9	6.7	12.8	10.9	12.1	16.9	41.1	39.0
< Secondary	11.2	26.2	8.0	10.4	12.9	11.0	15.4	41.0	32.4
Income		***			***	*		***	***
Low (1–5 decile)	10.2	28.9	7.5	12.0	9.3	11.4	17.6	39.8	30.2
High (6–10 decile)	12.6	36.7	6.6	14.8	14.7	14.7	19.3	51.2	40.7
Occup. of Chief Income Earner		*		***	***		*	**	***
Prof. | Mngr.	13.6	37.4	7.9	20.6	17.2	15.5	22.3	49.2	41.5
Intermediate	10.9	32.0	8.6	10.4	13.4	10.8	19.1	44.6	35.2
Manual	10.3	27.1	5.1	9.4	8.3	12.3	14.7	39.0	27.0
Other	8.6	36.5	6.3	9.7	7.8	14.6	13.3	36.9	28.9
Employment Stat.	***	**		*	***	**		***	*
Full-time	13.9	37.0	6.6	14.5	14.0	14.0	19.9	48.9	39.6
Part-time	16.9	29.1	6.2	13.2	13.8	14.3	19.3	40.4	35.0
Education	0.0	35.8	2.7	18.2	36.1	22.2	22.0	58.4	30.0
Unemployed	8.1	16.7	8.9	7.4	8.1	7.9	9.1	33.6	26.1
Retired | Disabled	7.5	28.8	8.7	14.9	7.7	14.3	17.2	38.0	36.8
Caring	8.2	31.3	7.8	8.9	8.2	7.4	17.9	39.0	25.6
Citizenship Stat.									
Migrant	13.4	35.1	8.2	11.2	9.2	12.2	18.4	44.8	40.6
Native	10.9	32.9	7.1	13.1	12.7	13.0	18.8	44.6	35.8

Note: % based on respondents selecting points 6–10 on the 0–10 scale; Q: On a scale from 0 to 10, where 0 means 'much worse' and 10 means 'much better'; *N* = 14,795.
* $p < 0.05$ ** $p < 0.01$ *** $p < 0.001$

generally the least likely to express satisfaction with government action on unemployment. Thus, those in the most at-risk positions of unemployment in terms of SES are clearly those least satisfied with government action in this policy domain.

Additionally, there are also important differences by employment status as one might expect, with those in unemployed, retired or disabled and caring situations generally less happy with government action on unemployment than those in full- or part-time employment or in education. Finally, there are no significant differences based on citizenship status. Migrants are not less likely to be satisfied with government policies than nationals.

Moving on to group differences in satisfaction with government action on precarious employment (table 4.3), we can see that here, too, that there are some significant gender differences across countries. Specifically, women were less satisfied than men in Poland, Italy, France, the UK and Switzerland. This supports the idea that women, who tend to be concentrated in lower-end occupations, are also more at risk of precarious modes of employment. Age group differences are only significant in four of the nine countries and young people, contrary to one might expect, are on the whole more positive than older generations, with the exception of the UK, where retirees are most positive. This pattern follows that for unemployment as well as for economic evaluations as seen in chapter 2, whereby youth generally tend to be the most positive with the exception of the UK, where retirees are the most satisfied.

With the SES indicators, education and income differences here appear less marked than for satisfaction with unemployment, but there are significant class differences in six of the nine countries. The education differences are most marked in Germany, Italy, Sweden and the UK, where individuals with lower levels of education are much less satisfied with government action on precarious employment. Equally, individuals with lower incomes are much less satisfied with government action on unemployment in Germany, Sweden, Switzerland and the UK. There are also significant differences by class in six of the nine countries, once again with those in manual employment least likely to be satisfied with government action on precarious employment.

Additionally, as expected, we find significant differences by employment status in most countries—six out of nine—showing that, in most countries, the unemployed in particular, but also those in retired or disabled groups and those in caring roles, are less satisfied with government policies on precarious employment than those in full-time, part-time employment and, generally, those in education. Finally, migrants were only more likely to be satisfied with government action on precarious employment in the UK.

In sum, this descriptive analysis provides a number of relevant findings on citizens' satisfaction with government policy in various areas, including on unemployment and precarious work. We found that there is a close link between satisfaction with welfare policies and the severity of crisis experiences at the national level, with countries like Greece that were particularly hard hit consistently scoring the lowest. On the other hand, countries like Germany and Switzerland that suffered a weaker crisis show higher levels satisfaction. However, respondents in some countries such as Sweden,

Table 4.3. Satisfaction with government action on precarious employment, by country and social category (% better)

	FR	*DE*	*GR*	*IT*	*PL*	*ES*	*SE*	*CH*	*UK*
Gender	*			**	***			***	*
Female	13.9	21.3	10.0	13.2	8.3	11.2	23.6	34.6	21.8
Male	18.1	24.1	7.9	18.3	13.3	11.6	26.1	43.2	26.1
Age	***	*						***	**
18–34	22.8	27.4	9.5	17.0	11.6	12.4	26.1	47.1	25.5
35–64	14.6	21.2	8.6	14.8	10.1	10.9	25.6	35.4	21.5
65+	12.8	21.0	11.5	20.4	10.1	12.5	20.2	36.9	29.6
Education		**		*			***		*
University+	16.6	22.6	9.7	20.5	11.8	13.2	29.9	41.6	21.5
Secondary	16.1	25.1	8.3	15.3	9.5	11.6	25.7	36.4	27.5
< Secondary	14.5	15.9	8.9	13.6	12.9	9.5	16.4	40.3	22.4
Income		***					*	***	*
Low (1–5 decile)	14.6	18.2	9.7	14.8	9.1	11.1	21.7	34.9	21.3
High (6–10 decile)	17.2	26.5	7.0	17.6	11.7	11.7	26.3	44.6	25.6
Occup. of Chief Income Earner		*		***	**	*	***	**	
Prof. | Mngr.	16.6	26.8	9.8	24.8	12.6	13.7	31.1	44.1	26.0
Intermediate	16.5	20.7	9.3	13.4	12.8	10.9	23.9	38.0	23.2
Manual	15.5	20.9	8.6	10.3	8.1	8.0	19.0	34.2	18.7
Other	11.7	21.2	7.3	12.1	5.6	13.9	17.2	32.4	25.3
Employment Stat.	**			**	***	**	**	***	
Full-time	18.3	24.9	8.6	17.2	10.9	12.1	28.2	43.4	24.5
Part-time	21.2	23.5	8.6	16.2	10.8	17.5	19.9	34.0	27.0
Education	13.3	23.8	8.0	21.8	38.9	12.7	34.0	51.7	25.0
Unemployed	8.1	11.1	10.2	8.6	11.3	6.6	22.7	33.6	14.5
Retired | Disabled	12.6	18.3	8.7	19.0	7.3	9.1	18.3	33.1	23.2
Caring	14.8	20.3	7.8	12.4	6.1	9.5	21.4	28.0	20.9
Citizenship Stat.									*
Migrant	16.4	26.2	8.2	12.4	8.0	9.3	27.2	40.7	29.0
Native	15.7	22.1	9.1	16.0	10.8	11.6	24.1	37.7	23.0

Note: % based on respondents selecting points 6–10 on the 0–10 scale; Q: On a scale from 0 to 10, where 0 means 'much worse' and 10 means 'much better'; N = 14,795.
* $p < 0.05$ ** $p < 0.01$ *** $p < 0.001$

France and Poland were particularly dissatisfied with government welfare policies relative to the severity of the crisis compared to other countries, whereas those in the UK were more positive than one might have expected on the whole given that they experienced deep austerity cuts. With respect to group differences, we found gender, SES and employment status differences for both policy areas, with the first two being more marked. On the other hand, for age and citizenship status we did not find particularly marked differences, although where these were significant, the direction went opposite to expectations, with the young being more satisfied, with the exception of the UK.

CORRELATES OF SATISFACTION WITH GOVERNMENT POLICY ON UNEMPLOYMENT AND PRECARIOUS WORK

In the previous section we examined descriptive patterns. However, in order to assess which variables are most important for predicting whether someone has positive evaluations of government policies with respect to unemployment and precarious work, we need to include the different variables into models which control for the other variables at the same time. To do so, we conduct step-wise models as in the previous chapters by introducing different types of factors in turn: first we include gender, then age, then the SES variables (education, income and occupational class), next we include employment status, then citizenship status, the extent to which the respondent had to reduce their consumption of staple goods as a result of the crisis, the extent to which the crisis impacted on their work situation and, finally, the three social capital measures also used in previous chapters (social trust, how often the respondent met with friends, and the respondent's associational membership) as they have been shown to link with greater satisfaction.

As in previous chapters, we take into account country differences by estimating multilevel regression models that treat country variation as random effects. The results of this analysis are shown in tables 4.4 and 4.5, respectively for satisfaction with government action on unemployment and on precarious work. We ran eight models, each including, in turn, the variables or groups of variables discussed above. All the models have been set at the same number of cases so as to makes statistical tests comparable across models.

Starting with unemployment (table 4.4), we can see in model 1 that women are less likely than men to be satisfied with government policy in this area. Adding age group in model 2 shows that older age groups are less likely to be positive about government policy on unemployment relative to younger ones. The effect of gender is strengthened, thus, suggesting that it is particularly young men that are more positive about government policy on unemployment.

Model 3 adds the SES variables and shows only weak differences by education level, with the least educated less likely than those with education levels of university or higher to be satisfied with unemployment policy. There are strong income and class differences, wherein those with the lowest incomes and those in intermediate, manual and other (mainly, farming) classes are less likely to be satisfied with government action on unemployment.

Model 4 includes employment status and shows that particularly the unemployed, retired or disabled are less happy with government policy on unemployment relative to those in full-time work. Model 5 includes migrant status and shows that there are no differences in this respect.

When we add reduced consumption in model 6, we observe an important decline in the effect of low income, suggesting that it is particularly those who experienced strong deprivation on a low income that were least satisfied with government action on unemployment. In this way, our models show that those sectors of the population in more vulnerable and precarious situations are the least happy with government welfare policies, specifically those in relation to employment. This is not surprising, given that these are the groups in society most at risk of entering the ranks of the unemployed or of having experienced previous spells of unemployment either themselves or in their families. Similarly, model 7 includes a variable examining the impact of the crisis on one's work situation and shows that this variable, too, has an important effect on satisfaction with unemployment policy and is closely linked with deprivation and reduced consumption, as well as with being in caring roles. Controlling for this variable, in fact, makes the effect of being in a caring role significant with respect to being much less likely than those in full-time work to be satisfied with unemployment policy.

Finally, model 8 includes the three social capital indicators. Social trust is closely linked to satisfaction with government policy on unemployment and so is associational membership. Moreover, social capital reduces the effect of the class variable, suggesting that this effect is linked to the level and extent of social and community bonds.

Moving on to satisfaction with government policy on precarious work (table 4.5), we can see in model 1 that women are less likely than men to be satisfied in this regard. Adding age group in model 2 shows that older age groups are less likely to be satisfied than the younger age groups. This finding seems to go against the idea of precarisation being a problem particularly for youth or, alternatively, that youth do not blame the government for this issue as much. Moreover, including age group reinforces the effect of gender, suggesting that older women are particularly less satisfied with government action in this respect.

Model 3 further includes the SES variables and shows that they are important predictors of dissatisfaction with government action on precarious employment. Individuals with a lower income are more likely to be dissatisfied with welfare policies for precarious work, which is likely to be linked to the

Table 4.4. Multi-level regression models on satisfaction with government action on unemployment

Model	*(1)*	*(2)*	*(3)*	*(4)*	*(5)*	*(6)*	*(7)*	*(8)*
Sociodemographic characteristics								
Gender (female)	−0.35***	−0.37***	−0.35***	−0.34***	−0.34***	−0.33***	−0.34***	−0.32***
	(0.04)	(0.04)	(0.04)	(0.04)	(0.04)	(0.04)	(0.05)	(0.05)
Age groups (ref. 18–34)	–	−0.26***	−0.28***	−0.23***	−0.23***	−0.24***	−0.24***	−0.29***
35–64	–	(0.05)	(0.05)	(0.05)	(0.05)	(0.05)	(0.05)	(0.05)
65+	–	−0.16*	−0.21**	0.01	0.01	−0.05	−0.07	−0.18
	–	(0.08)	(0.08)	(0.10)	(0.10)	(0.10)	(0.10)	(0.10)
Education group (ref. university +)								
Secondary	–	–	−0.07	−0.07	−0.06	−0.06	−0.07	−0.01
	–	–	(0.05)	(0.05)	(0.05)	(0.05)	(0.05)	(0.05)
< secondary	–	–	−0.12*	−0.10	−0.10	−0.08	−0.10	−0.00
	–	–	(0.06)	(0.06)	(0.06)	(0.06)	(0.06)	(0.07)
Income (low, 1–5 decile)	–	–	−0.24***	−0.21***	−0.21***	−0.12**	−0.12*	−0.13**
	–	–	(0.05)	(0.05)	(0.05)	(0.05)	(0.05)	(0.05)
Occup. of chief income earner (ref. prof. | mngr.)								
Intermediate	–	–	−0.18***	−0.17**	−0.17**	−0.16**	−0.17**	−0.14**
	–	–	(0.05)	(0.05)	(0.05)	(0.05)	(0.05)	(0.05)
Manual	–	–	−0.41***	−0.40***	−0.40***	−0.38***	−0.38***	−0.32***
	–	–	(0.07)	(0.07)	(0.07)	(0.07)	(0.07)	(0.07)
Other	–	–	−0.38***	−0.35***	−0.35***	−0.33***	−0.34***	−0.27**
	–	–	(0.09)	(0.09)	(0.09)	(0.09)	(0.09)	(0.09)
Employment status (ref. full-time)								
Part-time	–	–	–	−0.04	−0.05	−0.02	−0.01	−0.04
	–	–	–	(0.06)	(0.06)	(0.06)	(0.07)	(0.07)
In education	–	–	–	0.13	0.13	0.13	0.12	0.10
	–	–	–	(0.11)	(0.11)	(0.11)	(0.11)	(0.11)

Unemployed	–	–	–	−0.39***	−0.39***	−0.31***	−0.30**	−0.30**
	–	–	–	(0.09)	(0.09)	(0.09)	(0.09)	(0.09)
Retired | Disabled	–	–	–	−0.29***	−0.29***	−0.28***	−0.31***	−0.30***
	–	–	–	(0.08)	(0.08)	(0.08)	(0.08)	(0.08)
Caring	–	–	–	−0.20	−0.20	−0.20	−0.24*	−0.23*
	–	–	–	(0.11)	(0.11)	(0.11)	(0.11)	(0.11)
Citizenship status	–	–	–	–	0.05	0.07	0.07	0.06
(migrant)	–	–	–	–	(0.06)	(0.06)	(0.06)	(0.06)
Objective grievances								
Reduced consumption	–	–	–	–	–	−0.72***	−0.55***	−0.48***
	–	–	–	–	–	(0.09)	(0.10)	(0.10)
Crisis impacted on working situation	–	–	–	–	–	–	−0.43***	−0.42***
	–	–	–	–	–	–	(0.10)	(0.10)
Social capital								
Social trust	–	–	–	–	–	–	–	1.42***
	–	–	–	–	–	–	–	(0.09)
Met friends at least 1x per wk.	–	–	–	–	–	–	–	0.03
	–	–	–	–	–	–	–	(0.05)
Associational	–	–	–	–	–	–	–	0.11*
membership	–	–	–	–	–	–	–	(0.05)
Constant	−1.31***	−1.12***	−0.75**	−0.75**	−0.76**	−0.62**	−0.52*	−1.29***
	(0.25)	(0.26)	(0.25)	(0.25)	(0.25)	(0.23)	(0.23)	(0.23)
Log lik.	−6,933.67	−6,920.39	−6,857.71	−6,841.03	−6,840.66	−6,809.50	−6,800.84	−6,664.52
AIC	13,873.33	13,850.79	13,737.43	13,714.05	13,715.31	13,655.00	13,639.69	13,373.04
BIC	13,896.14	13,888.80	13,821.05	13,835.69	13,844.55	13,791.84	13,784.12	13,540.29
Sigma u	0.75	0.76	0.74	0.73	0.72	0.67	0.66	0.64
Rho	0.15	0.15	0.14	0.14	0.14	0.12	0.12	0.11

Standard errors in parentheses; $N = 14{,}795$.
* $p < 0.05$ ** $p < 0.01$ *** $p < 0.001$

Table 4.5. Multilevel regression models on satisfaction with government action on precarious employment

Model	*(1)*	*(2)*	*(3)*	*(4)*	*(5)*	*(6)*	*(7)*	*(8)*
Sociodemographic characteristics								
Gender (female)	−0.23***	−0.26***	−0.24***	−0.23***	−0.23***	−0.22***	−0.23***	−0.21***
	(0.04)	(0.04)	(0.04)	(0.05)	(0.05)	(0.05)	(0.05)	(0.05)
Age groups (ref. 18–34)	–	−0.30***	−0.32***	−0.26***	−0.26***	−0.26***	−0.26***	−0.31***
35–64	–	(0.05)	(0.05)	(0.05)	(0.05)	(0.05)	(0.05)	(0.05)
65+	–	−0.23**	−0.28***	−0.00	0.00	−0.04	−0.06	−0.16
	–	(0.08)	(0.08)	(0.10)	(0.10)	(0.10)	(0.10)	(0.10)
Education group (ref. university +)								
Secondary	–	–	0.04	0.04	0.05	0.05	0.04	0.10*
	–	–	(0.05)	(0.05)	(0.05)	(0.05)	(0.05)	(0.05)
< secondary	–	–	−0.06	−0.03	−0.03	−0.02	−0.03	0.07
	–	–	(0.06)	(0.06)	(0.06)	(0.07)	(0.07)	(0.07)
Income (low, 1-5 decile)	–	–	−0.17***	−0.14**	−0.14**	−0.08	−0.08	−0.09
	–	–	(0.05)	(0.05)	(0.05)	(0.05)	(0.05)	(0.05)
Occup. of chief income earner (ref. prof. | mngr.)								
Intermediate	–	–	−0.21***	−0.20***	−0.20***	−0.20***	−0.20***	−0.18**
	–	–	(0.05)	(0.05)	(0.05)	(0.05)	(0.05)	(0.05)
Manual	–	–	−0.42***	−0.40***	−0.40***	−0.39***	−0.39***	−0.33***
	–	–	(0.07)	(0.07)	(0.07)	(0.07)	(0.07)	(0.07)
Other	–	–	−0.43***	−0.40***	−0.40***	−0.39***	−0.39***	−0.33***
	–	–	(0.09)	(0.09)	(0.09)	(0.09)	(0.09)	(0.09)
Employment status (ref. full-time)								
Part-time	–	–	–	0.01	0.00	0.03	0.03	0.00
	–	–	–	(0.06)	(0.06)	(0.07)	(0.07)	(0.07)
In education	–	–	–	0.14	0.14	0.14	0.12	0.10
	–	–	–	(0.11)	(0.11)	(0.11)	(0.11)	(0.11)

Unemployed	–	–	–	−0.32***	−0.32***	−0.26**	−0.26**	−0.25**
	–	–	–	(0.09)	(0.09)	(0.09)	(0.09)	(0.09)
Retired | Disabled	–	–	–	−0.35***	−0.35***	−0.34***	−0.37***	−0.36***
	–	–	–	(0.08)	(0.08)	(0.08)	(0.08)	(0.08)
Caring	–	–	–	−0.22	−0.22*	0.23*	−0.26*	−0.24*
	–	–	–	(0.11)	(0.11)	(0.11)	(0.12)	(0.12)
Citizenship status	–	–	–	–	0.10	0.11*	0.12*	0.10
(migrant)	–	–	–	–	(0.06)	(0.06)	(0.06)	(0.06)
Objective grievances								
Reduced consumption	–	–	–	–	–	−0.54***	−0.39***	−0.33**
	–	–	–	–	–	(0.09)	(0.10)	(0.10)
Crisis impacted on working situation	–	–	–	–	–	–	−0.38***	−0.38***
	–	–	–	–	–	–	(0.10)	(0.11)
Social capital								
Social trust	–	–	–	–	–	–	–	1.30***
	–	–	–	–	–	–	–	(0.09)
Met friends at least 1x	–	–	–	–	–	–	–	0.05
per wk.	–	–	–	–	–	–	–	(0.05)
Associational	–	–	–	–	–	–	–	0.12**
membership	–	–	–	–	–	–	–	(0.05)
Constant	−1.42***	−1.19***	−0.91***	−0.92***	−0.94***	−0.83***	−0.74***	−1.47***
	(0.19)	(0.20)	(0.19)	(0.19)	(0.19)	(0.18)	(0.17)	(0.18)
Log likelihood	−6,872.83	−6,855.26	−6,807.98	−6,789.87	−6,788.36	−6,770.75	−6,763.88	−6,646.35
AIC	13,751.65	13,720.53	13,637.97	13,611.75	13,610.71	13,577.51	13,565.77	13,336.71
BIC	13,774.46	13,758.54	13,721.59	13,733.38	13,739.95	13,714.34	13,710.20	13,503.95
Sigma u	0.56	0.57	0.55	0.54	0.53	0.49	0.48	0.45
Rho	0.09	0.09	0.09	0.08	0.08	0.07	0.06	0.06

Standard errors in parentheses; $N = 14{,}795$.

* $p < 0.05$ ** $p < 0.01$ *** $p < 0.001$

fact that individuals in these social structural positions are more vulnerable to being in unstable employment arrangements. Moreover, individuals in intermediate, manual and other (mainly, farming) classes are also less likely than those in professional classes to be satisfied with government action on precarious employment. Model 4 further includes employment status and shows that, particularly, those who are unemployed, retired or disabled, relative to those in full-time work are less likely to be satisfied with government action on precarious employment. Moreover, the inclusion of employment status erodes the effect of income, suggesting that the unemployed and retired or disabled with low incomes are particularly likely to be dissatisfied in this respect. In contrast, adding citizenship status in model 5 does not yield any significant effects.

When reduced consumption is included in model 6, we can see it has a negative effect on satisfaction, and citizenship status becomes significant, suggesting that migrants that did not have to undergo deprivations were more likely to be satisfied with government policy in this area. Moreover, the inclusion of reduced consumption in model 6 erodes the effect of unemployed in particular, suggesting that those unemployed people that suffered deprivation in the crisis are even more likely to be dissatisfied with government policy on precarious work. These groups may have experienced precarious work themselves and, as such, may be relating their personal experiences of insecure work conditions to their negative evaluations of government action in this area. Similarly, model 7 includes the variable on whether the crisis had deteriorated work conditions and shows that this also has an important negative effect on policy satisfaction with precarious work and, also, leads to a decline in the effect of reduced consumption, showing that these two negative experiences are associated with each other.

Finally, model 8 includes the social capital variables and shows that social trust is linked to greater policy satisfaction whereas meeting with friends is not. There is also a positive effect of associational membership on policy satisfaction when all the other variables are accounted for.

CONCLUSION

This chapter examined the effects of the Great Recession on Europeans' policy evaluations in the field of unemployment and precarious work. We looked at the extent of Europeans' satisfaction with government policy on unemployment and on precarious employment, as well as with policy satisfaction on the economy, more widely, and on poverty, education and healthcare. Unemployment, precarious employment, the economy and other types of social spending have been the focus of political debate during the crisis, as governments have been challenged on whether they have done enough to tackle unemployment and whether spending cuts were justified as a political response to the economic crisis. While governments implemented austerity policies, many were left wondering whether a spending injection such as that applied in America, lifting the country out of recession, should not have also been the chosen policy in Europe. Moreover, anti-austerity movements lead to very large protests across the continent, protesting austerity cuts to public services (Giugni and Grasso 2015a). In a situation of economic crisis, where the poor are particularly vulnerable to exacerbating economic conditions, cuts to public spending further deteriorated the living standards of those at the bottom who relied on these. In this way, social policy was one of the main battlegrounds in the context of the crisis, where both old and new actors from within and outside the political institutional realm opposed their views against each other.

This chapter examined citizen satisfaction with welfare policies related to unemployment and precarious work in particular.

We showed how satisfaction, with these as well as other government policies, is closely linked to the extent to which countries experienced the crisis, but also that, in some countries, such as France, Poland and Sweden, respondents were more negative in their policy appraisals than would have been expected given the level of crisis experienced in their countries. We investigated, in this way, how policy satisfaction varies by country but we also looked at how it varies between different social groups. Both for satisfaction with unemployment policy and that with precarious work, women are less likely to be satisfied as well as those with lower incomes, those in less advantaged social classes and in more precarious employment situations. Additionally, reduced consumption and deteriorating work situations are linked with lower levels of satisfaction with government policy, whereas more social capital seems to be linked to higher levels of satisfaction.

Unemployment and precarious work are two of the most visible negative repercussions of the crisis. Of course, reforms allowing greater flexibility in labour contracts had begun much earlier, but the Great Recession accelerated and exacerbated these trends, and soaring unemployment in many countries has further increased the number of individuals in insecure and vulnerable social positions. Our analysis has shown that, on the whole, Europeans are not particularly satisfied with government policy action and, in particular, with respect to unemployment and precarious work. In a context of diminishing democratic capabilities to deliver social support and welfare policies fit for advanced societies, it is perhaps not too surprising that Europeans are not satisfied with government action in these areas. This chapter has shown that those with greater resources, who have been better able to weather the crisis, are more positive about government policy in these areas. However, these individuals are less likely to have experienced precarious work or spells of unemployment and, as such, are likely to have more positive views of these policy areas than those who have first-hand experience of being in these vulnerable positions. As we shall see in the next chapter, sociodemographic factors and levels of vulnerability also impact on Europeans' views in another contested political field in times of crisis, namely, immigration.

Chapter Five

Immigration and the Populist Challenge

This chapter looks at the effects of the Great Recession in the field of immigration and ethnic relations politics and how this has impacted on the views and political behaviours of Europeans. Together with unemployment, welfare and social spending, this is another key political issue that became particularly salient during the economic crisis. Migration and the way it is understood represents one of the fundamental conflicts where both traditional and new political actors confront each other in many contemporary democracies, leading to polarising debates and political contention, both inside and outside the institutionalised arenas. In this context, migrants are often treated by certain political entrepreneurs as scapegoats for wider social and economic problems and particularly so in times of economic hardship, when resources become more scarce and social groups are more likely to compete or feel they need to compete for resources.

Amongst individuals, one's stand on immigration has been shown to be key in explaining the support of extreme-right parties (Ivarsflaten 2008; Lubbers et al. 2002; Ford and Goodwin 2010). Questions about the place of newcomers in host societies—their rights and duties, and their integration—have become a main battleground for several parties, in particular, and for political contention in the public domain, more generally, albeit with key differences regarding how immigration and diversity are contested in different countries owing to specific national conceptions of citizenship (Koopmans et al. 2005).

In the recent context, it would seem that political views over immigration may have become less accepting, and this can be seen to contribute to an increased polarisation amongst both political elites and amongst the citizenry. Two series of events are often seen as having contributed to the development of polarisation on the issue. Firstly, the terrorist attacks by Muslim Jihadists that hit Europe in recent years and have directed attention to the so-called

Muslim question, that is, the supposed correlation between the increasing number of Muslims in European countries and such incidents. Secondly, what has been seen as an increasing emergency relating to the inflow of migrants and refugees from sub-Saharan Africa to Europe through various routes—above all, often tragically, through the Mediterranean route—which has furthermore brought to the fore suggestions, at least amongst certain political sides, that many of those landing in Europe should be returned to their home countries, that they are not 'real' refugees, and more generally a denial of their rights to move freely and to resettle.

Thus, the economic crisis can be understood to have been intermeshed with a crisis of European cultural identity—leading some to embrace the 'clash of civilizations' thesis (Huntington 1996)—as well as with a so-called 'refugee crisis' that found both the European Union and its member states unprepared and challenged in proposing concrete and feasible solutions. Moreover, both issues have been exploited by radical right and populist parties for electoral gains. In fact, mobilising and politicising the immigration issue has proved to be crucial for the rise of the radical right and to be part of a 'winning formula', which combines a critique of immigration with an embrace of wider authoritarianism and market liberalism (Kitschelt 1995), and has allowed it to make a significant electoral breakthroughs in many European countries.

To be sure, the increasing saliency of political debates and mobilisation around issues pertaining to immigration and ethnic relations preceded the economic crisis. Research on the mobilisation of social and cultural cleavages has shown that the structure and meaning of political conflicts in Europe have changed as a result of the rise of a new integration-demarcation cleavage brought about by increasing globalisation (Hutter 2014b; Kriesi et al. 2006, 2008, 2012). However, the economic crisis has further contributed to these structural and long-term transformations, spurring the rise of new political actors and mobilisations.

Indeed, recent years in particular have witnessed the rise of populist movements and parties making electoral breakthroughs (Bornschier 2017; Judis 2016; Kriesi 2014b; Kriesi and Pappas 2015; Mudde 2013; van Kessel 2015). Along with their anti-establishment and nationalist stance, these parties have made immigration their main battleground in their right-wing variants, particularly since the start of the refugee crisis in 2015. These movements and parties have been protagonists of a 'populist right round' of political mobilisation that has characterised the European political space since the 1990s and have focussed on issues pertaining to immigration, along with Europe and global justice (Hutter 2014b). Populist parties on the right in particular have benefitted much from the intermeshing of the economic crisis with the 'Muslim' question and that of the refugee crisis. The 'us the people against them the elites' ideology has been nurtured by the negative effects of the economic crisis amongst large sectors of the population. Populist right-wing parties can thus be seen in many contexts to have made of migrants the scapegoats for wider economic woes. On the other hand, perhaps as a reaction to these trends, a number of people and social movements have, on the contrary, exhibited solidary attitudes and behaviours towards migrants, although, in general, this does not seem to have directly translated into electoral gains by leftist parties.

In such a context, Europeans' views with respect to migrants—including xenophobic attitudes—as well as populist attitudes take on special importance and will be the object of study in this chapter. The next section discusses the literature on the relationship between attitudes to migration and economic crises. We then focus on a specific aspect of such a relationship: the linkage between the Great Recession and the rise of populisms, particularly of the right with its anti-immigration stance. The following two sections show the results of our empirical analysis, which is executed in two steps. The first step deals with our dependent variables, looking at how immigration and populist attitudes vary amongst individuals in various social groups across European countries. As we do in the other chapters, we then present in a second step multilevel regression models aimed at examining which factors are associated with such attitudes, once other relevant variables are controlled for in the models.

MIGRATION AND THE ECONOMIC CRISIS

Scholars have paid increasing attention to anti-immigrant feelings and views in recent years (see Ceobanu and Escandell 2010 and Hainmueller and Hopkins 2014 for reviews in sociology and political science, respectively).[1] This also includes studies focussing specifically on Europe (Lahav 2004; Schneider 2008; Sides and Citrin 2007). As a result, there is a wealth of scholarship on public attitudes towards immigrants and immigration. This body of work points to a number of determinants, or correlates, of such attitudes, in particular of anti-immigrant and even xenophobic attitudes. Such determinants bear both on individual characteristics and predispositions as well as on the larger sociopolitical and historical context (Quillian 1995). In other words, explanations of anti-immigrant attitudes refer to either the individual or the contextual level (Ceobanu and Escandell 2010). Regarding the latter, group threat theory, which focusses on intergroup competition and the related actual or perceived threat, has long attracted attention from scholars (Blumer 1958; Coser 1956; Fetzer 2000; Jackson et al. 2001; Scheepers et al. 2002).

Consistent with the overall aims of this book, here we focus on the individual level. We should also note, as Ceobanu and Escandell (2010) do, that studies on this topic often use different terms to refer to similar things, such as ethnic exclusionism, ethnic discrimination, anti-immigrant prejudice, xenophobia, prejudice against ethnic minorities, immigrant derogation, anti-immigrant sentiment, ethnic prejudice, anti-foreigner sentiment, anti-minority attitudes and, perhaps, still others. Here, we speak of attitudes towards migrants in general and of anti-immigrant or xenophobic attitudes when referring to views that are especially hostile towards them.

As far as individual-level explanations are concerned, sociologists and political scientists concur in saying that research on attitudes towards immigrants and immigration has followed two main paths: (1) a path stressing the self-interests of certain groups in society as well as the competition between natives and migrants over certain resources; and (2) a path emphasising group-related identities, values, attitudes and symbols (Ceobanu and Escandell 2010; Hainmueller and Hopkins 2014).[2] These two theoretical perspectives emphasise different explanatory factors, although they sometimes point to the very same factors but provide different interpretations for their impact.

Explanations stressing socioeconomic correlates and self-interest certainly belong to the first strand of micro-level theories. In this vein, research has shown the impact of one's socio-economic location and interests on attitudes towards immigrants and immigration (Pettigrew 2000; Sides and Citrin 2007). This would stem from the competition that occurs in the labour market and for residential space, as well as the resulting need to legitimate one's social position (Olzak 1992). More recent research has also stressed the role of material self-interest as operating through taxes and transfers rather than simply through labour market competition (Campbell et al. 2006; Dustmann and Preston 2007).

In this perspective, attitudes towards immigrants and immigration depend on material self-interest. Most work has focussed on labour-market competition (Mayda 2006; Scheve and Slaughter 2001). In particular, this strand suggests that the influx of low-skilled immigrants increases the supply of low-skilled labour, hence placing those working in those sectors in competition with and under threat by foreign workers (Scheve and Slaughter 2001). As a result, workers with lower skill levels and, more generally, from lower socioeconomic strata—including the unemployed—are more likely to display negative attitudes towards immigration because of the competition they face from immigrants with similar statuses (Esses et al. 2001; Quillian 1995; Semyonov et al. 2006, 2008). This explanation is consistent with scholarship on the electoral support for radical right parties, which shows that hostility towards immigration and anti-immigrant feelings tend to be concentrated among blue-collar and unskilled workers, especially those in the private sector (Ivarsflaten 2005). These are typically also identified as the 'losers of globalisation' (Kriesi et al. 2006, 2008, 2012) according to what has been seen as the emerging integration-demarcation cleavage who have much at stake when confronted with the threat—actual or perceived—posed by immigration. This research strand would therefore predict that individuals from the lower social strata, with low income and low education levels are more likely to be hostile to immigrants and, therefore, to display negative attitudes towards them, other things being equal. Furthermore, individuals who have suffered most from the negative consequences of the crisis and austerity measures should be more prone to hold anti-immigrant views as the competition with foreigners over jobs or residential space appears to be particularly strong in times of economic recession, when economic insecurity increases (Burns and Gimpel 2000).

In spite of their popularity, explanations stressing self-interest have largely failed to provide strong and consistent proof of their validity (Hainmueller and Hopkins 2014). This might be due to the fact that what matters is not so much 'objective' conditions and grievances as such, but rather 'subjective' perceptions of such conditions. In other words, xenophobic attitudes might be driven by feelings of relative deprivation, especially when the latter are associated with the threat posed by the influx of immigrants. However, pocketbook economic concerns do not seem to be a main driver of xenophobic attitudes but, rather, as Hainmueller and Hopkins (2014: 242) note, 'considered as a whole, the literature suggests that symbolic threats are likely to be more influential in shaping immigration attitudes'. Symbolic factors and personal contact—the latter being inversely correlated to xenophobic attitudes—may have a stronger impact than socioeconomic aspects or material interests (McLaren 2003; Sides and Citrin 2007; Wilkes et al. 2008; see, further, Ceobanu and Escandell 2010).

In this vein, the second strand of micro-level theories stresses the role of identities and values, and more generally that of symbolic interests as well as sociopsychological factors and dynamics. As Hainmueller and Hopkins (2014) point out, this is a rather heterogeneous approach that includes different strands, with one of them stressing perceived threats to national identity, and others emphasising prejudice and stereotyping.

Values and personal identifications surely play an important role in this perspective (Davidov et al. 2008; Sides and Citrin 2007). Thus, while approaches stressing competition and self-interest most often point to the role of non-attitudinal predictors of xenophobic attitudes such as social location or the level of skills to be valued in the labour market, sociopsychological approaches tend to focus on a variety of attitudinal predictors. As summarised by Ceobanu and Escandell (2010), these pertain to perceptions about the consequences of immigration, perceptions about the size of immigrant populations, political-ideological orientations, and attachments and identifications with the national community or supranational entity such as the European Union. Given that our study relates to the effects of the Great Recession, in our analysis we also examine sociotropic concerns. We look, in particular, at the evaluations of the state of the economy in relative terms (as compared to a previous period) as well as evaluations of the role of the government in dealing with the economic crisis. This is in line with sociopsychological approaches, which have stressed perceptions of sociotropic effects on the receiving country as a whole (Hainmueller and Hopkins 2014). While the literature points mainly to cultural sociotropic effects (Card et al. 2012; Sniderman and Hagendoorn 2007; Sniderman et al. 2004), evidence also exists for the role of economic sociotropic threats and concerns (Citrin et al. 1997; see, further, Hainmueller and Hopkins 2014).

As discussed, research on attitudes towards immigrants and immigration has mainly stressed two kinds of explanatory factors: individual self-interest and egotropic concerns, on the one hand, and symbolic and—sometimes economic, but mostly cultural—sociotropic concerns, on the other. Indeed, as Hainmueller and Hopkins (2014: 225) have aptly summarised in their review article,

> These two literatures have developed largely in isolation from one another, yet the conclusions that emerge from each are strikingly similar. Consistently, immigration attitudes show little evidence of being strongly correlated with personal economic circumstances. Instead, research finds that immigration attitudes are shaped by sociotropic concerns about its cultural impacts—and to a lesser extent its economic impacts—on the nation as a whole.

Interestingly, while, as we have seen, most often the two research traditions point to different explanatory factors, sometimes the very same factor is stressed, only with a different interpretation of its effect. Education is perhaps the most relevant case in point. A number of studies have shown that a higher educational level leads to less hostile views about immigrants and immigration (Hainmueller and Hiscox 2007; Hello et al. 2002; Quillian 1995; Wagner and Zick 1995). The reasons for the existence of such an effect, however, may be multiple. While many take education as an indicator of skill level and, therefore, conclude that individuals with lower education hold more anti-immigrant attitudes because they are in competition for jobs, residential space or other resources (Ford and Goodwin 2010), others maintain that this is primarily due to differences in cultural values and beliefs about immigration's sociotropic impacts (Hainmueller and Hiscox 2010) and that education has primarily a (cultural) 'liberalising' effect (Chandler and Tsai 2001; Coenders and Scheepers 2003), therefore casting serious doubts on the idea that the labour market position is a strong predictor of immigration attitudes (Hainmueller et al. 2011).

THE POPULIST CHALLENGE

As we have noted, the Great Recession has brought forth the 'populist challenge' (Kriesi 2014b; Mény and Surel 2002). An increasing number of scholars have analysed populist mobilisations and parties recently (Bornschier 2017; Judis 2016; Kriesi 2014b; Kriesi and Pappas 2015; Mudde 2013; Pauwels 2014; van Kessel 2015). While xenophobia and populism are by no means coterminous, they are closely related to each other inasmuch as those parties that emphasise the immigration issue in order to make electoral gains often also feature populist discourse and appeals, particularly on the Right. It is perhaps not by chance that labels such as 'radical right', 'extreme right', 'nationalist' or 'populist right' are often used interchangeably by both scholars and pundits to refer to such parties. These include many examples of parties that have made important electoral gains in recent years, but also parties that existed before the economic crisis, such as the Front National in France or Jobbik in Hungary, perhaps two of the most well-known examples of this kind of party in Western and Eastern Europe, respectively. Most European countries have a right-wing populist party whose importance may vary depending on a number of factors. As a result, research has most often focussed on right-wing populism (see Mudde 2013 for a comparative overview).

The increasing electoral strength of challenger and populist parties during the Great Recession relates, to a large extent, to the fact that many Europeans today are not fully satisfied with current opportunities for political choice or with mainstream political elites. Just as we examine xenophobic attitudes, here we focus on populist attitudes amongst the populations of the nine countries covered by our study as well as how they can be explained at the individual level of analysis.[3] Before we do so, however, we need to clarify what we mean by 'populism', as this is quite a fuzzy term which is sometimes used to designate different things. Indeed, populism can be and is defined in different ways. Yet, two views are perhaps prevailing in the literature. The first view sees populism as a specific kind of discourse (Levitsky and Roberts 2011; Weyland 2001). This may include a focus on communication style or strategy. The second and most common view stresses the ideological dimension of populism (Mudde 2004; Mudde and Rovira Kaltwasser 2013, 2017). In this perspective, populism is a "thin" ideology 'that considers society to be ultimately separated into two homogeneous and antagonistic groups, "the pure people" versus the "corrupt elite", and which argues that politics should be an expression of the *volonté générale* (general will) of the people' (Mudde 2004: 543; see, further, Mudde and Rovira Kaltwasser 2013). In other words, such an ideational approach to populism stresses the existence of two homogeneous groups—the people and the elite—in an antagonistic relationship with each other, the primacy of popular sovereignty, and a positive valorisation of the people while the elites are negatively described (Kriesi 2014b). Rooduijn (2014) points to four characteristics that constitute the core elements of populism: an emphasis on the central position of the people, a criticism of the elite, the perception of the people as a homogeneous entity and the proclamation of a serious crisis.

The ideational definition has the advantage of seeing populism not only as a right-wing phenomenon, as it is often done, but also considers left-wing and centrist populism. The latter, in fact, has become particularly relevant in the context of the economic crisis. The cases of *Syriza* in Greece, the *Movimento 5 Stelle* in Italy and *Podemos* in Spain are probably the most prominent examples. Unlike the populist parties of the right, which usually result from a transformation of previous, more moderate and centrist parties—like the Swiss People's Party—or emerge directly in the traditional form of a new political party, those from the left or center can often be characterised as 'movement-parties' (della Porta et al. 2017), at least in their *statu nascenti*.

The rise of populism in Western Europe, of course, has a variety of reasons: some are more structural, others more conjunctural. Discussing all such reasons is beyond the scope of this chapter. However, it is important to stress what are seen as some key structural preconditions for the populist challenge. Ultimately, the rise of populism can be traced back to the crisis of representation and the progressive erosion of the representative function of political parties (Katz and Mair 1995, 2009). Such erosion of the parties' representative function, furthermore, has been brought about, among other things, by two large-scale structural processes: (1) the increasing importance of the European and global levels in the contemporary multilevel governance structures, leading to a denationalisation of politics and policymaking; and (2) the increasing mediatisation of politics, which contributes to a 'depoliticisation' of politics' (Kriesi 2014b). This has meant the rise of a 'partyless democracy' (Mair 2002) favouring the mobilisation of populist challengers:

> As party leaderships become increasingly remote from the wider society, and as they also appear increasingly similar to one another in ideological or policy terms, it simply becomes that much easier for populist protestors to rally against

> the supposed privileges of an undifferentiated political class. As party democracy weakens, therefore, the opportunities for populist protest clearly increase. (Mair 2002: 88)

Such a populist protest, in turn, may take different forms, such as the rise of new challengers in the party system, the radical rejection of the party system as such and the expansion of conflict beyond the party system—that is, outside the electoral arena and into the protest arena instead (Kriesi 2014b).[4]

To be sure, populism is a phenomenon which predates the Great Recession, both in Europe and in other continents such as, in particular, Latin America. As far as the old continent is concerned, this applies especially to right-wing populism, but to some extent also to left-wing populism. The economic crisis, however, is likely to have exacerbated such previous trends. In other words, the Great Recession has helped populist parties to become more effective political challengers of the existing mainstream. As such, the economic crisis is likely to have created a fertile ground for the rise of support of populist views among various sectors of the citizenry. More generally, populism is often linked to contexts and perceptions of crisis. As Taggart (2004: 275) has noted, 'populism is a reaction to a sense of extreme crisis. Populism is not the politics of the stable, ordered polity but comes as an accompaniment to change, crisis and challenge'. Deep economic crises as well as the hardship they bring may thus provide further fertile conditions for the development of support for populist parties.

In this chapter we focus on xenophobic and populist attitudes as well as, in the final stage, attachment to populist parties. Unlike attitudes on immigrants and immigration, which are the object of an abundant and long-standing literature, populist attitudes are less often studied (see for e.g. Akkerman et al. 2014; Rico and Anduiza 2017). Scholarship has tended to focus on electoral support for populist parties. Yet, focussing on populist attitudes amongst the population has a number of advantages, as compared to explaining vote choice (Rico and Anduiza 2017). This includes allowing populism to vary across individuals regardless of their vote choice, allowing 'to separate populism from features that might regularly occur together *with* it, but are not part *of* it' (Mudde and Rovira Kaltwasser 2017: 2), and allowing focus on demand-side factors, not only on supply-side factors as the bulk of existing works have done so far (Mudde 2007; van Kessel 2013).

Our analysis of populist attitudes will follow the one on xenophobic attitudes. In both cases we first show descriptively how such attitudes vary across the nine countries covered by our study. Then, in a second, more explanatory step, we examine a number of correlates of xenophobic and populist attitudes. We will start from the socioeconomic correlates—also in order to ascertain who is most likely to hold such views—then add in our models predictors pertaining to the grievances produced by the crisis—both in their subjective and objective manifestations—the evaluations of the role of the government in the crisis and, more generally, the economy, political attitudes and values, and finally the amount of social capital as measured by the level of social trust as well as interpersonal and associational networks. Given the focus of this book on the impact of the economic crisis, we devote attention to this aspect.

XENOPHOBIC AND POPULIST ATTITUDES IN THE WAKE OF THE ECONOMIC CRISIS

In the first part of our empirical analysis, we examine xenophobic and populist attitudes as they are captured by our survey conducted in the wake of the economic crisis.[5] To be sure, neither in these descriptive analyses nor in the more explanatory ones below can we establish, without doubt, a single causal direction of effect between the crisis and such attitudes. What we can do here, however, is ascertain the extent to which Europeans in the nine countries included in our study hold xenophobic and populist views and, above all, how such views vary across those countries. This is important because it allows us to grasp the prevalence of xenophobic and populist attitudes and also gives a sense of the potential electoral base for radical right parties in Europe.

In order to capture xenophobic and populist attitudes, we created two indexes that will be used in the analyses below.[6] The xenophobic attitudes index is made of two items, based on the following two survey questions: 'Would you say it is generally bad or good for [respondent's country]'s economy that people come to live here from other countries? Please state your answer on this scale, where 0 means 'bad' and 10 means 'good'; and 'Would you say that [respondent's country]'s cultural life is generally undermined or enriched by people coming to live here from other countries? Please state your answer on this scale, where 0 means 'undermined' and 10 means 'enriched'. The former is meant to capture the economic dimension of anti-immigrant attitudes and opinions, while the latter refers to their cultural dimension. Both items were then combined to form a xenophobic attitudes scale ranging from 0 to 10 (Cronbach's alpha = 0.86).

Populist attitudes are captured through a battery of eight items. The question read as follows: 'To what extent do you agree or disagree with each of the following statements?' Eight response items were then offered (with the following response options: disagree strongly, disagree, neither, agree, and agree strongly). The first six have been proposed by Akkerman et al. (2014), based on statements designed to tap into core ideas that make up the populist discourse such as people-centrism, anti-elitism, the antagonism between the people and the elite, and the primacy of popular sovereignty (see further Rico and Anduiza 2017): 'The politicians in [respondent's country]'s parliament need to follow the will of the people'; 'The people, and not politicians, should make our most important policy decisions'; 'The political differences between the elite and the people are larger than the differences among the people'; 'I would rather be represented by a citizen than by a specialised politician'; and, 'What people call "compromise" in politics is really just selling out on one's principles'. To these six items, we added two additional ones meant to capture the anti-elitist dimension of populism: 'The particular interests of the political class negatively affect the welfare of the people', and, 'Politicians always end up agreeing when it comes to protecting their privileges'. All eight items were then combined to form a populist attitudes scale ranging from 0 to 4 (Cronbach's alpha = 0.88).

Table 5.1 shows the mean values on the two scales referring to xenophobic attitudes as well as the combined index. Looking at the average scores, most of the respondents stand somewhere around the middle, between score 4 and score 6. This holds for both individual items as well as for the combined index.

Here, however, we are mostly interested in variations across countries, including ascertaining whether countries hardest hit by the economic crisis

Table 5.1. Attitudes towards immigrants by country (means)

	FR	*DE*	*GR*	*IT*	*PL*	*ES*	*SE*	*CH*	*UK*
Would you say its generally bad or good for [country]'s economy that people come to live here from other countries?	4.31	5.87	3.77	4.35	4.47	5.41	4.81	5.65	4.96
Would you say that [country]'s cultural life is generally undermined or enriched by people coming to live here from other countries?	4.70	5.78	4.09	4.79	4.73	5.96	5.51	5.57	4.90
Combined index	4.52	5.81	3.95	4.57	4.60	5.69	5.16	5.61	4.92

Note: 0–10 scales, from 'bad' to 'good', respectively from 'undermined' to 'enriched'; Cronbach's alpha for the combined index = 0.86

show higher levels of xenophobic attitudes amongst the population than countries less severely hit. Looking at the combined index, we can see higher levels of xenophobic—or anti-migrant—attitudes in Greece and, to a lesser extent, also in France, Italy and Poland (lower values on these scales reflect stronger xenophobic views). From a 'grievance theory' or 'ethnic competition' perspective, the cases of Greece and Italy may be, at least in part, explained by the strong influx of immigrants from sub-Saharan Africa in recent years given these two countries have been at the forefront of the so-called 2015 refugee crisis. For France and Poland, the explanation might be different, relating to the specific political situation in those countries, most notably a growing radical right party or, in the French case, tense minority-majority ethnic relations following the latest terrorist attacks.

Countries such as Germany, Spain, Switzerland and, to some extent, Sweden and the UK, in contrast, are characterised by lower average levels of xenophobic attitudes. Three of these countries (Germany, Sweden and Switzerland) have been largely—though not entirely—spared the worse negative effects of the Great Recession. This might suggest that there is a link between the severity of the economic crisis and the presence of xenophobic attitudes. However, in this group of countries we also find the UK and especially Spain, two countries that have been harder hit by the crisis, hence casting doubts about this kind of simplistic explanation.

Do these distributions vary if we look at the two more specific items? In general, they do not, as the ranking of the nine countries remains basically the same whether we consider the economic or the cultural dimension of these attitudes. Interestingly, in most countries the economic dimension displays a higher average level of xenophobic attitudes than the cultural dimension, the exceptions being Germany, Switzerland, and the UK, where culturally based anti-immigrant views are predominant. This casts some doubts about the thesis that, when it comes to anti-immigrant sentiments, the main stake is a cultural rather than economic one, such as threatening the national—or European, whatever this is understood to mean—cultural identity and Western values (Ford and Goodwin 2010). At least in the wake of the economic crisis and in most of the countries included in this study, individuals seem more concerned with immigrants having a negative impact on the country's economy than on its cultural life.

Table 5.2 shows cross-national differences concerning populist attitudes (in this case, higher values on the scales mean stronger populist views). Starting once again from the combined index, we can see that the overall level of populism amongst the population is quite high, ranging between 2.5 and 3 on a 0 to 4 scale. This must be taken with some caution, as we do not have a baseline to which we can compare these figures over time, but it points to an

Table 5.2. Populist attitudes by country (means)

	FR	*DE*	*GR*	*IT*	*PL*	*ES*	*SE*	*CH*	*UK*
Politicians in [country]'s parliament need to follow the will of the people	2.99	2.94	3.24	2.99	3.20	3.24	3.11	2.88	3.05
People, not politicians, should make our most important policy decisions	2.79	2.59	2.80	2.77	2.73	2.80	2.44	2.65	2.35
Political differences between the elite and the people are larger than differences among the people	2.79	2.60	2.94	2.96	3.09	2.94	2.54	2.51	2.69
I would rather be represented by a citizen than by a specialised politician	2.87	2.38	2.76	2.79	2.64	2.60	2.26	2.39	2.31
Elected officials talk too much and take too little action	3.11	2.87	3.15	3.27	3.25	3.20	2.84	2.73	2.87
What people call 'compromise' in politics is really just selling out on one's principles	2.69	2.40	2.70	2.72	2.31	2.36	2.40	2.19	2.36
Particular interests of the political class negatively affect the welfare of the people	3.04	2.60	3.15	3.21	2.94	3.18	2.47	2.44	2.57
Politicians always end up agreeing when it comes to protecting their privileges	3.20	2.94	3.18	3.35	3.11	3.27	2.54	2.75	2.93
Combined index	2.93	2.66	2.99	3.01	2.91	2.95	2.57	2.57	2.64

Note: 0–4 scales, from 'disagree strongly' to 'agree strongly'. Cronbach's alpha for the combined index = 0.88.

increasing gap between the people and political elites as well as to a strong detachment and disaffection from politics more generally (Dalton and Wattenberg 2002; Grasso 2016a; Hay 2007; Mair 2006).

Cross-country variations are not very large but, still, we can observe some differences. Overall, in terms of the combined index, we discern two groups of countries: France, Greece, Italy, Poland and Spain which display higher levels of populist attitudes amongst the population than in Germany,

Sweden, Switzerland and the UK. As we can see, this largely reflects the pattern observed earlier regarding xenophobic attitudes, with only the exception of Spain which, in this case, clusters differently. This shows once again that populist views are more widespread in the countries that have been hardest hit be the economic crisis, but also that the correlation between the crisis and populism is far from perfect. Quite logically, these are also countries that have witnessed the rise of populist parties in recent years, mostly from the Right but, in some cases, also from the Left or center.

Moving to the more specific items, we see that, in general, people are particularly sensitive to members of parliament having to follow the will of the people (first item), elected officials talking too much and taking too little action (fourth item), the particular interests of the political class negatively affecting the welfare of the people (seventh item) and politicians always ending up agreeing when it comes to protecting their privileges (eighth item). This holds especially true in the three southern European countries and also in Poland, although the anti-elite dimension of populism (last two items) is somewhat less relevant in the latter country, while it takes on particular importance in France as well. Additionally, even in those countries where the overall level of populist attitudes is lower—namely, Germany, Sweden, Switzerland and the UK—most respondents are concerned about the fact that politicians should follow the will of the people.

In sum, this brief descriptive analysis suggests that a sizeable share of Europeans—at least those living in the nine countries covered by our study—hold xenophobic or at least anti-immigrant views and, even more so, populist views in the wake of the Great Recession. Even those who do not directly express xenophobia or populism are often worried about the potential negative effects of immigration on both their country's economy and cultural life and are critical of the political elites—not to say detached and alienated from politics, in general, and institutional politics in particular. At the same time, there are important cross-national differences. In general, those countries that have been hardest hit by the economic crisis and its negative effects display a higher average level of xenophobic and populist attitudes. However, we should be cautious before establishing a direct correlation between the severity of the crisis, on the one hand, and the rise of xenophobic and populist attitudes, on the other. While the grievances relating to the crisis and its effects might play a role, there are clearly other factors of relevance when it comes to explaining why people become hostile to migrants as well as more inclined to oppose the 'people' to the 'elites'. This leads us to investigate more thoroughly the factors associated with xenophobic and populist attitudes in the next section.

CORRELATES OF XENOPHOBIC AND POPULIST ATTITUDES

The second part of our empirical analysis in this chapter examines a number of explanations for xenophobic and populist attitudes as discussed earlier. This leads us to inquire into a number of factors that are associated with such attitudes. To do so we conduct a series of multilevel regression models on both types of attitudes as dependent variables. We include in our models most of the independent variables we used in previous chapters, with some changes relating to the specific aspects we are dealing with here. The predictors included in the models below form seven clusters: the sociodemographic characteristics also included in previous chapters (gender, age, education, income, occupation, employment status and citizenship status), subjective grievances (perceptions of the crisis, sociotropic evaluations of the state of the economy, egotropic or pocketbook evaluations in terms of retrospective and prospective feelings of relative deprivation), objective grievances (perceptions of how the crisis has impacted one's personal life in general and the workplace),[7] evaluations of the role of the government in the economic crisis (how it has dealt with it and blame assignment), political attitudes and values (political interest and efficacy as well as left-right and libertarian-authoritarian values), and social capital variables (social trust, meeting friends and associational membership).[8] Each cluster of factors is introduced stepwise in a subsequent model. By doing so, we can not only see the direct effect of a given variable but also the extent to which such an effect depends on the variables introduced in the following model(s). All the independent variables have been standardised as either dummies or 0 to 1 scales. Additionally, for these analyses we have reversed the coding of the xenophobic attitude scale so that higher values mean higher levels of xenophobia and of negative views of immigration. All the models have been set at the same number of cases so as to makes statistical tests comparable across models.

Table 5.3 shows the results for xenophobic attitudes. The first model refers to sociodemographic characteristics, allowing us to examine how anti-migrant attitudes vary depending on gender, age, education, income, occupation, employment status and citizenship status. These are the very same aspects that we considered in chapters 2, 3 and 4 when we looked at inequality, resilience and unemployment. All these variables are significantly correlated with the positioning of respondents on the xenophobic attitude scale, except for gender and income.[9] This suggests that the development of anti-immigrant attitudes is, to a large extent, socially embedded. To begin with, they depend on age. Specifically, younger people (the reference category for age group)

Table 5.3. Multilevel regression models on xenophobic attitudes (fixed part only)

Model	*(1)*	*(2)*	*(3)*	*(4)*	*(5)*	*(6)*	*(7)*
Sociodemographic characteristics							
Gender (female)	0.03	−0.02	−0.02	−0.01	−0.02	0.20***	0.12**
	(0.04)	(0.04)	(0.04)	(0.04)	(0.04)	(0.04)	(0.04)
Age groups (ref.: 18-34) 35–64	−0.02	−0.11*	−0.19***	−0.19***	−0.19***	−0.22***	−0.02
	(0.05)	(0.05)	(0.05)	(0.05)	(0.05)	(0.05)	(0.04)
65+	−0.22**	−0.27**	−0.42***	−0.41***	−0.38***	−0.64***	−0.22**
	(0.08)	(0.08)	(0.08)	(0.08)	(0.08)	(0.08)	(0.07)
Education group (Ref.: University and above)							
Secondary	0.48***	0.48***	0.49***	0.49***	0.49***	0.30***	0.20***
	(0.05)	(0.05)	(0.05)	(0.05)	(0.05)	(0.05)	(0.04)
< secondary	0.90***	0.86***	0.86***	0.87***	0.85***	0.57***	0.44***
	(0.07)	(0.06)	(0.06)	(0.06)	(0.06)	(0.06)	(0.05)
Income (low, 1st to 5th decile)	−0.01	−0.09	−0.13**	−0.13**	−0.12*	−0.00	0.02
	(0.05)	(0.05)	(0.05)	(0.05)	(0.05)	(0.04)	(0.04)
Occupation of chief wage earner (Ref.: Professional or managerial)							
Intermediate	0.28***	0.25***	0.23***	0.23***	0.23***	0.18***	0.14**
	(0.06)	(0.06)	(0.06)	(0.06)	(0.06)	(0.05)	(0.04)
Manual	0.50***	0.45***	0.41***	0.41***	0.40***	0.31***	0.19***
	(0.07)	(0.07)	(0.07)	(0.07)	(0.07)	(0.06)	(0.05)

Other	0.48***	0.41***	0.38***	0.38***	0.35***	0.21**	0.07
	(0.09)	(0.08)	(0.08)	(0.08)	(0.08)	(0.07)	(0.07)
Unemployed	0.18*	0.06	0.02	0.02	0.02	0.09	0.07
	(0.08)	(0.08)	(0.08)	(0.08)	(0.08)	(0.07)	(0.06)
Citizenship status (migrant)	−0.58***	−0.55***	−0.54***	−0.54***	−0.53***	−0.49***	−0.45***
	(0.06)	(0.06)	(0.06)	(0.06)	(0.06)	(0.05)	(0.05)
Subjective grievances	–						
Serious crisis	–	0.35***	0.32***	0.32***	0.23***	0.25***	0.13**
	–	(0.06)	(0.06)	(0.06)	(0.06)	(0.05)	(0.05)
Sociotropic evals. last yr.	–	−2.15***	−1.56***	−1.56***	−1.09***	−1.04***	−0.64***
	–	(0.11)	(0.12)	(0.12)	(0.13)	(0.12)	(0.11)
Pocketbook retrospective	–	–	−0.22*	−0.22	−0.19	−0.37***	−0.17
evals. 5 yrs.	–	–	(0.11)	(0.11)	(0.11)	(0.10)	(0.09)
Pocketbook prospective	–	–	−1.16***	−1.16***	−1.09***	−0.85***	−0.61***
evals. 1 yr.	–	–	(0.12)	(0.12)	(0.12)	(0.11)	(0.10)
Objective grievances							
Reduced consumption	–	–	–	−0.01	−0.02	0.06	0.01
	–	–	–	(0.10)	(0.10)	(0.09)	(0.08)
Impact of crisis on working	–	–	–	0.01	−0.02	0.14	0.11
situation	–	–	–	(0.10)	(0.10)	(0.09)	(0.08)
Evals. of govt's role							
Satisfaction with	–	–	–	–	−0.95***	−1.08***	−0.60***
government	–	–	–	–	(0.10)	(0.09)	(0.08)
Blames the national	–	–	–	–	−0.04	−0.12**	−0.10*
government	–	–	–	–	(0.05)	(0.04)	(0.04)

(continued)

Table 5.3. *(continued)*

Model	*(1)*	*(2)*	*(3)*	*(4)*	*(5)*	*(6)*	*(7)*
Political attitudes & values							
Political interest	–	–	–	–	–	–0.05	–0.01
	–	–	–	–	–	(0.03)	(0.03)
Internal political efficacy	–	–	–	–	–	–0.25***	–0.17**
	–	–	–	–	–	(0.06)	(0.05)
External political efficacy	–	–	–	–	–	0.45***	0.15**
	–	–	–	–	–	(0.06)	(0.05)
Left–right scale (subjective)	–	–	–	–	–	1.90***	1.51***
	–	–	–	–	–	(0.08)	(0.08)
Left–right values	–	–	–	–	–	1.56***	0.97***
	–	–	–	–	–	(0.12)	(0.11)
Libertarian–authoritarian	–	–	–	–	–	3.92***	2.80***
values	–	–	–	–	–	(0.12)	(0.11)
Social capital							
Social trust	–	–	–	–	–	–	–4.14***
	–	–	–	–	–	–	(0.08)
Meets friends at least every	–	–	–	–	–	–	–0.02
wk.	–	–	–	–	–	–	(0.04)
Associational membership	–	–	–	–	–	–	–0.10**
	–	–	–	–	–	–	(0.04)
Constant	4.38***	5.30***	5.86***	5.86***	6.05***	2.62***	4.96***
	(0.21)	(0.17)	(0.17)	(0.17)	(0.18)	(0.18)	(0.18)
Log likelihood	–31,321.769	–31,062.486	–30,997.404	–30,997.404	–30,952.894	–29,394.240	–28,034.936

Standard errors in parentheses. $N = 13,280$.
* $p < 0.05$ ** $p < 0.01$ *** $p < 0.001$

tend to have more hostile views about migrants than older age groups, in particular those who are in the oldest age group. Education, in contrast, is negatively correlated with xenophobic attitudes, as the most highly educated respondents (the reference category for education) are more open towards migrants than less educated ones, attesting to the fact that higher levels of education may well have a 'liberalising' effect (Chandler and Tsai 2001; Coenders and Scheepers 2003), favouring more open views about immigrants owing to cultural values and beliefs about immigration's sociotropic impacts (Hainmuller and Hiscox 2007). Or perhaps, more highly educated people feel less threatened by immigration as they feel more secure in their social position.

Xenophobic attitudes are also linked to social class. As work on the electoral support to radical right parties has shown (Ivarsflaten 2005), hostility towards immigration and anti-immigrant feelings tend to be concentrated among blue-collar and unskilled workers, especially those in the private sector. This is confirmed in our data, as all occupational categories are more likely to display higher scores on the xenophobic attitudes scale, as compared to professional and managers (the reference category). Similarly, the unemployed are also more likely to hold anti-immigrant views than the employed. It is important to stress that this is net of the other sociodemographic characteristics since, for example, the average level of education is likely to be lower amongst jobless people. In contrast and quite unsurprisingly, migrants tend to be less hostile towards immigration and therefore have more open views than natives in this regard.

All these effects of sociodemographic characteristics remain significant once we control for the other variables in subsequent models, although their magnitude changes. We observe in particular a decreasing effect of age, education, occupation, employment status and citizenship status when passing from the first to the last model. In the case of employment status, the effect disappears altogether as we include the first two subjective grievance variables in the models, suggesting that the fact that jobless people hold a tougher view vis-à-vis migrants, stems, at least in part, from their negative perception of the economic situation in their country. As to the other variables, their effect diminishes above all when we include political attitudes and values and, also, when we add the social capital variables, suggesting that the effect of education and occupation on xenophobic attitudes is, in part, explained by the degree of interest in politics, feelings of political efficacy, positioning on the left-right and libertarian-authoritarian scales as well as by the respondents' social trust and embeddedness. The reduction of the effects of citizenship status, in contrast, is more homogeneously distributed across models, while age shows a more complex behaviour as its effect appears and disappears depending on which variables we include in the models.

Thus, the propensity to hold anti-immigrant views is rooted in people's social characteristics. However, what about the other clusters of factors which we mentioned in our theoretical discussion? The next set of factors—included in models 2, 3 and 4—refer to the role of grievances, both in their subjective and objective dimensions. We have seen in chapter 2 how feelings of relative deprivation are linked to the structural location of individuals and in chapter 3 how they relate to their capacity for resilience. Overall, here we find support for the idea that xenophobic attitudes are associated with subjective grievances but not with objective ones, and hence that perceptions of relative deprivation rather than actual conditions appear to be what matters. Furthermore, both sociotropic and pocketbook perceptions seem to matter. Concerning the sociotropic dimension (model 2), those who believed that their country was facing a very serious economic crisis scored higher on the xenophobic attitudes index. Similarly, there is a particularly strong negative correlation between believing that the state of the national economy has improved over the year prior to the interview and holding anti-immigrant views. In other words, although we should be careful to assign a causal meaning to such a correlation, sociotropic feelings of relative deprivation are linked to a more hostile stance towards migrants. Concerning the egotropic dimension (model 3), both retrospective (past five years) and prospective (future) feelings of relative deprivation are associated with higher scores on the xenophobic attitudes index. In other words, the more one believes their own household's economic situation has deteriorated, the more one tends to hold anti-immigrant views. In contrast, as we said, objective grievances (model 4) do not seem to matter at all.

Model 5 adds the evaluations of the role of the government in dealing with the crisis. This is an aspect that we have dealt with in a slightly different fashion in chapters 2 and 3 and which we will investigate further in chapters 7 and 8 with respect to its impact on political engagement. Here we wish to ascertain whether xenophobic attitudes are enhanced by people's degree of satisfaction with how their national government is dealing with the economy as well as by whether they hold that government responsible for the global financial crisis. There is an inverse relationship between satisfaction with the way the government is dealing with the crisis and anti-immigrant attitudes: the more satisfied, the less xenophobic the views. The effect of blaming the national government, in contrast, is not statistically significant. However, it becomes so once we include political attitudes and values in model 6. We should also note that, when we control for satisfaction with the government and blaming the government, the effects of the subjective grievance variables are reduced, suggesting that part of those effects are linked to people negatively evaluating the role of the government in the crisis and, more generally, in dealing with the economy.

Moving on to political attitudes and values, model 6 shows that they matter both directly and indirectly. While xenophobic attitudes do not seem to be related to the level of political interest, they are associated with political efficacy as well as with different types of political values. The two forms of political efficacy, however, have contrasting effects: internal efficacy is negatively correlated to anti-immigrant views, whereas external efficacy has a positive effect. This relates to the fact that the latter captures the presence of political cynicism on the part of respondents (Agger et al. 1961). Therefore, more politically cynical individuals are likely to hold more negative views about the place of migrants in their country. Furthermore, quite unsurprisingly, xenophobic attitudes are related to a positioning on the right of the left-right scale as well as on the authoritarian pole of the libertarian-authoritarian scale. In brief, right-authoritarian individuals are more likely to hold xenophobic views than left-libertarians, as might have been expected.

Controlling for political attitudes and values also leads to a reduction in the effects of some other variables, pointing to explanations as to why those variables have an effect on xenophobic attitudes. This is the case, for example, for education and, to a more limited extent, occupation, meaning that these sociodemographic characteristics impinge upon people's political attitudes and values and that this, in turn, is linked to different views about the place of migrants in the country. Similarly, there is a reduction in the effect of prospective pocketbook relative deprivation. This suggests that the impact of relative deprivation depends on political attitudes and values. On, the other hand, the effect of retrospective deprivation increases when we include the political variables.

Finally, model 7 refers to the social capital variables. Social trust clearly has a strong negative effect on xenophobic views, that is, the higher the level of trust, the weaker the anti-immigrant attitudes. We also observe a negative effect of associational membership, meaning that those who are members of voluntary associations tend to hold less xenophobic views, perhaps also because they are more likely to meet with migrants within those associations to which they belong. Even if the third social capital variable—meeting with friends—is not statistically significant, these findings overall would point to the important role played by social capital in supporting a more positive stance towards migrants and migration more generally. In this perspective, individuals are less likely to consider migrants as threats if one possesses a stronger social capital.

The inclusion of the social capital variables leads to a reduction in the effects of some of the other variables. For example, when we added the political variables, we observed an erosion in the effects of education, occupation and, here, also of age, suggesting that the structural roots of anti-immigrant attitudes may be related to the amount of social capital possessed by individuals. Most importantly, we also see a reduction in the effects of all variables referring to subjective grievances and the effect of retrospective deprivation disappears altogether. This suggests that the impact of subjective grievances on xenophobic views is linked to a large extent on the amount of individual-level social capital. In other words, a lack of social capital may explain why more aggrieved people often hold more xenophobic views. The same also applies to the evaluation of the role of the government and, more specifically, to satisfaction with the way the government deals with the economy. Finally, inclusion of the social capital variables also weakens the effect of the political variables on anti-immigrant attitudes, suggesting they are linked in terms of their effect on xenophobic attitudes.

Let us now turn to populist attitudes, albeit in a more succinct fashion. The results are shown in table 5.4 and bear some similarities but also important differences with those pertaining to xenophobic attitudes. Starting with the sociodemographic characteristics in model 1, we can see that all of them are significantly associated with populist views, except for citizenship status. Specifically, older, less educated, poorer people from lower social strata—more specifically, from occupations other than professionals and managers—are more populist than younger, more educated, richer people from the upper class. This reflects, for the most part, what we found earlier for xenophobic attitudes, although gender had no effect—in contrast, citizenship status did—and older respondents tended to be less xenophobic than younger ones. Also, the magnitude of the effects is larger in the case of xenophobic attitudes.

Most of the effects of sociodemographic variables remain significant across models, except for having less than secondary education, lower income and unemployment status. Adding the grievance variables in models 2, 3 and 4, in particular, does little to reduce the effects of the sociodemographic characteristics. However, the effect of unemployment status disappears, suggesting that being unemployed leads to populist views in part because this status is associated with stronger grievances, in this case relating to the perception of the economic crisis. Concerning this latter aspect, respondents who believed there was a serious crisis and those who thought the state of the economy had deteriorated relative to a year earlier—the sociotropic dimension—tend to hold stronger populist views (model 2). Similarly, just as they have been shown to impinge on xenophobic views, retrospective and prospective relative deprivation—the egocentric dimension—is significantly associated with stronger populist attitudes (model 3). We should also note that the effect of sociotropic deprivation is somewhat reduced once we include egocentric deprivation in the model. Finally, while populism seems related to subjective grievances, it seems to be uncorrelated with objective grievances (model 4).

Table 5.4. Multilevel regression models on populist attitudes (fixed part only)

Model	*(1)*	*(2)*	*(3)*	*(4)*	*(5)*	*(6)*	*(7)*
Sociodemographic characteristics							
Gender (female)	−0.05***	−0.07***	−0.07***	−0.07***	−0.07***	−0.05***	−0.05***
	(0.01)	(0.01)	(0.01)	(0.01)	(0.01)	(0.01)	(0.01)
Age groups (ref.: 18-34)	0.16***	0.12***	0.10***	0.11***	0.12***	0.09***	0.09***
35–64	(0.01)	(0.01)	(0.01)	(0.01)	(0.01)	(0.01)	(0.01)
65+	0.09***	0.07***	0.05*	0.07***	0.10***	0.04	0.05**
	(0.02)	(0.02)	(0.02)	(0.02)	(0.02)	(0.02)	(0.02)
Education group (Ref.: University and above)							
Secondary	0.04**	0.04**	0.04***	0.05***	0.05***	0.03*	0.03*
	(0.01)	(0.01)	(0.01)	(0.01)	(0.01)	(0.01)	(0.01)
< secondary	0.07***	0.05***	0.06***	0.06***	0.05***	0.02	0.02
	(0.02)	(0.02)	(0.02)	(0.02)	(0.02)	(0.01)	(0.01)
Income (low, 1st to 5th decile)	0.05***	0.03*	0.01	0.00	0.00	0.01	0.01
	(0.01)	(0.01)	(0.01)	(0.01)	(0.01)	(0.01)	(0.01)
Occupation of chief wage earner (Ref.: Professional or managerial)							
Intermediate	0.08***	0.07***	0.07***	0.07***	0.06***	0.05***	0.05***
	(0.01)	(0.01)	(0.01)	(0.01)	(0.01)	(0.01)	(0.01)
Manual	0.15***	0.14***	0.13***	0.13***	0.12***	0.08***	0.07***
	(0.02)	(0.02)	(0.02)	(0.02)	(0.02)	(0.02)	(0.02)
Other	0.11***	0.09***	0.08***	0.08***	0.07***	0.06***	0.06**
	(0.02)	(0.02)	(0.02)	(0.02)	(0.02)	(0.02)	(0.02)

(continued)

Table 5.4. (*continued*)

Model	*(1)*	*(2)*	*(3)*	*(4)*	*(5)*	*(6)*	*(7)*
Unemployed	0.05*	−0.00	−0.02	−0.03	−0.03	−0.02	−0.03
	(0.02)	(0.02)	(0.02)	(0.02)	(0.02)	(0.02)	(0.02)
Citizenship status (migrant)	−0.01	0.00	0.00	−0.00	0.00	0.01	0.01
	(0.02)	(0.02)	(0.02)	(0.02)	(0.02)	(0.01)	(0.01)
Subjective grievances							
Serious crisis	–	0.23***	0.22***	0.22***	0.16***	0.11***	0.11***
	–	(0.01)	(0.01)	(0.01)	(0.01)	(0.01)	(0.01)
Sociotropic evals. last	–	−0.78***	−0.66***	−0.65***	−0.35***	−0.27***	−0.26***
year	–	(0.03)	(0.03)	(0.03)	(0.03)	(0.03)	(0.03)
Pocketbook retrospective	–	–	−0.14***	−0.11***	−0.08**	−0.06*	−0.06*
evals. 5 yrs.	–	–	(0.03)	(0.03)	(0.03)	(0.03)	(0.03)
Pocketbook prospective	–	–	−0.13***	−0.13***	−0.09**	−0.04	−0.04
evals. 1 yr.	–	–	(0.03)	(0.03)	(0.03)	(0.03)	(0.03)
Objective grievances							
Reduced consumption	–	–	–	0.08**	0.08**	0.05*	0.05*
	–	–	–	(0.03)	(0.02)	(0.02)	(0.02)
Impact of crisis on working situation	–	–	–	0.09***	0.07**	0.03	0.04
	–	–	–	(0.02)	(0.02)	(0.02)	(0.02)
Eval. of govt's role							
Satisfaction with govt.	–	–	–	–	−0.50***	−0.42***	−0.41***
	–	–	–	–	(0.03)	(0.02)	(0.02)
Blames the national	–	–	–	–	0.14***	0.11***	0.11***
govt.	–	–	–	–	(0.01)	(0.01)	(0.01)

Political attitudes & values							
Political interest	–	–	–	–	–	−0.00	−0.00
	–	–	–	–	–	(0.01)	(0.01)
Internal political efficacy	–	–	–	–	–	0.25***	0.26***
	–	–	–	–	–	(0.02)	(0.02)
External political efficacy	–	–	–	–	–	0.62***	0.61***
	–	–	–	–	–	(0.01)	(0.01)
Left–right scale	–	–	–	–	–	−0.15***	−0.15***
	–	–	–	–	–	(0.02)	(0.02)
Left–right values	–	–	–	–	–	−0.04	−0.06
	–	–	–	–	–	(0.03)	(0.03)
Libertarian–authoritarian values	–	–	–	–	–	0.11***	0.10**
	–	–	–	–	–	(0.03)	(0.03)
Xenophobic attitudes	–	–	–	–	–	0.27***	0.18***
						(0.02)	(0.02)
Social capital							
Social trust	–	–	–	–	–	–	−0.19***
	–	–	–	–	–	–	(0.02)
Meets friends at least every wk.	–	–	–	–	–	–	−0.00
	–	–	–	–	–	–	(0.01)
Associational membership	–	–	–	–	–	–	−0.02
	–	–	–	–	–	–	(0.01)
Constant	2.61***	2.90***	3.01***	2.94***	2.94***	2.43***	2.56***
	(0.06)	(0.04)	(0.04)	(0.04)	(0.04)	(0.05)	(0.05)
Log likelihood	−13,456.367	−12,778.935	−12,742.618	−12,724.911	−12,410.984	−11,293.713	−11,260.876

Standard errors in parentheses; $N = 13,280$.
* $p < 0.05$ ** $p < 0.01$ *** $p < 0.001$

Populist attitudes are also associated with the respondents' evaluations of the role of the government in the crisis, as we can see in model 5. Specifically, those individuals who are satisfied with the way the government deals with the economy hold weaker populist views, while the populist attitudes of those who hold the national government most responsible for the global financial crisis are stronger.

As we can see in model 6, populist attitudes also correlate with political attitudes and values, albeit to a lesser extent than for xenophobic views and, at times, in different directions. Thus, the greater the feelings of efficacy, the stronger the populist views. Furthermore, populism is related to authoritarian values. We also observe a statistically significant effect of left-right self-placement, but controlling for all the other variables it is leftist individuals that appear to hold stronger populist views. Indeed, populism is not necessarily a right-wing phenomenon but, rather, it largely cross-cuts traditional political cleavages, giving us both a—now predominant—right-wing populism as well as a left-wing populism (Giugni and Lorenzini 2020). It should also be noted that including the political variables leads some of the other variables to disappear or to become smaller. Thus, among the sociodemographic variables, as we said earlier, the effect of having the lowest level of education disappears while that of being in a manual occupation is somewhat reduced. Most importantly, most if not all the grievance variables witness a change in their effect once we control for the political variables. The effects of prospective relative deprivation and of the impact of the crisis on working situations, in particular, disappear altogether, while those of the other variables find themselves more or less strongly reduced. This suggests that part of the explanation of why grievances seem to strengthen populist attitudes lies in a lack of political resources.[10]

Finally, model 7 adds the social capital variables. The impact of this kind of factors on populist attitudes is somewhat weaker than the one we observed in the case of xenophobic views. Only social trust is significantly and negatively associated with populist attitudes, while meeting with friends as well as associational membership are not. Also, unlike xenophobic views, including the social capital variables—social trust, in this case—does not fundamentally alter the effects of the other variables. The only exception are xenophobic attitudes, whose effect is reduced when we control for social capital.

To complete this part of the analysis on the correlates of xenophobic and populist attitudes in the context of the Great Recession we would like to take a further step by briefly scrutinise the impact of these two kinds of attitudes on the ways in which respondents relate to party politics. The vast literature on electoral behaviour has pointed to a variety of factors that are associated

Table 5.5. Multilevel logistic regression models on attachment for radical right parties (fixed part only)

Model	*(1)*	*(2)*
Xenophobic & populist attitudes		
Xenophobic attitudes	3.65***	2.52***
	(0.12)	(0.15)
Populist attitudes	1.36***	1.19***
	(0.17)	(0.21)
Sociodemographic characteristics		
Gender (female)	–	−0.26***
	–	(0.06)
Age groups (Ref.: 18-34) 35–64	–	−0.07
	–	(0.07)
65+	–	−0.31**
	–	(0.11)
Education group (Ref.: University and above)		
Secondary	–	0.19**
	–	(0.07)
< secondary	–	0.25**
	–	(0.09)
Income (low, 1st to 5th decile)	–	0.18**
	–	(0.06)
Occupation of chief wage earner (Ref.: Professional or managerial)		
Intermediate	–	0.04
	–	(0.08)
Manual	–	0.12
	–	(0.09)
Other	–	−0.01
	–	(0.11)
Unemployed	–	0.00
	–	(0.11)
Citizenship status (migrant)	–	−0.14
		(0.08)
Subjective grievances		
Serious crisis	–	0.27***
	–	(0.08)
Sociotropic evals. last year	–	0.06
	–	(0.18)
Pocketbook retrospective evals. 5 yrs.	–	0.03
	–	(0.15)
Pocketbook prospective evals. 1 yr.	–	0.24
	–	(0.16)
Objective grievances		
Reduced consumption	–	0.25
	–	(0.14)

(continued)

Table 5.5. (*continued*)

Model	*(1)*	*(2)*
Impact of crisis on working situation	–	0.03
	–	(0.13)
Evals. of govt's role		
Satisfaction with govt.	–	−0.07
	–	(0.14)
Blames the national govt.	–	−0.04
	–	(0.06)
Political attitudes & values		
Political interest	–	0.29***
	–	(0.04)
Internal political efficacy	–	−0.24**
	–	(0.09)
External political efficacy	–	0.21*
	–	(0.09)
Left–right scale	–	3.29***
	–	(0.13)
Left–right values	–	0.34
	–	(0.18)
Libertarian–authoritarian values	–	1.48***
	–	(0.19)
Social capital		
Social trust	–	−0.08
	–	(0.14)
Meets friends at least every wk.	–	−0.05
	–	(0.06)
Associational membership	–	0.13*
	–	(0.06)
Constant	−5.35***	−8.59***
	(0.63)	(0.67)
Log likelihood	−4,503.087	−3,932.038

Standard errors in parentheses; $N = 13{,}280$.
* $p < 0.05$ ** $p < 0.01$ *** $p < 0.001$

with voting for the extreme or radical right (Ford and Goodwin 2010) and, amongst them, xenophobic and populist attitudes play an important role. Here we focus on party attachment, which is a more stable measure than voting, and investigate the impact of these attitudes on respondents' attachments to radical right parties by means of multilevel logistic regression models. As table 5.5 shows, these attitudes have a statistically significant and strong effect on attachment to the radical right. This holds both in model 1, where the two variables are taken on their own, and in model 2, which controls for all other variables included in the analyses so far. Thus, net of sociodemographic characteristics, subjective grievances, objective grievances, evaluations of the role of the government in the economic crisis, political attitudes and values, and social capital, the more one holds xenophobic and populist views, the more likely one is to be attached to radical right parties.

While it is not our focus here, it is also worth noting the effects of the other variables. Our evidence suggests that, concerning the sociodemographic characteristics, men, younger respondents, less educated individuals and people with lower incomes are more likely to feel attached to radical right parties. Only one of the grievance variables shows a statistically significant effect, namely the perception that there is a serious crisis: respondents who believe so are more likely to be attached to the radical right. This adds support for those who argue that the economic crisis has strengthened the position of radical right and populist parties. Moreover, political attitudes and values have a strong impact on attachment for the radical right. Quite obviously, respondents who place themselves on the right of the political spectrum are much more likely to feel attached to this kind of party, and the same holds for those with more authoritarian values. Moreover, attachment to the radical right also depends on political interest and efficacy: the stronger the political interest, the weaker the feeling of internal efficacy, and the stronger the feeling of external efficacy—or political cynicism—the more likely one is to support radical right parties. Finally, there is only weak evidence of an impact of social capital, but we can see that associational membership is significantly and positively associated with attachment to radical-right parties, possibly since people who feel attached to these parties are also more likely to engage in related socio-political organisations.

CONCLUSION

In this chapter we have examined Europeans' attitudes towards immigrants and immigration in the wake of the Great Recession as well as populist attitudes and attachment to radical right parties. While immigration was a key political issue well before the economic crisis, it became more central during the years of the crisis, also due to the so-called 'refugee crisis' of 2015. Populism—both as a discourse and as a 'thin' ideology—precedes the economic crisis. Yet, populism often arises as a response to a sense of deep crisis (Taggart 2004) and populist attitudes are likely to be sustained by economic hardship (Rico and Anduiza 2017). As a result, during the years of the economic crisis we have witnessed the rise of various populist parties and movements, in particular across Europe (Bornschier 2017). Studying the cross-national variations and the correlates of both xenophobic and populist attitudes across countries in relation to the intensity of the economic crisis is an important step toward understanding the relationship between economic hardship and individuals' support of anti-immigrant and populist parties.

The literature on attitudes towards immigrants and immigration—xenophobic attitudes, as we have called them here—as well as that on populist attitudes, points to a variety of contextual and individual factors that may account for their emergence and rise. As we have seen, for example, works on immigration follow two main approaches: one focussing on self-interest and group competition, and one that stresses symbolic factors, including identities and values (Ceobanu and Escandell 2010; Hainmueller and Hopkins 2014). Similarly, works on electoral support of populist parties point to multiple determinants of such attitudes which reflect explanations of vote choice in general, including sociodemographic characteristics, self-interest, political attitudes and individual values (Rico and Anduiza 2017). Our main interest in the context of this book, however, is to look at how economic hardship and deprivation inked to the economic crisis may influence Europeans' views on immigrants and immigration as well as their likelihood of embracing a populist stance. In this regard, both kinds of attitudes seem to be influenced by egotropic concerns such as self-interest and individual vulnerability and grievances as well as by sociotropic evaluations of the state of the economy and how the government is dealing with the crisis. However, while there is evidence of both kinds of explanations, the literature on immigration attitudes and on populist attitudes suggests that sociotropic concerns are more important in this respect (Ceobanu and Escandell 2010; Hainmueller and Hopkins 2014; Rico and Anduiza 2017).

Our findings support this conclusion, albeit perhaps not in such a straightforward way. After having shown that a sizeable share of the population in the nine countries covered by our study, in the wake of the Great Recession, hold xenophobic and populist views but that, at the same time, such views vary in important ways between those countries, seemingly in relation to the severity of the crisis, our analysis of the correlates of the two types of attitudes is in line with previous studies. Concerning immigration attitudes, our analysis has shown, first, that the propensity to hold anti-immigrant views is rooted in people's social characteristics. It also suggests that both sociotropic and pocketbook perceptions seem to matter; perceptions of relative deprivation rather than actual conditions are what matter in this respect. At the same time, we also have evidence that part of the effect of grievances is due to people negatively evaluating the role of the government in the crisis and, more generally, in dealing with the economy—that is, of sociotropic concerns. Furthermore, we have seen that political attitudes and values also matter and that the inclusion of these variables reduces the effect of other variables, which suggests that the effect of sociodemographic characteristics and of relative deprivation are related, in part, to political attitudes and values. Finally, we showed the important role played by social capital in softening people's views of immigrants and immigration, both directly and indirectly. The impact of subjective grievances on xenophobic views, in particular, largely depends on the amount of social capital possessed by individuals.

Populist attitudes are similarly linked to sociodemographic characteristics, suggesting that the more vulnerable groups are not only more likely to hold negative attitudes towards immigrants and immigration but also to have populist attitudes. Furthermore, both sociotropic and pocketbook evaluations matter in this case, too. Yet, once again, subjective grievances rather than objective ones are what appear to really matter in this respect. Populist attitudes, furthermore, are also associated with the evaluation of the role of national governments in the crisis, as people who are unsatisfied with the way government deals with the economy tend to hold stronger populist views. Also, just as xenophobic attitudes are related to political attitudes and values, so too are populist attitudes, but to a somewhat lesser extent. Finally, while the impact is weaker than it is on xenophobic attitudes, we also found some evidence for the role of social capital on populist attitudes, but only as far as social trust is concerned. All this reflects on the strong impact of both types of attitudes on attachment to radical right parties, suggesting that xenophobic and populist attitudes are strong predictors of partisanship and support for such parties in the context of the Great Recession, although other factors are likely to play a role as well.

These last two chapters have focussed on two key political fields during the Great Recession, namely unemployment (chapter 4) and immigration (chapter 5). In both cases, we have examined how individuals' views with respect these two issues and political fields vary across countries and how they can be explained by a number of factors and, in particular, by the effect of the economic crisis on living conditions and perceptions. In this chapter, furthermore, we also discussed and analysed the role of populist attitudes, as populist parties and movements have been on the rise throughout the Great Recession. The next two chapters are devoted to an analysis of political participation in the context of the crisis. We examine the interplay of hardship and deprivation, on the one hand, and political opportunities for action, on the other—both in general (chapter 6) and more specifically with regard to the attribution of blame for the negative effects of the crisis (chapter 7). These chapters show how the impact of the economic crisis on political participation depends on perceptions of political opportunities.

Chapter Six

Protest Participation and Economic Crisis[1]

The economic crisis that started in 2008 has led to rising unemployment and shrinking economic growth across Europe and the rest of the world (De Grauwe and Ji 2013). Almost ten years on, there is great variation in the economic conditions of different European nations. Particularly in those countries hardest hit by economic recession, large protests took place as national governments were blamed for the deteriorating conditions (Rüdig and Karyotis 2013b; Giugni and Grasso 2015a; Grasso and Giugni 2013, 2016a). All of these observations raise important questions with respect to the relationship between protest behaviour and micro- and macro-level deprivation. They also motivate an interrogation of the nature of the link with a perceived imbalance between expected standards of living and the realities of current economic conditions as a result of the economic crisis.

The literature on social movements has been split between those that emphasise the importance of resources in political involvement and those that, instead, see grievances as an important spur for action. Since the 1970s, objective material conditions and deprivation have largely been dismissed as explanations for political action (Useem 1998; Buechler 2004). Earlier scholars such as Smelser (1962), Gurr (1970) and, to some extent, Piven and Cloward (1977) had seen negative material conditions, expressed in grievances, as a precondition spurring individuals to contentious political action. However, the main strands of research on mobilisation that have since emerged, including 'resource mobilisation theory' (RMT) (e.g. McCarthy and Zald 1973), political process (e.g. Tilly 1978; McAdam 1982; Kriesi et al. 1995) and new social movement theory (Touraine 1981; Melucci 1989), have viewed material hardship as largely unimportant or only relevant to the extent that social movements could frame it in ways to mobilise action.

The sudden rise of protest movements during the recent economic crisis has brought to the fore once more the question of whether grievance theories may play a role in explaining collective action. Scholars have started to re-examine the impact of grievances on protest behaviour (e.g. Rüdig and Karyotis 2013b; Bernburg 2015). However, most studies only examine the effect of these factors on mobilisation from either an individual or a macro-level perspective and do not consider the interaction of individual- and contextual-level factors. (Kern et al. (2015) is a recent exception but, here, change in economic conditions is examined and the focus is not on protest specifically). To address this gap in the literature, we examine the interplay of micro-level grievances and macro-level factors for protest behaviour. In particular, we argue that the extent of the effect of individual deprivation on protest is conditional upon the presence of contextual macroeconomic and policy factors which broaden out perceived political opportunities.

The high levels of variation in the current economic contexts of European nations and the differences in policy responses across national governments provide an excellent test case for investigating these macro-micro interactions. While subjective perceptions of relative deprivation have been shown to be important for mobilisation to contentious political action (Klandermans et al. 2008), we argue that individuals also take cues from the general economic environment and that state policies will also have an impact on mobilisation (see Giugni and Grasso (2015b), for example, in relation to the environmental movement). We theorise that the impact of feelings of relative deprivation on engagement in protest activities is moderated by macroeconomic and political contextual factors (Giugni and Grasso 2016). To investigate this proposition, we analyse data from an original cross-national survey conducted in 2015 in the context of the 'Living with Hard Times' (LIVEWHAT) project (grant agreement no. 613237) coordinated by the University of Geneva (Marco Giugni) and funded by the European Commission under the auspices of the Seventh Framework Programme. We specify multilevel models with cross-level interactions and show that micro- level deprivation interacts with contextual factors to spur protest behaviour. In what follows, we first review previous research, then detail the data and methods used in our study, present our results and, finally, discuss their wider implications for the discipline and for theorising about protest in times of crisis.

PREVIOUS RESEARCH

As citizens struggle to cope with the negative effects of the economic crisis, attention has been drawn to related issues of fairness and the distribution of resources in society. Recent years have seen a growth in studies on inequality (Nolan and Whelan 2011; Musterd and Ostendorf 2013; Dorling 2014; Piketty 2014; Atkinson 2015). While less has been written on the political ramifications of these developments, some social movement scholars have recently sought to 'bring capitalism back into protest analysis' (della Porta 2015). With the economic crisis still unfolding and growing inequality across the globe, it is time to re- examine the debate in political science, sociology and social movement studies over whether deprivation leads to an increase or a decrease in protest participation.

Grievance theories see material deprivation as instrumental to social movement mobilisation (Useem 1998; Buechler 2004). Various feelings such as psychological strain, alienation and other negative emotions are understood to emerge from it, leading people to challenge the political order (Opp 1988). Kornhauser's (1959) mass society theory emphasised concerns over anomie and egoism present in Emile Durkheim's classic work and suggested that the breakdown of mid-level groups and social anchors would lead individuals to gravitate to collective behaviour as one of the only few available sources of social belonging in modernity. Smelser (1962) combined strain and breakdown theories focussing on dissolution of social cohesion during periods of change into a structural- functionalist theory of collective behaviour. An important variant in the grievance tradition is relative deprivation theory (Gurr 1970). Here the strain is understood at the individual level and pertains to comparisons either with some reference group or oneself against past or future selves (Buechler 2004). Relative deprivation theory in particular emphasises the gap between expectations and experienced reality (Geschwender 1968; Davies 1962).

While stressing the primacy of perceptions of illegitimate deprivation, Thompson (1971) and Scott (1976) also saw a role for structural breakdown in explanations of protest. Piven and Cloward (1977) combined political factors and the stress of structural changes wrought by the Great Depression in their explanation of social unrest. While some elements of strain and breakdown theories persisted in these works and those of Useem (1980), Goldstone (1986, 1991a, 1991b) and Snow et al. (1998), among others, a large number of scholars challenged grievance-related explanations as they did not seem particularly useful to make sense of the new social movements emerging since the 1960s and 1970s. For example, Tilly et al. (1975) emphasised group solidarity as the key factor explaining collective action. More generally, resource mobilisation theory emphasised the rationality of social movements as following the patterns of more institutional types of action (McCarthy and Zald 1973, 1977; Oberschall 1973; Tilly 1978). Since grievances were understood as constant over time they were discounted as explanatory factors for mobilisation and the focus moved on to that which varied—that is, resources (McCarthy and Zald 1977). Individual-level studies also supported resource-based accounts, and education, occupation and income were seen as major drivers of participation (Verba et al. 1995).

One of the clearest challenges to the idea that grievances led to protest came from political process theory (Tilly 1978; McAdam 1982). Political opportunity structures, central to this approach, were understood in terms of the institutional features of the political system and the set-up of the configurations of power relative to challengers such as social movements. Political process theory emphasised the importance of resources and political opportunities, but also the subjective dimension of protest and framing (Eisinger 1973; Kitschelt 1986; Tarrow 1994; McAdam 1996; Kriesi 2004; Meyer 2004). The key insight was perhaps the suggestion that the subjective understanding of the status quo as something that could be challenged provided the rational basis for protest (McAdam 1982). For example, McVeigh (2009) noted how declining power altered individuals' perceptions of their circumstances and provided opportunities for constructing new mobilising frames.

While the emphasis tends to be placed on the social construction of grievances as critical for protest (Klandermans et al. 2008), some prominent studies have noted how 'objective' grievances can also be relevant (Snow et al. 1998; McVeigh 2009). Snow et al.'s 'disruption of the quotidian' framework emphasises the role of interference with normal routines in the tradition of Piven and Cloward (1977). Disruptions could be nuclear disasters or threats to the neighbourhood. Deprivation that leads to changes in routines can become a quotidian disruption (Snow and Soule 2009). Protest could result from deprivation without an equal decline in expectations (Thomassen 1989).

More recently, the economic crisis has spurred further studies of the impact of economic hardship on political participation. However, none of these studies looks specifically at the relationship between protest and relative deprivation, and most of them focus on just the individual or macro-level and. Thus. cannot test for cross-level interactions between the two. Caren et al. (2017) use newspaper reports of contentious acts across one hundred and fifty-seven countries between 1960 and 2001 and find a significant negative relation between contentious acts and economic growth. Laurence and Lim (2012) show that the economic crisis depressed volunteering in the US and the UK (see also Clarke and Heath 2014; Lim and Laurence 2015). Using 2004 International Social Survey Programme data, Dodson (2015) finds evidence that the mobilising effects of economic uncertainty are strongest among the most vulnerable. Kern et al. (2015) use European Social Survey data for 2002 through 2010 to show a direct effect of unemployment change between 2009 and 2010 on a scale measure of non-institutionalised participation. However, they find no significant cross-level interaction for 'double-deprivation theory' (Foster and Matheson 1995: 1168): the expectation that in countries particularly hit by the crisis 'the personal becomes political' so that individuals who suffer become particularly motivated to action.

In this chapter we build on the idea from political process theory that grievances matter to the extent that they are socially constructed and subjectively perceived in order to develop our argument that deprivation felt by individuals in times of crisis will be more likely to lead to protest behaviour, under certain contextual conditions, or to political opportunities. Following Bermeo and Bartels (2014), we suggest that the policies implemented by national governments may also interact with individual-level relative deprivation to spur political action. This argument develops from political opportunity theory since policies are an important component of political opportunities (Meyer 2004).

Our argument, we hope, also contributes to the literature by examining how economic and political factors configuring the political opportunity structures, in turn, interact with deprivation to enhance the protest potential of grievances. Case studies of marginalised groups such as the homeless (Snow et al. 2005), militias (Van Dyke and Soule 2002), the Ku Klux Klan (McVeigh 2009) or the unemployed (Giugni 2008) provide mixed support for the influence of economic threat on mobilisation. Research to date has examined how institutional structures allow marginalised groups, such as the unemployed, opportunities to mobilise (Chabanet and Faniel 2012; Giugni 2008). Studies have shown that mobilisation of the unemployed is higher where cultural contexts support it and where elites are more open to these types of demands. Generally, contexts characterised by higher levels of social spending are more encouraging of the protest of those who are relatively more deprived. Higher levels of social spending denote more social democratic political cultures where inequality and poverty are constructed as social and political problems. In turn, this leads individuals to understand their deprivation as susceptible to political solutions through political participation. On the other hand, liberal or neoliberal contexts tend to be characterised by more individualised understandings of poverty, thus depressing protest action. Taken together, these considerations contribute to the theoretical argument that we develop and test in this chapter in keeping with the political opportunity approach that suggests that the effect of individual relative deprivation will be emphasised under certain contextual dynamics.

To summarise, we expect that relative deprivation will spur engagement in protest activism to a greater extent where it occurs in concomitance with macro-level external conditions in terms of more open political opportunity structures. The former could be seen to be reflected in high unemployment rates or slow economic growth, while the latter can be seen in particular in higher levels of social spending or higher rates of taxation. We understand these conditions to be conducive to the politicisation of individual deprivation, thus spurring political action to a greater degree than simply the direct effect. By developing and testing a theory on the interrelation between relative deprivation, macroeconomic context and political opportunity structures, our research also heeds the calls to develop scholarship on micro-macro linkages for explaining protest (Opp 2009).

DATA AND METHODS

We use data from an original cross-national survey (N = 18,370) conducted in 2015 in the context of the 'Living with Hard Times' (LIVEWHAT) project funded by the European Commission under the auspices of their Seventh Framework Programme. The survey was conducted in each of the nine European countries included in the project (France, Germany, Greece, Italy, Poland, Spain, Sweden, Switzerland and the UK) by a specialised polling agency (YouGov) using online panels with the methodologies available in each country and quota balanced in order to match national population statistics in terms of region, sex, age and education level. We also include macro-level data from 2014 from the World Bank on unemployment and gross domestic product (GDP) growth as well as from the Organisation for Economic Cooperation and Development (OECD) on government social spending and tax wedges. Descriptive statistics for all the variables are presented in table 6.1. Once all missing values are removed, the final sample is 17,667 (Ns for each country are reported in table 6.2).

Our dependent variable is a dichotomous one, measuring whether someone had participated in protests in the last twelve months. Since studies have shown that protest participation has features distinct from other types of political action that could reasonably be classed in the 'unconventional' realm (Grasso 2011, 2014, 2016a), we do not create scales of activities but rather focus on this 'modal' expression (Tarrow 1996) of social movement activism, also as exemplified by the anti-austerity demonstrations taking place as a result of the crisis. As an alternative, scales for non-institutional participation (e.g. Kern et al. 2015) could be problematic, particularly at the cross-national level, since they include very different types of political action that are likely to have different relationships with deprivation. Additionally, some

Table 6.1. Variable descriptive statistics

Variable	*Mean*	*SD*	*Min.*	*Max.*
Protest participation	0.11	0.31	0.0	1.0
Relative deprivation	0.45	0.50	0.0	1.0
Age	44.82	14.81	18.0	88.0
Gender (male)	0.47	0.50	0.0	1.0
Education level (< upper secondary)	0.24	0.43	0.0	1.0
Occupation (manual)	0.24	0.43	0.0	1.0
Unemployed	0.12	0.32	0.0	1.0
Political interest	0.64	0.48	0.0	1.0
Internal political efficacy	0.49	0.40	0.0	1.0
External political efficacy	0.48	0.36	0.0	1.0
Left-right values	5.24	1.84	0.0	10.0
Libertarian-authoritarian values	4.47	1.88	0.0	10.0
Organisational memberships	1.25	2.38	0.0	12.0
Unemployment rate 2014	11.93	7.75	4.5	26.5
GDP growth 2014	1.53	1.13	−0.4	3.4
Social spending 2014	25.20	3.88	19.4	31.9
Tax wedge 2014	39.83	8.47	22.3	49.3
Relative deprivation x unemployment	6.61	9.24	0.0	26.5
Relative deprivation x GDP growth	0.58	0.99	−0.4	3.4
Relative deprivation x social spending	11.55	12.92	0.0	31.9
Relative deprivation x tax wedge	18.39	20.82	0.0	49.3

N = 17,667.

actions, such as petitioning, are extremely popular whereas other forms, such as demonstrating, are practiced by much smaller fractions of the population. Moreover, since we want to understand the impact of the economic context in 2014 on participation in 2015, we limited the indicator to participation in the last year. Table 6.2 shows the proportion of individuals that said they had demonstrated in the last twelve months in each country. As we can see, there is a reasonable degree of variation, part of which appears to be related to the severity and extent of the crisis. Countries where the crisis had deeper effects saw greater levels of protest (e.g. Greece).

The key independent variable for subjective feelings of relative deprivation is retrospective to the last five years so that the deterioration of conditions relative to expectations should have at least begun to occur prior to protest participation in the last twelve months and, as such, the time-ordering of independent and dependent variables respects the requirements of causality. Respondents were asked whether they felt that the economic situation of their household was much better or much worse than it was five years ago. We dichotomise this measure following previous research (Rüdig and Karyotis 2013b) in a dummy for whether individuals felt the economic situation of

Table 6.2. Variable distributions, by country

	All	*FR*	*DE*	*GR*	*IT*	*PL*	*ES*	*SE*	*CH*	*UK*
Protest participation (%)	10.50	14.40	6.70	22.00	11.30	5.90	17.20	7.30	5.90	4.00
Relative deprivation (%)	45.70	51.90	27.40	84.50	56.40	43.20	55.10	22.50	34.60	34.10
Age (mean)	44.80	48.10	44.30	45.10	47.10	44.20	45.10	45.30	45.90	47.40
Gender (male; %)	48.90	50.30	48.10	49.00	48.00	48.00	49.00	50.30	49.00	48.50
Education (low; %)	27.60	27.30	17.00	36.70	45.60	14.50	48.10	21.20	15.90	22.40
Occupation (manual; %)	25.10	25.40	20.60	23.80	24.60	32.60	25.50	28.20	23.60	21.50
Unemployed (%)	12.00	9.10	4.30	30.20	16.40	11.00	19.70	6.40	6.50	5.00
Political interest (%)	62.90	56.60	65.20	62.10	58.00	73.20	56.10	64.30	57.40	73.20
Internal political efficacy 0–1 (mean)	0.48	0.40	0.52	0.48	0.46	0.50	0.42	0.41	0.47	0.63
External political efficacy 0–1 (mean)	0.48	0.39	0.46	0.36	0.57	0.64	0.50	0.45	0.44	0.48
Left-right values 0–10 (mean)	5.30	5.50	5.20	4.80	5.40	5.00	4.70	5.50	5.40	5.80
Libertarian-authoritarian 0–10 (mean)	4.50	4.80	4.10	4.70	4.90	5.40	3.80	3.70	4.50	4.60
Organisational memberships 0–12 (mean)	1.20	1.10	0.60	1.70	1.90	1.00	1.20	1.60	1.30	0.80
Unemployment rate 2014 (%)	11.80	10.30	5.00	26.50	12.70	9.00	24.40	8.00	4.50	6.10
GDP growth 2014 (%)	1.50	0.20	1.60	0.80	–0.40	3.40	1.40	2.30	1.90	2.60
Social spending 2014 (%)	25.20	31.90	25.80	240	28.60	20.60	26.80	28.10	19.40	21.70
Tax wedge 2014 (%)	39.80	48.40	49.30	40.40	48.20	35.60	40.70	42.50	22.30	31.10
N	17,667	1,934	1,967	2,030	1,978	1,947	1,988	1,916	1,969	1,938

their household had become worse. Table 6.2 also shows the proportion of individuals who said the economic situation had become worse in each country. Here too, there is a good amount of variation.

Our key macroeconomic variables aim to examine both negative and positive indicators of economic context. On the one hand, high unemployment levels are perhaps the most pernicious consequence of the current economic crisis in Europe. Countries like Greece and Spain, where unemployment is highest, are those that in general have suffered the most from the current economic crisis. On the other hand, we also examine GDP growth as this is perhaps the clearest measure that a country is doing well and is coming out of recession. Both variables are taken for 2014 in order to examine conditions prior to participation but not too far back in time.

On the policy side, we include two measures: the government expenses for social policies (as a percentage of the GDP) and the tax wedge (as a percentage of labour cost). These two variables reflect also a definition of austerity policies as reducing government spending, especially in the social realm, and increasing taxation, especially on labour. Most importantly for our present purpose, they are meant to capture the output side of political opportunity structures. Again, both variables are taken for 2014.

We also include in our models the usual sociodemographic controls (for more information, see Grasso et al. 2017; Grasso 2013; Dunn et al. 2014; Saunders et al. 2012): age, gender (male), education level (less than upper secondary), occupation (manual) and employment status (whether the respondent is unemployed). Furthermore, we include a number of controls for political attitudes and resources: political interest, internal and external political efficacy (the external political efficacy scale is reversed), left-right values, libertarian-authoritarian values and number of organisational memberships (descriptive statistics and distributions by country for all dependent and independent variables are provided in tables 6.1 and 6.2).

Our dependent variable is measured at the individual level but we have independent variables at both the individual and the country levels. Moreover, we are interested in the interactions between these two levels since our argument refers to differences in how individual subjective feelings of deprivation relate to individuals' protest behaviour according to country-level economic and political contexts. For this reason, we specify multilevel models with random intercept coefficients to take into account the two-level nature of the data (country and individual). This model is useful to correct for the within-country dependence of observations (intra-class correlation), and adjusts both within and between parameter estimates in relation to the clustered nature of the data (Snijders and Bosker 1999). Since our dependent variable is dichotomous, we estimate logistic multilevel models with a Gaussian link function.

FINDINGS

We specify ten models reported in table 6.3: model 1 is the empty model; model 2 includes the key individual-level independent variable measuring relative deprivation and only the individual-level control variables; model 3 includes the first macro-level indicator—unemployment rate in 2014; model 4 includes GDP growth in 2014; model 5 includes social spending in 2014; and model 6 includes tax wedge in 2014. Models 7 through 10 include, in turn, each of the four macro-level variables from models 3 through 6 and the relevant cross-level interaction with individual relative deprivation.

Model fit improves with the inclusion of the individual-level variables as signalled by the reduction in log likelihood. There is also an improvement with the inclusion of the macro-level factors and their cross-level interactions with relative deprivation, particularly unemployment in models 3 and 7. Across models 1 through 6 (models 7 through 10 include cross-level interactions) relative deprivation has a positive effect on protest participation. Model 2 including all the individual-level controls shows that there is no significant effect of low education level or having a manual occupation on participation. However, being unemployed has a negative and significant effect across models. In other words, at the individual level there is very little evidence for grievance theory: being unemployed reduces chances of demonstrating (this also goes against the predictions of biographical availability in some specifications). Also in line with the resources/SES and civic voluntarism model (Verba et al. 1995), having a greater political interest, having stronger internal and external efficacy (the direction of the items in the scale is negative so the effect of external efficacy is also positive), being more left-wing (relative to right-wing) and also being more libertarian (relative to more authoritarian) all have a significant and positive effect on protest; as expected, organisational membership also has a strong positive effect.

What happens when we consider the macro-level economic factors? When the first contextual variable—unemployment—is included in model 3, we can see that there is a positive and significant effect of this macroeconomic context variable on demonstrating. Individuals in countries with higher unemployment are more likely to have engaged in protests in the last twelve months. At first glance, this provides some evidence for grievance theory: at the macro-level, countries with worse economic conditions are more likely to experience protest. However, the inclusion of this macro-level variable in model 3 does not remove the individual-level effect of relative deprivation found previously. Subjective feelings of relative deprivation still have an impact regardless of whether individuals are living in countries with high or low unemployment levels. This suggests that individuals examine their own

Table 6.3. Multi-level logistic regression models predicting protest participation (last 12 months)

Model	*(1)*	*(2)*	*(3)*	*(4)*
Intercept	−2.22	−1.57	−2.36	−0.94
	(0.20)***	(0.26)***	(0.28)***	(0.29)**
Micro-level				
Relative deprivation	–	0.16	0.16	0.16
	–	(0.06)**	(0.06)**	(0.06)**
Age	–	−0.01	−0.01	−0.01
	–	(0.00)***	(0.00)***	(0.00)***
Gender (male)	–	0.00	0.00	0.00
	–	(0.05)	(0.05)	(0.05)
Education (< upper	–	−0.07	−0.07	−0.07
secondary)	–	(0.07)	(0.07)	(0.07)
Occupation (manual)	–	0.06	0.06	0.06
	–	(0.06)	(0.06)	(0.06)
Unemployed	–	−0.25	−0.25	−0.25
	–	(0.08)**	(0.08)**	(0.08)**
Political interest	–	0.76	0.76	0.76
	–	(0.07)***	(0.07)***	(0.07)***
Internal political efficacy	–	0.78	0.78	0.78
	–	(0.08)***	(0.08)***	(0.08)***
External political	–	−0.18	−0.18	−0.18
efficacy	–	(0.08)*	(0.08)*	(0.08)*
Left–right values (0–10)	–	−0.18	−0.18	−0.18
	–	(0.02)***	(0.02)***	(0.02)***
Libertarian–authoritarian	–	−0.18	−0.18	−0.18
values (0–10)	–	(0.02)***	(0.02)***	(0.02)***
Organisational	–	0.17	0.17	0.17
memberships (0–12)	–	(0.01)***	(0.01)***	(0.01)***
Macro-level				
Unemployment rate	–	–	0.07	–
2014	–	–	(0.02)***	–
GDP growth 2014	–	–	–	−0.41
	–	–	–	(0.14)**
Social spending 2014	–	–	–	–
	–	–	–	–
Tax wedge 2014	–	–	–	–
	–	–	–	–
Cross-level interactions				
Relative deprivation x	–	–	–	–
Unemployment	–	–	–	–
Relative deprivation x	–	–	–	–
GDP growth	–	–	–	–
Relative deprivation x	–	–	–	–
Social spending	–	–	–	–
Relative deprivation x	–	–	–	–
Tax wedge	–	–	–	–
Sigma u	0.59	0.64	0.38	0.45
Rho	0.10	0.11	0.04	0.06
Log likelihood	−5,877.43	−5,121.12	−5,116.57	−5,118.06

Notes: N = 17,667; No. of groups = 9.

(5)	*(6)*	*(7)*	*(8)*	*(9)*	*(10)*
−3.89	−3.12	−2.25	−0.98	−3.54	−2.96
(1.19)**	(0.91)***	(0.28)***	(0.30)***	(1.22)**	(0.92)**
0.16	0.16	−0.10	0.24	−0.64	−0.25
(0.06)**	(0.06)**	(0.11)	(0.09)**	(0.40)	(0.32)
−0.01	−0.01	−0.01	−0.01	−0.01	−0.01
(0.00)***	(0.00)***	(0.00)***	(0.00)***	(0.00)***	(0.00)***
0.00	0.00	−0.00	0.00	0.00	0.00
(0.05)	(0.05)	(0.05)	(0.05)	(0.05)	(0.05)
−0.07	−0.07	−0.07	−0.07	−0.07	−0.07
(0.07)	(0.07)	(0.07)	(0.07)	(0.07)	(0.07)
0.06	0.06	0.06	0.06	0.06	0.06
(0.06)	(0.06)	(0.06)	(0.06)	(0.06)	(0.06)
−0.24	−0.24	−0.25	−0.25	−0.25	−0.25
(0.08)**	(0.08)**	(0.08)**	(0.08)**	(0.08)**	(0.08)**
0.76	0.76	0.76	0.76	0.76	0.76
(0.07)***	(0.07)***	(0.07)***	(0.07)***	(0.07)***	(0.07)***
0.78	0.78	0.78	0.78	0.78	0.78
(0.08)***	(0.08)***	(0.08)***	(0.08)***	(0.08)***	(0.08)***
−0.18	−0.18	−0.18	−0.18	−0.18	−0.18
(0.08)*	(0.08)*	(0.08)*	(0.08)*	(0.08)*	(0.08)*
−0.18	−0.18	−0.18	−0.18	−0.18	−0.18
(0.02)***	(0.02)***	(0.02)***	(0.02)***	(0.02)***	(0.02)***
−0.18	−0.18	−0.18	−0.18	−0.18	−0.18
(0.02)***	(0.02)***	(0.02)***	(0.02)***	(0.02)***	(0.02)***
0.17	0.17	0.17	0.17	0.17	0.17
(0.01)***	(0.01)***	(0.01)***	(0.01)***	(0.01)***	(0.01)***
–	–	0.06	–	–	–
–	–	(0.02)***	–	–	–
–	–	–	−0.38	–	–
–	–	–	(0.14)**	–	–
0.09	–	–	–	0.08	–
(0.05)*	–	–	–	(0.05)+	–
–	0.04	–	–	–	0.04
–	(0.02)+	–	–	–	(0.02)
–	–	0.02	–	–	–
–	–	(0.01)**	–	–	–
–	–	–	−0.06	–	–
–	–	–	(0.05)	–	–
–	–	–	–	0.03	–
–	–	–	–	(0.02)*	–
–	–	–	–	–	0.01
–	–	–	–	–	(0.01)
0.54	0.55	0.39	0.46	0.54	0.55
0.08	0.09	0.04	0.06	0.08	0.08
−5,119.49	−5,119.78	−5,113.27	−5,117.37	−5,117.41	−5,118.92

household situation with respect to their expectations of where they should have been and this mechanism operates independently of wider comparisons.

When GDP growth is included in model 4, there is a negative and significant direct effect of this economic context variable on protest. Individuals in countries with lower GDP growth are more likely to have engaged in protests in the last twelve months. Again, this might be seen as providing evidence for grievance theory: at the macro-level, countries with lower levels of economic growth are more likely to experience protest. However, the inclusion of this macro-level variable in model 4 does not remove the individual-level effects found previously. Subjective feelings of relative deprivation still have an impact regardless of whether individuals are living in countries with high or low GDP growth. Once more, this supports the idea that individuals primarily examine their own household situation with respect to their expectations of where they should have been and that wider comparisons do not explain away the effect of subjective feelings of relative deprivation.

Turning to macro-level political factors, we observe a similar pattern as for the economic context. When social spending is included in model 5, it has a positive effect on demonstration activities. We interpret this as signalling more open political opportunity structures. Again, the inclusion of this macro-level political factor does not erode the effect of relative deprivation, meaning that the latter still has an impact regardless of whether individuals are living in countries with diverse levels of spending.

When including tax wedge in model 6 there is a small but significant (p :-: 0.10) effect: the greater the tax wedge, the greater the protest. This is in line with Bermeo and Bartels' (2014) hypothesis that people react to austerity policies rather than directly to the negative effects of the economic crisis. At the same time, however, the inclusion of this macro-level factor once again does not change the effect of relative deprivation. In other words, the latter plays a role net of this measure.

The main goal of this research, developing on previous work in the literature, was to combine the individual- and macro-level perspectives on protest mobilisation in times of crisis. To extend this framework, models 7 through 10 include cross-level interactions between each of our macro-level variables and relative deprivation at the individual level in turn. Our results, as presented in model 7, show that in countries with higher unemployment rates, the effect of feelings of relative deprivation on participation is increased. This suggests that individual-level subjective perceptions of relative deprivation are amplified by the wider national economic context. Individuals feeling that their conditions have deteriorated in the last five years in countries such as Greece or Spain are likely to have experienced worse deterioration than individuals in countries such as Germany and Switzerland that have had fewer negative experiences of the recent economic crisis. These results thus show that while deprivation at the individual level has a positive effect on protest participation regardless of the economic context, at higher levels of unemployment the effect of deprivation is magnified relative to contexts with lower unemployment. In turn, this suggests that this type of contextual fact may serve to politicise individual deprivation, as we discuss in more detail in the final section.

We find this conditional effect also for the political context in terms of the political opportunity structure offered by social democracies with more extensive welfare states. These results are shown in model 9. In contrast, neither GDP growth (model 8) nor tax wedge (model 10) condition the effect of individual relative deprivation in this respect while they do have a direct effect on protest participation.

Model 7, with one cross-level interaction for relative deprivation and unemployment, showed that the coefficient for relative deprivation is -0.10 and not significant, which means that there is no difference between those who are relatively more or less deprived when the unemployment rate is 0. The positive and statistically significant coefficient for the interaction term between relative deprivation and unemployment (0.02) suggests that the gap between those who are relatively more or less deprived increases as unemployment goes up. For every percentage point increase in the unemployment rate, the gap in the log-odds of protesting increases by 0.02. At what point do the relatively deprived start protesting at higher levels than those who do not feel deprived? These estimates suggest that the two groups start departing

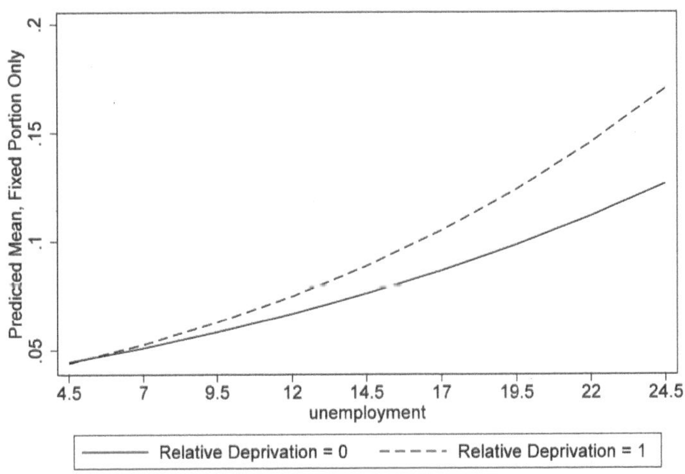

Figure 6.1. Plot of the cross-level interaction between relative deprivation and unemployment

when unemployment reaches a level of 5 percent (i.e. -0.10 / 0.02 = -5)—that is, quite low. For social spending, in model 9, the positive and statistically significant coefficient for the interaction term between relative deprivation and social spending (0.03) suggests that the gap in protesting between those who are relatively more or less deprived also increases as social spending rises. For every percentage point increase in social spending, the gap in the log-odds of protesting between the two groups increases by 0.03; the relatively deprived start protesting at higher levels than those who are less deprived when social spending is over 21.33 percent of GDP (-0.64 / 0.03 = -21.33). To visualise these patterns more clearly, figures 6.1 and 6.2 plot the cross-level interaction effects between relative deprivation and both unemployment and social spending, in turn.

These graphs clearly show that the effect of personal deprivation is amplified in contexts of high unemployment (i.e. over 5 percent) and in contexts where there are relatively higher levels of social spending as a proportion of GDP (i.e. greater than 21.33 percent). We interpret both these findings in light of political opportunity structure theory: a situation of high unemployment opens up the political space for individual levels of deprivation to become understood at a more collective level and therefore to become the basis for political mobilisation. Similarly, for social spending, we argue that contexts where social spending is higher are already contexts where the opportunity structure, with respect to protest, is more open. In countries where social spending is lower, neoliberal approaches to welfare and the individualisation of poverty and deprivation tend to be normalised. On the other hand,

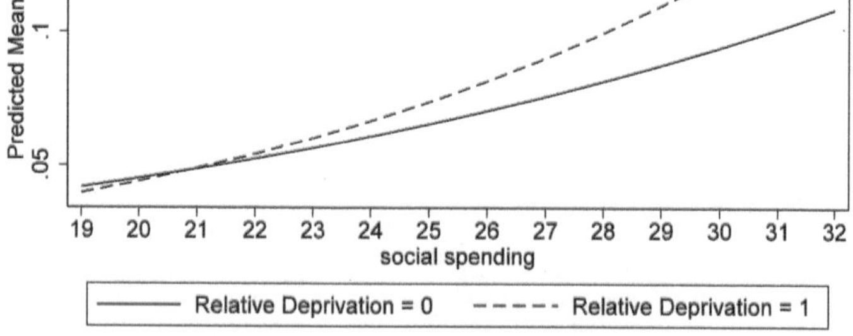

Figure 6.2. Plot of the cross-level interaction between relative deprivation and social spending

in contexts where social spending is higher there tends to be a greater receptivity to understanding poverty and inequality as social and political problems that can be redressed through collective action.

DISCUSSION AND CONCLUSION

Our study shows the value of examining the cross-context conditionality of grievances and opportunities for individual-level protest participation. We show that individuals who feel that their conditions have deteriorated are more likely to take to the streets. We thus find evidence supporting Snow et al.'s (1998) thesis that the mismatch between current standards of living and expectations has some role to play for mobilising individuals, net of their objective economic position in society. This is an important result since it shows that when understood in subjective and relative terms grievances *do* have an impact on mobilisation. Linking these subjective feelings to the wider economic and political context, we find that not only do individual-level feelings of relative deprivation have a direct effect on the propensity to have protested in the last year, but that this effect is greater in contexts characterised by either higher unemployment rates or higher levels of social spending. We interpret both findings in terms of their role for opening up political opportunities for protest among those who felt a deterioration of living standards in the current crisis. While grievance theories and political opportunity approaches appear to be at odds with each other, the significant results for the cross-level interactions between relative deprivation and macro- level factors show that context conditions the extent of the effect of individual deprivation on political action. We argue that this evidence for contextual influences on the effect of individual-level deprivation for protest can be interpreted in terms of political opportunity theory.

Both grievances and political opportunities, if specified correctly, are shown to contribute to our understanding of political action. Indeed, the results of this study illustrate how it is their dynamic interaction which explains differential protest behaviour. More specifically, our findings show that in contexts of higher unemployment, deprived individuals protest at higher rates than less deprived individuals. We understand higher levels of unemployment as providing a context where individuals are more likely to understand their own relative deprivation in a politicised way. For example, higher unemployment is more likely to become discussed as a wider social ill affecting society and therefore leading individuals, and particularly those who feel deprived, to become more likely to realise that deteriorating living standards are not just their own, individualised private problem, but rather a generalised, national one shared by many others in different forms (e.g. as loss of income, loss of employment, having to make cut backs in consumption, etc.). In this way, a context of higher unemployment can play a role in politicising private lived experience, resulting in outward political action. We argue that individuals take cues from their wider environment and that these lead them to become more likely to act on their subjective feelings of deprivation by taking to the streets to protest against the government. On this reading, a visibly deteriorated economic context is understood as providing fertile ground for the subjective understanding of one's deprivation as something that can be challenged and redressed collectively and politically.

Our results also show that the difference between citizens who feel that their conditions deteriorated and those who do not, in terms of taking to the streets, are greater in contexts marked by higher levels of social spending. We interpret this finding by a similar logic. In times of crisis in particular, contexts with higher levels of social spending are those where political opportunities for protest would be perceived as more open, thus leading the more deprived to be more likely to take the streets. Our results show how individuals in more social democratic arrangements appear to be more likely to react politically when they feel that the crisis has impacted them negatively. These findings support the results of scholarship suggesting that welfare state provisions and citizenship rights represent critical resources for groups organising for collective action. While specific case studies have shown that the mechanism relates to the movement in question—for example, the mobilisation of the unemployed is linked to the extent of unemployment benefits (Giugni 2008), whereas the mobilisation of immigrants is linked to the type and level of citizenship rights (Giugni and Passy 2004; Koopmans et al. 2005)—here we generalise this finding to show that the welfare state, as captured by higher levels of social spending, encourages mobilisation.

In more neoliberal contexts characterised by lower levels of social spending, on the other hand, those who feel deprived are more likely to understand their situation in individualised terms and therefore to be less likely to be spurred to collective, political action. While both the deprived and less deprived are less likely to take to the streets in countries with less generous levels of social spending, citizens who feel more deprived in more generous welfare states are more likely to take to the streets than citizens who feel less deprived. We suggest that this is because more generous welfare states are more receptive to their demands since issues relating to material deprivation are more widely understood as political problems needing collective solutions, not personal concerns that should be privately dealt with. While other studies provide some evidence that welfare states could be demobilising (e.g. Dodson 2015), our study with data from 2015 suggests the opposite.

Further studies should explore this question in even greater detail and develop analyses to further disentangle which individual- and aggregate-level factors interact with welfare state provisions to explain the individual-level decision to become engaged in protest.

The findings of our study emphasise the importance of examining the macro-level economic and political contexts alongside individual-level deprivation, resources, attitudes and networks for understanding the wider drivers of protest action. This is in line with previous research showing that the mobilisation of resource-poor groups is more likely when economic conditions have deteriorated (Baglioni et al. 2008; Piven and Cloward 1977). More generally, our results suggest that individuals respond rationally to the experience of crisis, both at the individual and aggregate levels, by expressing their voice politically though protest. Feelings of deprivation are an important spur to the voicing of what could easily be seen as increasing grievances in times of crisis and we show that these individual-level influences are amplified under given contextual circumstances. Our study has highlighted, in particular, that at least in the context of economic crisis, protest behaviour is higher among those individuals that have felt a deterioration in their circumstances. This is net of all other characteristics that could be reasonably expected to foster protest behaviour at the individual level.

At the aggregate level, we have also shown that protest is also higher in contexts with lower GDP growth and a higher tax wedge, but these types of contexts did not amplify the impact of individual relative deprivation on protest behaviour. On the other hand, contexts characterised by greater unemployment and higher social spending levels also experienced higher levels of protest while at the same time also increasing the impact of individual- level relative deprivation. Protest in times of crisis is thus shown to be more prevalent among individuals who feel deprived in contexts with higher and therefore likely more politicised unemployment levels and more open political opportunity structures afforded by the welfare state. By extension, this means that there are more political responses to the crisis where the political opportunity conditions exist for the political expression of grievances among more deprived groups. On the one hand, higher levels of unemployment appear to lead individual problems of deprivation to become more clearly collectivised in the popular and political imagination; on the other hand, higher levels of social spending, suggesting a greater concern for the economic welfare of citizens and particularly the more marginalised and more deprived groups, appear to provide the legitimatisation and political space for the demands of protestors in times of crisis.

Our study has shown that the extent to which individuals will mobilise in demonstrations during times of crisis depends on their feeling a deterioration in their living standards and also on the ways in which the wider environment contributes to the framing of opportunities (Gamson and Meyer 1996). This further suggests that protest mobilisation is borne out of the complex interaction of factors at different levels, in turn impacting on each other. Research tends to be split between those examining individual-level influences on protest behaviour and those examining macro-level relations. Our findings suggest that, besides looking for direct effects of the micro- and macro-level on protest, greater attention needs to be paid to their dynamic interaction for understanding the decision to become politically active, particularly in times of economic crisis.

Chapter Seven

Blame and Contention[1]

The economic crisis starting in 2008 has led to unemployment growth and shrinking GDP across Europe. About ten years since its onset, there is great variation in the economic conditions of different countries in Europe. In countries where the crisis hit hardest, Greece and Spain, unemployment is still well over 20 percent . On the other hand, where the crisis only had mild effects, as in Germany and Switzerland, it is under 5 percent. In the UK and Poland, GDP grew at 2.6 and 3.4 percent, respectively, whereas in Italy the economy shrunk by 0.4 percent in 2014. Previous research has shown that the economic downturn affected citizens' support for government intervention (Malhotra and Margalit 2010; Margalit 2013; Popp and Rudolph 2011) and fuelled political protests and a variety of social movements (Bennett 2012; Skocpol and Williamson 2013). Particularly in those countries worst hit, large protests took place as European governments were blamed for the negative economic context (Giugni and Grasso 2015a, 2018a). What were the ways in which European citizens aimed to make their voices heard and criticise government handling of the crisis? Which types of citizens disengaged while others engaged in a variety of political activities? Political science literature has long shown how voters use their judgment about circumstances around them to hold politicians accountable (Fiorina 1981) as well as that citizens use a wide array of institutional and non-institutional modes of engagement (Grasso 2018; Pattie et al. 2004). However, research has tended to either focus on understanding the causes for voter turnout (Lewis-Beck and Stegmaier 2000, 2007; Lewis-Beck and Paldam 2000; Lewis-Beck 1988) or looking at other more contentious political activities such as participating in protests or engaging in social movement activism (Bernburg 2015; Grasso and Giugni 2016b; Rüdig and Karyotis 2013b). Moreover, most studies of political participation tend to focus on the classic sociological explanations of participation (Brady et al. 1995; Wolfinger and Rosenstone 1980), disregarding the effects of political attitudes and economic perceptions, blame assignment, and policy-related approval. An effort to fill both gaps has recently been made by Levin et al. (2015) in their study on California before the 2010 General Election. These authors have shown the impact of perceptions of economic conditions, policy-oriented evaluations, and blame assignment on involvement in a variety of political activities. In this chapter, we take a broader comparative perspective in analysing the extent to which perceptions of the government's role in the economic crisis impacted on different forms of political behaviour of European citizens. We focus in particular on different types of political expressions of dissatisfaction with the current situation, from more mainstream to more confrontational types of political actions: voting against the incumbent, attending public meetings, participating in demonstrations, and participating in strikes. Although voting against the incumbent is not always the result of dissatisfaction with performance rather than a more proactive support of an alternative party or candidate, the four types of political behaviour analysed in this study can all be theorised as at least potential political expressions of dissatisfaction with the current state of things.

We are particularly interested in examining the impact of two kinds of predictors of political behaviour in the context of economic crisis stressed by previous research: evaluations of the way in which the government deals with one of the most politicised aspects of the crisis—namely unemployment—and blame assignment, more precisely attributing blame for the country's economic difficulties to the government. The latter two aspects in particular capture people's perceptions of the role of the government in the crisis. We suggest, first, that government performance evaluations and blame assignment have a differential effect on distinct forms of political behaviour. Second, we suggest that the way in which people frame the crisis—in terms of blame assignment and satisfaction with the way the government is dealing with it—conditions the effect of the perceptions of one's own economic situation on political behaviour. In addition to investigating the main effects of these two predictors, therefore, we focus our analysis also on the way in which they interact with feelings of relative deprivation.

We focus on nine European countries and analyse data collected by means of an original survey in 2015. These countries shared the experience of the economic crisis to different degrees. Most countries suffered polarisation over disagreements on how to handle the economy and whether to introduce austerity policies or not. Moreover, in some countries voters punished incumbents. At a time where the political context is rife with diverse sources of dissatisfaction, the drivers of political participation may differ in relevant ways between different types of political actions as well as across different kinds of citizens. Exploring these dynamics in a comparative context leads to our chapter's novel contribution to existing research. More specifically, we aim to add to the existing literature on political behaviour in three ways. First, we examine the effect of perceptions of the government's role in the economic crisis on different forms of political behaviour, from the more mainstream to the more confrontational, hence allowing for a differentiated approach to the study of political behaviour. Second and relatedly, we study these effects across electoral and non-electoral forms of political behaviour. These aspects have been widely studied in previous research with respect to voting behaviour (Lewis-Beck and Stegmaier 2000, 2007; Lewis-Beck and Paldam 2000; Lewis-Beck 1988), but not so much in the context of non-institutionalised forms of political participation. Thus, we heed recent calls to bridge the gap between the study of electoral politics and that of protest politics (Heaney and Rojas 2014; Hutter 2014b; Kriesi 2014a; McAdam and Tarrow 2010). Third, continuing a research agenda we begun elsewhere (Giugni and Grasso 2016), we aim to disentangle the way in which deprivation interacts with individual perceptions on the broader political and economic environment to impact on political behaviour in times of crisis. In this chapter specifically, we aim to examine how evaluations of the way in which the government deals with unemployment and blame assignment condition the impact of relative deprivation, developing our understanding of the decision to become politically active.

PREVIOUS RESEARCH AND HYPOTHESES

The literature on the impact of the economy on political activity is extensive but often narrowly focussed (Levin et al. 2015). Economic voting theory suggests that individuals reward incumbents when the economy is doing well but punish them when the economy is doing badly (Duch 2007; Hellwig 2010; Lewis-Beck and Paldam 2000; Lewis-Beck and Stegmaier 2000, 2007). Studies have examined both 'pocketbook' evaluations of one's own individual or household concerns, including unemployment or whether one struggles to make ends meet and more 'sociotropic' concerns about economic adversity affecting one's community or nation, including dissatisfaction with the state of the economy, unemployment, or inflation (Lewis-Beck 1988). By and large, the literature has found very little evidence of a relationship between individual economic problems and voting (Kinder and Kiewiet 1979; Kiewiet 1983; Alvarez and Nagler 1995; Lewis-Beck and Stegmaier 2000).

On the other hand, studies have found that macroeconomic conditions as well as evaluations of how the incumbent has handled the economy do affect voter choice (Lewis-Beck and Stegmaier 2000, 2007; Lewis-Beck and Paldam 2000; Lewis-Beck 1988). This seems at odds with the availability of information: individuals are much more likely to be privy to facts about their own or their household's economic situation than the national economy or government handling of it (Lohmann 1994). Some have explained it by suggesting that the reward–punishment hypothesis only works under conditions where individuals assign responsibility to the government for the situation or think that the government should solve it (Feldman 1982). It also appears that individuals are less likely to hold government responsible for their own economic conditions but more likely to see government responsible for the national economic context (Brody and Sniderman 1977). Kaase and Marsh (1979) had already noted how feelings of deprivation become politicised only where problems appear collectively shared and when political authorities can be blamed or held responsible for the problem.

While the literature had distinguished between pocketbook and sociotropic concerns, it could be perhaps that citizens focus their gaze on specific aspects of the economy such as unemployment or poverty alleviation, rewarding or punishing incumbents depending on how they feel that they have dealt with that specific aspect—thus applying a sort of 'policy-oriented economic voting' (Kiewiet 1983; Lewis-Beck and Stegmaier 2000). However, even among studies examining economic perceptions on voting there has not been much work done to analyse the effect of evaluations of action in specific areas (Lewis-Beck and Stegmaier 2000). While scholars study the impact of economic issue preferences—that is, support for intervention in the economy—it is rarer to find studies of policies or government actions.

In a context of different levels of crisis, examining data from different European countries in 2015 allows us to examine the effect of evaluations of government action on unemployment specifically, perhaps the most politicised negative consequence of the current crisis. The economy has come back as one of the main concerns of European publics with the economic crisis. Many European countries were still in dire economic conditions by 2015, particularly those Southern European countries hardest hit by the crisis. In such a situation, levels of support for government tend to fall as they come to be blamed and held responsible for a negative economic context. Government responsibility for economic problems can be understood in different ways: for causing the problem, failing to solve it, or performing at sub-standard level (Iyengar 1991; Peffley 1984; Brody and Sniderman 1977). Blame assignment for economic problems could vary across countries as a function of the different economic conditions and whether one's preferred party is in power. Blame assignment is understood here to have an impact on political participation since it politicises political evaluations (Iyengar 1991; Peffley 1984; Sniderman and Brody 1977) and allows voter to engage in rational retrospective voting (Feldman 1982; Iyengar 1991). Moreover, by connecting personal and social problems to political judgments, blame assignment can act as a psychological cue with profound influences (Iyengar 1991), including on political behaviour.

This leads us to our first hypothesis:

> *H1*: Dissatisfaction with the way the government is dealing with unemployment and blaming the national government for the nation's economic difficulties should spur political participation (direct-effect hypothesis).

While previous research has focussed on the impact of evaluations of government performance and blame assignment on voting behaviour, little if any work has been done on how they affect other less institutionalised forms of participation. In our study, we also test for their effect on three further types of activities, namely attending public meetings, participating in demonstrations, and participating in strikes. Given the lack of previous work on these non-electoral forms of participation, we lack a firm ground upon which we can anchor specific hypotheses. However, given the different logics followed by these more contentious forms of political action as opposed to electoral behaviour, we expect perceptions of the government role in the economic crisis to vary across these types of political behaviour. In particular, we suggest that the impact of such perceptions should be stronger when it comes to electoral behaviour and, more specifically, for voting against the incumbent in the context of the crisis. The rationale behind this expectation is that the effect of such behaviour most directly affects those whom the people hold as responsible for the situation.

This leads us to our second hypothesis:

> *H2*: The effect of dissatisfaction with the way the government is dealing with unemployment and blame assignment should be strongest for voting against the incumbent since here the effect of the action will most directly punish the perceived culprits (differential-effect hypothesis).

Our first two hypotheses deal with the direct impact of evaluations of the government role in the economic crisis on different types of political behaviour. We would like to add a third hypothesis concerning the interaction of such evaluations with the way individuals perceive their own economic situation. Particularly in the collective behaviour tradition, relative deprivation theory has typically stressed the role of individual grievances and hardship for political behaviour (Davies 1962; Geschwender 1968; Gurr 1970). Subjective perceptions of relative deprivation have been shown to be important in particular for mobilisation to contentious political action (Klandermans et al. 2008), but they are also likely to matter for other forms of expression of political dissatisfaction (Thomassen 1989). The recent economic crisis has revamped this research tradition and led to a number of studies testing the hypothesis that feelings of relative deprivation led to an increase in protest activities (Grasso and Giugni 2016a; Rüdig and Karyotis 2013b; Bernburg 2015).

We suggest that the impact of relative deprivation and, more generally, perceptions of one's own economic situation on political behaviour is conditional upon the perceptions of the government role in the economic crisis. More specifically, dissatisfaction with the way the government is dealing with unemployment and blame assignment are expected to condition the effect of relative deprivation on the four kinds of political behaviour under investigation. A recent study (Grasso and Giugni 2016a) has shown that the impact of individual subjective feelings of deprivation is conditional on contextual macroeconomic and policy factors. This study found that, while individual-level relative deprivation has a direct effect on the propensity to have protested in the last year, this effect is greater under certain macroeconomic and political conditions. By the same token, we may expect perceptions of such macroeconomic and political conditions to play a similar role.

This leads us to our third hypothesis:

> *H3*: Dissatisfaction with the way the government is dealing with unemployment and blame assignment should have a conditional effect on the relationship between relative deprivation and political behaviour, increasing its effect on participation (conditional-effect hypothesis).

In sum, we expect blame assignment and dissatisfaction with the way the government is dealing with unemployment to play an important role for explaining individuals' engagement in different types of political activities, both directly and indirectly through their conditional effect on the relationship between relative deprivation and political behaviour. Further, we expect these two variables to have a greater or lesser impact depending on the specific form of political behaviour at hand, with expected differences between more mainstream and more confrontational forms of political behaviour.

DATA AND METHODS

We use data from an original cross-national survey (N = 18,370) fielded in 2015 in the context of the 'Living with Hard Times' (LIVEWHAT) project

Table 7.1. Variable descriptive statistics

	Mean	*SD*	*Min.*	*Max.*
Intends to vote against incumbent	0.7089489	0.454260	0.00	1.0
Attended meeting last 12 mos.	0.0965642	0.295372	0.00	1.0
Participated in demonstration last 12 mos.	0.1110545	0.314209	0.00	1.0
Joined strike last 12 mos.	0.0558669	0.229671	0.00	1.0
Age (mean)	44.8187600	14.812040	18.00	88.0
Gender (male)	0.4720666	0.499233	0.00	1.0
Education (low)	0.2406181	0.427471	0.00	1.0
Occupation (manual)	0.2377314	0.425706	0.00	1.0
Unemployed	0.1172242	0.321696	0.00	1.0
Political interest	0.6431199	0.479093	0.00	1.0
Internal political efficacy	0.4939341	0.397554	0.00	1.0
External political efficacy	0.4792929	0.358678	0.00	1.0
Party attachment	2.5293490	1.025088	1.00	4.0
Left–right values	5.2392540	1.842704	0.00	10.0
Libertarian–authoritarian values	4.4653470	1.878585	0.00	10.0
Organisational memberships	1.2532410	2.383205	0.00	12.0
Unemployment rate 2014	11.9268300	7.752418	4.50	26.5
GDP growth 2014	1.5258110	1.124696	−0.40	3.4
Social spending 2014	25.2002800	3.878119	19.40	31.9
Tax wedge 2014	39.8340300	8.466294	22.25	49.3
Relative deprivation	0.4540669	0.497900	0.00	1.0
Unsatisfied how govt. deals with unemployment	0.8001924	0.399867	0.00	1.0
Blames govt. for economic difficulties	0.4829909	0.499725	0.00	1.0
Disproportionality index	9.5373920	5.579571	1.25	17.66

N = 17,667.

funded by the European Commission under the auspices of their Seventh Framework Programme. The survey was conducted by YouGov in each of the nine European countries included in the project: France, Germany, Greece, Italy, Poland, Spain, Sweden, Switzerland and the UK. Samples were matched to national statistics for age, gender, region, and education. Since the crisis impacted on the countries to different extents, we also include macro-level data from the World Bank on unemployment and GDP growth as well as from the OECD on government social spending and tax wedges as level-2 variables. Descriptive statistics for all the variables are presented in table 7.1. Once all missing values are removed, the final sample is 17,667 (*N*s for each country are reported in table 7.2).

We examine four dependent variables in this study. The first is a dichotomous variable for whether respondents intend to vote for the incumbent party or coalition if there were an election tomorrow. We coded 0 all those who

Table 7.2. Variable distributions, by country

	All	*FR*	*DE*	*GR*	*IT*	*PL*	*ES*	*SE*	*CH*	*UK*
Intends to vote against incumbent (%)	70.90	83.90	60.90	58.00	82.50	77.70	85.00	75.90	47.60	67.10
Attended meeting last 12 mos. (%)	9.70	5.30	7.90	12.70	13.90	8.50	12.80	9.10	7.60	8.80
Participation in demonstration last 12 mos. (%)	11.10	14.20	8.40	23.20	12.00	6.10	17.80	7.30	6.00	4.30
Joined strike last 12 mos. (%)	5.60	5.40	3.50	13.70	11.60	2.10	8.70	0.60	1.80	2.30
Relative deprivation (%)	45.40	52.60	27.30	84.60	55.70	41.80	54.30	22.50	33.00	34.80
Unsatisfied how govt. deals with unemployment (%)	80.00	89.40	68.40	93.20	87.80	88.30	87.90	83.00	57.00	65.00
Blames govt. for economic difficulties (%)	48.30	46.20	35.10	54.60	61.30	63.00	60.00	53.20	22.00	39.00
Age (mean)	44.80	48.70	44.20	39.90	44.20	41.50	43.00	47.20	43.80	51.20
Gender (male; %)	47.20	44.10	51.90	46.70	47.50	44.50	50.10	46.00	47.20	46.80
Education (low; %)	24.10	28.90	17.50	13.40	32.80	15.00	38.50	26.80	18.20	25.80
Occupation (manual; %)	23.80	24.50	20.90	19.40	22.70	32.30	24.10	27.40	24.10	18.90
Unemployed (%)	11.70	9.10	4.00	27.50	17.20	11.50	18.80	5.40	6.50	4.50

Political interest (%)	64.30	56.30	71.00	62.90	60.00	73.70	57.70	63.90	58.40	75.50
Internal political efficacy (mean)	0.49	0.39	0.59	0.49	0.48	0.51	0.45	0.40	0.48	0.66
External political efficacy (mean)	0.48	0.40	0.48	0.35	0.57	0.65	0.49	0.46	0.44	0.49
Party attachment (mean)	2.53	2.50	2.61	2.44	2.38	2.40	2.55	2.74	2.33	2.84
Left–right values (mean)	5.20	5.50	5.20	4.80	5.40	5.00	4.80	5.50	5.40	5.70
Libertarian–authoritarian values (mean)	4.50	4.90	4.00	4.70	4.80	5.40	3.70	3.70	4.50	4.50
Organisational memberships (mean)	1.30	1.00	0.70	1.60	2.00	1.10	1.20	1.60	1.30	0.80
Unemployment rate 2014 (%)	11.80	10.30	5.00	26.50	12.70	9.00	24.40	8.00	4.50	6.10
GDP growth 2014 (%)	1.50	0.20	1.60	0.80	-0.40	3.40	1.40	2.30	1.90	2.60
Social spending 2014 (%)	25.20	31.90	25.80	240	28.60	20.60	26.80	28.10	19.40	21.70
Tax wedge 2014 (%)	39.80	48.40	49.30	40.40	48.20	35.60	40.70	42.50	22.30	31.10
Disproportionality index	9.54	17.66	7.83	9.96	17.34	5.95	6.93	1.25	3.76	15.10
N	17,667	1,934	1,967	2,030	1,978	1,947	1,988	1,916	1,969	1,938

intended to vote for the incumbent and as 1 those who expressed alternative vote choices. The other three dependent variables are measures of participation based on dichotomous variables measuring whether someone had participated in various political activities in the last twelve months. Specifically, we look at attending public meetings, participating in demonstrations, and participating in strikes.

Past research has shown that protest participation has distinct features to other types of political action that could reasonably be classed in the 'unconventional' realm (Grasso 2014). As such one alternative is to not create scales of activities but rather focus on this 'modal' expression (Tarrow 1996) of social movement activism—particularly as exhibited by the anti-austerity demonstrations taking place as a result of the crisis. Constructing scales of activities has been applied in studies of participation but these could be problematic, particularly at the cross-national level, and adequate checks must be applied in order to ensure they do not confound very different types of political action (Grasso 2013, 2016a). Moreover, some actions such as petitioning are in some countries even more popular than voting, whereas other forms such as occupying are practised in most European countries only by very tiny fractions of the population (Grasso 2011, 2016b). In this study we therefore opted for measuring protest participation by looking at specific political activities separately. Moreover, since we want to understand the impact of the economic context in 2014 on participation in 2015, we limited the indicators to participation in the last year. On the other hand, for voting the question asked which respondents would vote for if there were an election tomorrow, namely, future intention to vote. Table 7.2 shows the proportion of individuals that said they had participated in the various activities in each country or that said they would not vote for the incumbent if there was an election tomorrow. Table 7.2 also shows that there is reasonable variation. Part of the variation appears to be related to the severity and extent of the crisis. Countries where the crisis had deeper effects such as Greece saw greater levels of protest activism.

Our key independent variable for subjective feelings of relative deprivation is retrospective to the last five years so that the deterioration of conditions relative to expectations should have at least begun to occur prior to political behaviour in the last twelve months and as such the time-ordering of independent and dependent variables respects the requirements of causality. This question asks respondents whether they felt that the economic situation of their household was much better or much worse than it was five years ago. We dichotomise this measure following previous research (Rüdig and Karyotis 2013b) in a dummy for whether individuals felt the economic situation of their household had become worse. Table 7.2 also shows the proportion of individuals that said the economic situation had become worse in each country. Table 7.2 shows that there is a good amount of variation also in this respect.

Perceptions of the government's role in the crisis are captured by two variables. On the one hand, to assess the impact of perceptions on specific policy issues, we asked the following question about support for government actions with respect to a specific policy area: unemployment. We coded as 1 those that were unsatisfied with the way the government was dealing with unemployment and 0 the others. On the other hand, to evaluate the influence of blame assignment, we asked the following question about responsibility for the problems: Which of the following do you think are most responsible for the [country]'s economic difficulties? We coded as 1 those selecting 'national government' and 0 all others (banks and financial actors, US, European Union, trade unions, migrants and others). Satisfaction with the government on unemployment and blaming the government for the state of the economy are only weakly correlated at 0.13 ($p < 0.000$).

Two macroeconomic variables aim to examine both negative and positive indicators of the economic context. They control for the potential impact that economic hardship, at the aggregate level, has on political behaviour, as posited for example by relative deprivation theory (Grasso and Giugni 2016a). On the one hand, high unemployment levels are perhaps the most pernicious consequence of the current economic crisis in Europe. Countries where unemployment is highest, are those that in general have suffered the most from the current economic crisis. On the other hand, we also examine GDP growth as this is perhaps the clearest measure that a country is doing well and is coming out of recession. Countries with positive and large GDP growth figures are understood to be out of recession and to have curbed the most pernicious effects of the economic crisis. Both variables are taken for 2014 in order to examine conditions prior to participation but not too far back in time. On the policy side, we include two variables linked to austerity policies: the government expenses for social policies (as a percentage of the GDP) and the tax wedge (as a percentage of labour cost). These two variables reflect the definition of austerity policies as reducing government spending, especially in the social realm, and increasing taxation, especially on labour. Research has pointed to the role of public policies as part of the political opportunity structure affecting protest participation (Giugni and Grasso 2015b; Meyer 2004). In this perspective, these two variables control for the potential impact of political opportunities. Again, both are for 2014. In addition, we also control for the effect of different political systems by including Gallagher's disproportionality index. This also captures the fact that voters in different systems might find it easier or harder to assign responsibility for specific policy outcomes to the incumbent, depending on the institutional setup.

We also include in our models the following classic individual-level controls (for more details see, e.g. Dunn et al. 2014; Grasso et al. 2017; Saunders et al. 2012): age, gender, education level (low), occupation (manual), employment status (whether the respondent is unemployed), political interest, internal and external political efficacy, party attachment, left–right values, libertarian–authoritarian values and number of organisational memberships (distributions by country for all dependent and independent variables are provided in table 7.2). Sociodemographic characteristics, political attitudes, and organisational involvement have long been shown to play an important role for political participation (Brady et al. 1995; Brady 1999), including party attachment for voting (Campbell et al. 1960). Moreover, research has often argued that more progressive values underpin extra-institutional political participation (Dalton et al. 2010; Welzel and Deutsch 2012).

Our dependent variable is measured at the individual level but we have independent variables at both the individual and the country level. For this reason, we specify multilevel models with random intercept coefficients to take into account the two-level nature of the data (country and individual). This model is useful to correct for the within-country dependence of observations (intraclass correlation) and adjusts both within and between parameter estimates in relation to the clustered nature of the data (Snijders and Bosker 1999). Since our dependent variables are dichotomous, we estimate logistic multilevel models with a Gaussian link function. Although the issue is the object of a debate among methodologists, we use multilevel modelling even if the number of level-2 units is towards the lower end. For this reason, we also ran fixed effects models to check for robustness of our results. The results from the latter were effectively the same as those from the multilevel models, so we present the random effects models as a more elegant way of displaying the results and allowing also for the inclusion of the level-2 controls. Moreover, since we hypothesise that the effect of relative deprivation is conditional upon perceptions of the government's role in the crisis—that is, the way people frame it in terms of blame assignment and satisfaction with the way the government is dealing with unemployment—we include in the models, in turn, two interaction terms aimed at capturing these effects.

RESULTS

Tables 7.3, 7.4, 7.5, and 7.6 show the results of our analysis. Each table refers to one of the four types of political behaviour under scrutiny: voting against the incumbent, attending public meetings, participating in demonstrations, and joining strikes. We focus our comments on the main effects of satisfaction with the way the government deals with unemployment and of blame assignment (models 3–5), as well as on the interactions of these two variables and feelings of relative deprivation (models 6 and 7). The main effects allow us to test our first and second hypotheses, while the interactions allow for examining the evidence for our third hypothesis.

Starting with the main effects, both satisfaction with the way the government deals with unemployment and blame assignment have a significant positive effect on the likelihood to vote against the incumbent (table 7.3). Results show that people do not vote for the incumbent when they suffer from poor economic conditions, they think the government is responsible for negative economic conditions in the country, and they are dissatisfied with how it has dealt with the unemployment. Perhaps most importantly, dissatisfaction with the way the government is dealing with the crisis—specifically, with regard to unemployment—has the largest effect, while reducing the effect of relative deprivation when included in the model, showing that perceptions of the government's role in the crisis underlie the key mechanism at work here.

Moving to the three non-electoral forms of participation, we see that people unsatisfied with the way the government deals with unemployment are more likely to attend political meetings, while blame assignment does not seem to matter (table 7.4). A similar pattern can be observed for participation in demonstrations (table 7.5). As far as the main effects of our two variables are concerned, dissatisfaction with the way the government deals with the crisis displays a significant effect, while blame assignment is not significant. This effect, however, is much less important than for not voting for the incumbent. Finally, joining strikes does not seem to be influenced by dissatisfaction with the way the government deals with the crisis nor by blame assignment, as neither of these two variables has a significant effect (table 7.6).

Thus, the analysis of the main effects provides some evidence supporting the first and second hypotheses. As we expected, we observe a direct effect on political behaviour of dissatisfaction with the way the government is dealing with unemployment and of blaming the national government for the nation's economic difficulties. However, such an effect varies across types of political behaviour, being strongest for the more institutionalised forms, and more specifically for voting against the incumbent, that is, for the electoral form. The more contentious forms of political behaviour are less influenced by perceptions of the role of the government in the economic crisis.

If we look at the interaction terms (third hypothesis), we observe a significant effect of the interaction between relative deprivation and dissatisfaction with the way the government deals with the crisis in the case of voting against

Table 7.3. Logistic multilevel regression predicting voting against the incumbent party or coalition if election tomorrow

Model	*(1)*	*(2)*	*(3)*	*(4)*	*(5)*	*(6)*	*(7)*
Age	–	–0.01***	–0.01***	–0.01***	–0.01***	–0.01***	–0.01***
	–	(0.00)	(0.00)	(0.00)	(0.00)	(0.00)	(0.00)
Gender (male)	–	0.11**	0.16***	0.11**	0.15***	0.15***	0.15***
	–	(0.04)	(0.04)	(0.04)	(0.04)	(0.04)	(0.04)
Education (low)	–	–0.03	–0.04	–0.02	–0.03	–0.03	–0.03
	–	(0.05)	(0.05)	(0.05)	(0.05)	(0.05)	(0.05)
Occupation (manual)	–	0.03	0.02	0.02	0.01	0.01	0.01
	–	(0.04)	(0.05)	(0.05)	(0.05)	(0.05)	(0.05)
Unemployed	–	0.03	0.03	0.02	0.02	0.02	0.02
	–	(0.06)	(0.06)	(0.06)	(0.06)	(0.06)	(0.06)
Political interest	–	–0.19***	–0.17***	–0.20***	–0.19***	–0.18***	–0.18***
	–	(0.05)	(0.05)	(0.05)	(0.05)	(0.05)	(0.05)
Internal political efficacy	–	–0.05	–0.01	–0.10	–0.04	–0.05	–0.05
	–	(0.05)	(0.06)	(0.05)	(0.06)	(0.06)	(0.06)
External political efficacy	–	0.50***	0.40***	0.42***	0.34***	0.33***	0.34***
	–	(0.05)	(0.05)	(0.05)	(0.05)	(0.05)	(0.05)
Party attachment	–	–0.48***	–0.47***	–0.48***	–0.47***	–0.47***	–0.47***
	–	(0.02)	(0.02)	(0.02)	(0.02)	(0.02)	(0.02)
Left–right values	–	–0.10***	–0.08***	–0.10***	–0.09***	–0.09***	–0.09***
	–	(0.01)	(0.01)	(0.01)	(0.01)	(0.01)	(0.01)
Libertarian–authoritarian values	–	–0.01	–0.01	–0.01	–0.01	–0.01	–0.01
	–	(0.01)	(0.01)	(0.01)	(0.01)	(0.01)	(0.01)
Organisational memberships	–	0.03**	0.04***	0.03***	0.05***	0.05***	0.05***
	–	(0.01)	(0.01)	(0.01)	(0.01)	(0.01)	(0.01)
Unemployment rate	–	0.02	0.01	0.01	0.00	0.00	0.00
	–	(0.01)	(0.01)	(0.01)	(0.01)	(0.01)	(0.01)

GDP growth	–	0.58***	0.55***	0.54***	0.52***	0.52***	0.52***
	–	(0.16)	(0.15)	(0.14)	(0.15)	(0.15)	(0.15)
Social spending	–	0.24***	0.23***	0.23***	0.22***	0.22***	0.22***
	–	(0.06)	(0.06)	(0.05)	(0.05)	(0.05)	(0.05)
Tax wedge	−0.02	–	−0.03	−0.03	−0.03	−0.03	−0.03
	(0.02)	–	(0.02)	(0.02)	(0.02)	(0.02)	(0.02)
Disproportionality index	–	0.06*	0.06*	0.06*	0.06*	0.06*	0.06*
	–	(0.02)	(0.02)	(0.02)	(0.02)	(0.02)	(0.02)
Relative deprivation	–	0.42***	0.30***	0.37***	0.27***	0.11	0.21***
	–	(0.04)	(0.04)	(0.04)	(0.04)	(0.09)	(0.05)
Unsatisfied with how govt.	–	–	0.99***	–	0.93***	0.87***	0.93***
deals with unemployment	–	–	(0.04)	–	(0.05)	(0.05)	(0.05)
Blames govt. for economic	–	–	–	0.64***	0.57***	0.57***	0.52***
difficulties	–	–	–	(0.04)	(0.04)	(0.04)	(0.05)
Relative deprivation X unsatisfied	–	–	–	–	–	0.21*	–
with how govt. deals with unemployment	–	–	–	–	–	(0.10)	–
Relative deprivation X blames	–	–	–	–	–	–	0.14
govt. for economic difficulties	–	–	–	–	–	–	(0.08)
Constant	0.97***	−3.75**	−4.00***	−3.58**	−3.83***	−3.81***	−3.83***
	(0.20)	(1.19)	(1.19)	(1.10)	(1.13)	(1.14)	(1.13)
Log likelihood	−10,015.67	−9,367.04	−9,124.05	−9,222.45	−9,013.22	−9,010.92	−9,011.62
AIC	20,035.33	18,774.09	18,290.10	18,486.90	18,070.43	18,067.84	18,069.24
BIC	20,050.89	18,929.68	18,453.47	18,650.27	18,241.58	18,246.77	18,248.17
Sigma u	0.61	0.30	0.30	0.27	0.28	0.28	0.28
Rho	0.10	0.03	0.03	0.02	0.02	0.02	0.02

Standard errors in parentheses; *N* = 17,667.
* $p < 0.05$ ** $p < 0.01$ *** $p < 0.001$

Table 7.4. Logistic multilevel regression predicting attending public meetings in last 12 months

Model	*(1)*	*(2)*	*(3)*	*(4)*	*(5)*	*(6)*	*(7)*
Age	–	0.00	–0.00	–0.00	–0.00	–0.00	–0.00
	–	(0.00)	(0.00)	(0.00)	(0.00)	(0.00)	(0.00)
Gender (male)	–	0.35***	0.36***	0.35***	0.36***	0.36***	0.36***
	–	(0.06)	(0.06)	(0.06)	(0.06)	(0.06)	(0.06)
Education (low)	–	–0.17*	–0.18*	–0.17*	–0.17*	–0.18*	–0.17*
	–	(0.07)	(0.07)	(0.07)	(0.07)	(0.07)	(0.07)
Occupation (manual)	–	–0.08	–0.09	–0.08	–0.09	–0.09	–0.09
	–	(0.07)	(0.07)	(0.07)	(0.07)	(0.07)	(0.07)
Unemployed	–	0.01	0.01	0.01	0.01	0.00	0.01
	–	(0.09)	(0.09)	(0.09)	(0.09)	(0.09)	(0.09)
Political interest	–	0.96***	0.96***	0.96***	0.96***	0.96***	0.96***
	–	(0.09)	(0.09)	(0.09)	(0.09)	(0.09)	(0.09)
Internal political efficacy	–	1.06***	1.07***	1.06***	1.07***	1.06***	1.07***
	–	(0.09)	(0.09)	(0.09)	(0.09)	(0.09)	(0.09)
External political efficacy	–	–0.13	–0.15	–0.14	–0.15	–0.16	–0.15
	–	(0.08)	(0.08)	(0.08)	(0.08)	(0.08)	(0.08)
Party attachment	–	0.38***	0.39***	0.39***	0.39***	0.39***	0.39***
	–	(0.03)	(0.03)	(0.03)	(0.03)	(0.03)	(0.03)
Left–right values	–	–0.06***	–0.05***	–0.06***	–0.05***	–0.05***	–0.05***
	–	(0.02)	(0.02)	(0.02)	(0.02)	(0.02)	(0.02)
Libertarian–authoritarian values	–	–0.07***	–0.07***	–0.07***	–0.07***	–0.07***	–0.07***
	–	(0.02)	(0.02)	(0.02)	(0.02)	(0.02)	(0.02)
Organisational memberships	–	0.18***	0.19***	0.18***	0.19***	0.19***	0.19***
	–	(0.01)	(0.01)	(0.01)	(0.01)	(0.01)	(0.01)
Unemployment rate	–	0.02*	0.02*	0.02*	0.02*	0.02*	0.02*
	–	(0.01)	(0.01)	(0.01)	(0.01)	(0.01)	(0.01)
GDP growth	–	–0.11	–0.11	–0.11	–0.11	–0.11	–0.11
	–	(0.10)	(0.10)	(0.10)	(0.10)	(0.10)	(0.10)

Social spending	–	−0.04	−0.05	−0.05	−0.05	−0.05	−0.05
	–	(0.04)	(0.04)	(0.04)	(0.04)	(0.04)	(0.04)
Tax wedge	–	0.01	0.01	0.01	0.01	0.01	0.01
	–	(0.02)	(0.01)	(0.01)	(0.01)	(0.01)	(0.01)
Disproportionality index	–	−0.01	−0.01	−0.01	−0.01	−0.01	−0.01
	–	(0.02)	(0.02)	(0.02)	(0.02)	(0.02)	(0.02)
Relative deprivation	–	0.13*	0.11	0.13*	0.11	−0.19	0.12
	–	(0.06)	(0.06)	(0.06)	(0.06)	(0.15)	(0.08)
Unsatisfied with how govt.	–	–	0.18*	–	0.18*	0.09	0.18*
deals with unemployment	–	–	(0.07)	–	(0.07)	(0.08)	(0.07)
Blames govt.	–	–	–	0.03	0.01	0.01	0.03
for economic difficulties	–	–	–	(0.06)	(0.06)	(0.06)	(0.08)
Relative deprivation X unsatisfied	–	–	–	–	–	−0.12	–
with how govt. deals with unemployment	–	–	–	–	–	(0.15)	–
Relative deprivation X blames	–	–	–	–	–	–	−0.03
govt.	–	–	–	–	–	–	(0.11)
for economic difficulties							
Constant	−2.28***	−4.01***	−4.05***	−4.01***	−4.04***	−3.99***	−4.05***
	(0.11)	(0.80)	(0.79)	(0.79)	(0.78)	(0.79)	(0.78)
Log likelihood	−5,552.05	−4,691.63	−4,688.33	−4,691.47	−4,688.30	−4,685.82	−4,688.25
AIC	11,108.09	9,423.27	9,418.65	9,424.93	9,420.59	9,417.64	9,422.50
BIC	11,123.65	9,578.86	9,582.02	9,588.30	9,591.74	9,596.56	9,601.43
Sigma	0.31	0.18	0.17	0.18	0.17	0.17	0.17
Rho	0.03	0.01	0.01	0.01	0.01	0.01	0.01

Standard errors in parentheses; $N = 17,667$
* $p < 0.05$ ** $p < 0.01$ *** $p < 0.001$

Table 7.5. Logistic multilevel regression predicting participating in demonstrations in last 12 months

	(1)	*(2)*	*(3)*	*(4)*	*(5)*	*(6)*	*(7)*
Age	–	−0.01***	−0.01***	−0.01***	−0.01***	−0.01***	−0.01***
	–	(0.00)	(0.00)	(0.00)	(0.00)	(0.00)	(0.00)
Gender (male)	–	−0.02	−0.01	−0.02	−0.01	−0.01	−0.01
	–	(0.05)	(0.05)	(0.05)	(0.05)	(0.05)	(0.05)
Education (low)	–	−0.08	−0.08	−0.07	−0.07	−0.07	−0.07
	–	(0.07)	(0.07)	(0.07)	(0.07)	(0.07)	(0.07)
Occupation (manual)	–	0.06	0.06	0.06	0.06	0.06	0.06
	–	(0.06)	(0.06)	(0.06)	(0.06)	(0.06)	(0.06)
Unemployed	–	−0.26**	−0.26**	−0.26**	−0.26**	−0.26**	−0.26**
	–	(0.08)	(0.08)	(0.08)	(0.08)	(0.08)	(0.08)
Political interest	–	0.67***	0.68***	0.67***	0.67***	0.67***	0.67***
	–	(0.07)	(0.07)	(0.07)	(0.07)	(0.07)	(0.07)
Internal political efficacy	–	0.73***	0.74***	0.72***	0.73***	0.73***	0.73***
	–	(0.08)	(0.08)	(0.08)	(0.08)	(0.08)	(0.08)
External political efficacy	–	−0.16*	−0.17*	−0.18*	−0.19*	−0.19*	−0.19*
	–	(0.08)	(0.08)	(0.08)	(0.08)	(0.08)	(0.08)
Party attachment	–	0.17***	0.17***	0.17***	0.17***	0.17***	0.17***
	–	(0.03)	(0.03)	(0.03)	(0.03)	(0.03)	(0.03)
Left–right values	–	−0.18***	−0.17***	−0.18***	−0.18***	−0.18***	−0.18***
	–	(0.02)	(0.02)	(0.02)	(0.02)	(0.02)	(0.02)
Libertarian–authoritarian values	–	−0.18***	−0.18***	−0.18***	−0.18***	−0.18***	−0.18***
	–	(0.02)	(0.02)	(0.02)	(0.02)	(0.02)	(0.02)
Organisational memberships	–	0.16***	0.16***	0.16***	0.16***	0.16***	0.16***
	–	(0.01)	(0.01)	(0.01)	(0.01)	(0.01)	(0.01)
Unemployment rate	–	0.05***	0.05***	0.05***	0.05***	0.05***	0.05***
	–	(0.01)	(0.01)	(0.01)	(0.01)	(0.01)	(0.01)
GDP growth	–	−0.24	−0.26	−0.26	−0.27	−0.27	−0.27
	–	(0.13)	(0.13)	(0.14)	(0.14)	(0.14)	(0.14)

Social spending	–	0.02	0.01	0.02	0.01	0.01	0.01
	–	(0.05)	(0.05)	(0.05)	(0.05)	(0.05)	(0.05)
Tax wedge	–	0.01	0.01	0.01	0.00	0.00	0.00
	–	(0.02)	(0.02)	(0.02)	(0.02)	(0.02)	(0.02)
Disproportionality index	–	–0.01	–0.01	–0.01	–0.01	–0.01	–0.01
	–	(0.02)	(0.02)	(0.02)	(0.02)	(0.02)	(0.02)
Relative deprivation	–	0.17**	0.14*	0.15**	0.13*	0.23	0.16*
	–	(0.06)	(0.06)	(0.06)	(0.06)	(0.14)	(0.08)
Unsatisfied with how govt.	–	–	0.21**	–	0.19*	0.23*	0.19*
deals with unemployment	–	–	(0.08)	–	(0.08)	(0.09)	(0.08)
Blames govt.	–	–	–	0.13*	0.11*	0.11*	0.14
for economic difficulties	–	–	–	(0.05)	(0.05)	–	(0.08)
Relative deprivation X unsatisfied	–	–	–	–	–	–0.12	–
with how govt. deals with unemployment	–	–	–	–	–	(0.15)	–
Relative deprivation X	–	–	–	–	–	–	–0.05
blames govt. for economic difficulties	–	–	–	–	–	–	(0.11)
Constant	–2.22***	–2.70**	–2.74**	–2.66*	–2.70**	–2.72**	–2.71**
	(0.20)	(1.03)	(1.03)	(1.05)	(1.05)	(1.05)	(1.05)
Log likelihood	–5,877.43	–5,094.72	–5,090.85	–5,091.94	–5,088.80	–5,088.51	–5,088.67
AIC	11,758.86	10,229.45	10,223.70	10,225.89	10,221.60	10,223.03	10,223.34
BIC	11,774.42	10,385.03	10,387.07	10,389.26	10,392.75	10,401.96	10,402.27
Sigma	0.59	0.24	0.24	0.25	0.25	0.25	0.25
Rho	0.10	0.02	0.02	0.02	0.02	0.02	0.02

Standard errors in parentheses; N = 17,667.
* $p < 0.05$ ** $p < 0.01$ *** $p < 0.001$

Table 7.6. Logistic multilevel regression predicting joining strikes in last 12 months

	(1)	*(2)*	*(3)*	*(4)*	*(5)*	*(6)*	*(7)*
Age	–	−0.02***	−0.02***	−0.02***	−0.02***	−0.02***	−0.02***
	–	(0.00)	(0.00)	(0.00)	(0.00)	(0.00)	(0.00)
Gender (male)	–	−0.00	−0.00	−0.00	−0.00	−0.00	−0.00
	–	(0.07)	(0.07)	(0.07)	(0.07)	(0.07)	(0.07)
Education (low)	–	−0.21*	−0.21*	−0.21*	−0.21*	−0.21*	−0.21*
	–	(0.09)	(0.09)	(0.09)	(0.09)	(0.09)	(0.09)
Occupation (manual)	–	0.00	0.00	0.00	0.00	0.00	0.01
	–	(0.09)	(0.09)	(0.09)	(0.09)	(0.09)	(0.09)
Unemployed	–	−0.53***	−0.53***	−0.53***	−0.53***	−0.53***	−0.54***
	–	(0.11)	(0.11)	(0.11)	(0.11)	(0.11)	(0.11)
Political interest	–	0.35***	0.35***	0.35***	0.35***	0.35***	0.35***
	–	(0.09)	(0.09)	(0.09)	(0.09)	(0.09)	(0.09)
Internal political efficacy	–	0.38***	0.38***	0.38***	0.38***	0.38***	0.38***
	–	(0.10)	(0.10)	(0.10)	(0.10)	(0.10)	(0.10)
External political efficacy	–	0.02	0.02	0.02	0.02	0.02	0.02
	–	(0.11)	(0.11)	(0.11)	(0.11)	(0.11)	(0.11)
Party attachment	–	0.09*	0.09*	0.09*	0.09*	0.09*	0.09*
	–	(0.04)	(0.04)	(0.04)	(0.04)	(0.04)	(0.04)
Left–right values	–	−0.16***	−0.16***	−0.16***	−0.16***	−0.16***	−0.16***
	–	(0.02)	(0.02)	(0.02)	(0.02)	(0.02)	(0.02)
Libertarian–authoritarian values	–	−0.08***	−0.08***	−0.08***	−0.08***	−0.08***	−0.08***
	–	(0.02)	(0.02)	(0.02)	(0.02)	(0.02)	(0.02)
Organisational memberships	–	0.16***	0.16***	0.16***	0.16***	0.16***	0.16***
	–	(0.01)	(0.01)	(0.01)	(0.01)	(0.01)	(0.01)
Unemployment rate	–	0.06***	0.06***	0.06***	0.06***	0.06***	0.06***
	–	(0.01)	(0.01)	(0.01)	(0.01)	(0.01)	(0.01)
GDP growth	–	−0.41***	−0.41***	−0.41***	−0.41***	−0.41***	−0.41***
	–	(0.11)	(0.11)	(0.11)	(0.11)	(0.11)	(0.11)

Social spending	–	−0.12**	−0.12**	−0.12**	−0.12**	−0.12**	−0.12**
	–	(0.04)	(0.04)	(0.04)	(0.04)	(0.04)	(0.04)
Tax wedge	–	0.04*	0.04*	0.04*	0.04*	0.04*	0.04*
	–	(0.02)	(0.02)	(0.02)	(0.02)	(0.02)	(0.02)
Disproportionality index	–	0.06***	0.06***	0.06**	0.06***	0.06***	0.06***
	–	(0.02)	(0.02)	(0.02)	(0.02)	(0.02)	(0.02)
Relative deprivation	–	0.23**	0.23**	0.22**	0.23**	0.14	0.15
	–	(0.08)	(0.08)	(0.08)	(0.08)	(0.19)	(0.11)
Unsatisfied with how govt.	–	–	−0.02	–	−0.03	−0.02	−0.02
deals with unemployment	–	–	(0.10)	–	(0.10)	(0.12)	(0.10)
Blames govt. for economic	–	–	–	0.03	0.03	0.03	−0.06
difficulties	–	–	–	(0.07)	(0.07)	(0.07)	(0.11)
Relative deprivation X unsatisfied	–	–	–	–	–	0.10	–
with	–	–	–	–	–	(0.21)	–
how govt. deals with							
unemployment							
Relative deprivation X blames	–	–	–	–	–	–	0.16
govt. for economic difficulties	–	–	–	–	–	–	(0.14)
Constant	−3.23***	−1.49	−1.49	−1.48	−1.48	−1.46	−1.47
	(0.34)	(0.92)	(0.92)	(0.92)	(0.92)	(0.92)	(0.91)
Log likelihood	−3,494.15	−3,169.75	−3,169.73	−3,169.68	−3,169.65	−3,169.52	−3,169.06
AIC	6,992.30	6,379.51	6,381.47	6,381.37	6,383.30	6,385.05	6,384.12
BIC	7,007.86	6,535.10	6,544.84	6,544.73	6,554.45	6,563.98	6,563.05
Sigma u	1.00	0.15	0.15	0.15	0.15	0.15	0.14
Rho	0.23	0.01	0.01	0.01	0.01	0.01	0.01

Standard errors in parentheses; N = 17,667.
* $p < 0.05$ ** $p < 0.01$ *** $p < 0.001$

the incumbent (table 7.4). This means that the effect of relative deprivation on economic voting is conditional upon believing that the government has not dealt with the crisis in a satisfactory way. We also observe a significant interaction term in the case of attending political meetings (table 7.4). Again, dissatisfaction with the way the government deals with the crisis significantly interacts with relative deprivation. Like for voting against the incumbent, although to a lesser extent, here the effect of relative deprivation seems to be conditional upon perceptions of the role of government in the crisis. More specifically, the effect of government performance on unemployment is significant also in the case of attending political meetings. In contrast, the interaction between relative deprivation and blame assignment is not significant either for voting against the incumbent nor for attending political meetings. Furthermore, none of the two interactive terms displays a statistically significant effect on participating in demonstrations and joining strikes, indicating that there is no conditional effect of perceptions of the government's role in the crisis on the relationship between feelings of relative deprivation and involvement in these more contentious forms of political behaviour. Our third hypothesis is therefore confirmed only in part, namely for the two more institutional form of political behaviour and in the case of the conditional role of

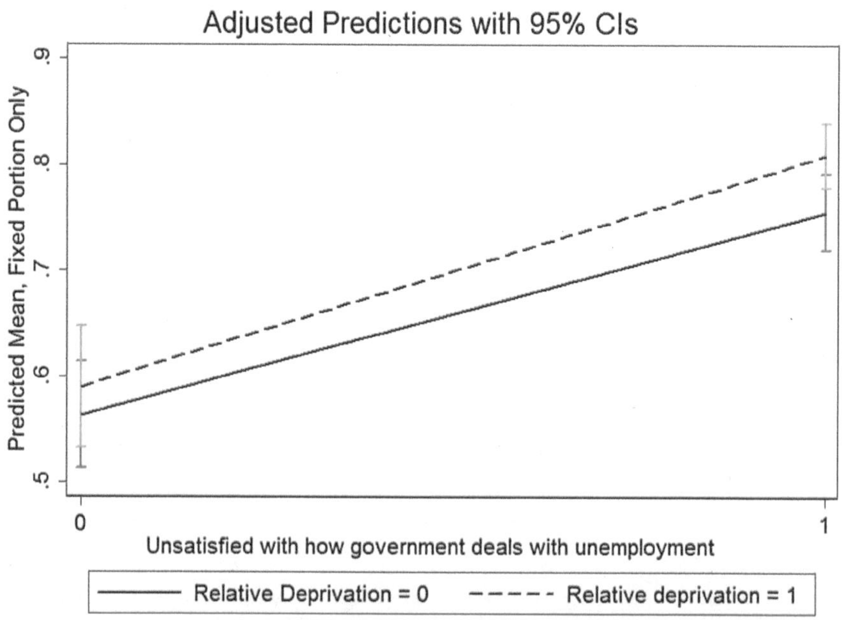

Figure 7.1. Plot of interaction between relative deprivation and dissatisfaction with how government deals with unemployment on voting against the incumbent

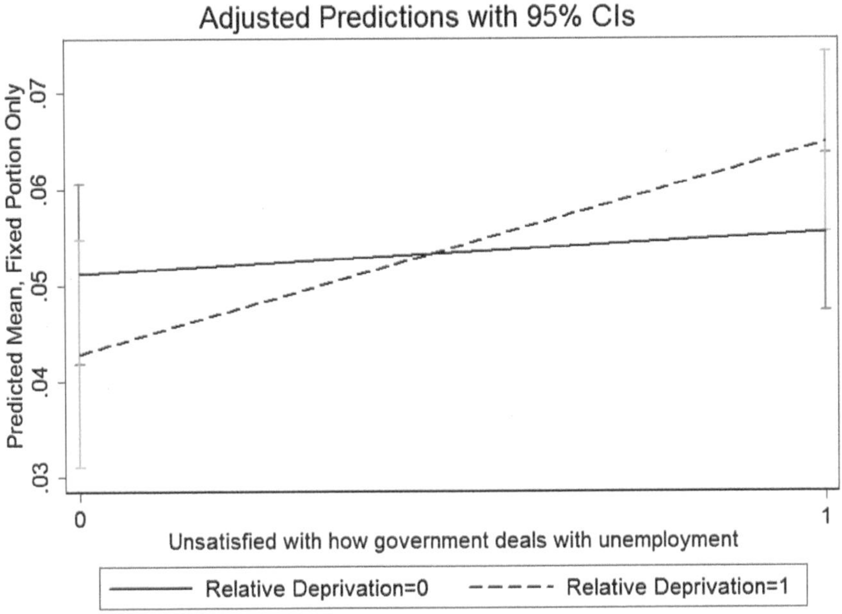

Figure 7.2. Plot of interaction between relative deprivation and dissatisfaction with how government deals with unemployment on attending public meetings

dissatisfaction with government performance, while blame assignment does not seem to matter here.

Conditional effects can be seen more clearly in figures 7.1 and 7.2, which show the plots of the two statistically significant interaction terms. Here we can better appreciate the direction and size of such effects. As we can see, the conditional role of perceptions of the role of government, while present both in the case of voting against the incumbent and in the case of attending political meetings, is particularly visible for the latter. This can be seen by comparing the slope for those who feel deprived with the slope for those who do not feel deprived. The latter is nearly flat, whereas the former shows a strong effect of relative deprivation on this form of political behaviour. In brief, overall, we can see that dissatisfaction with the way the government is dealing with unemployment matters both for those who feel deprived and for those who do not feel deprived. However, the former are more likely to engage than the latter, especially so when it comes to attending political meetings. This pattern, furthermore, is present only in the more institutionalised forms of political behaviour, whereas relative deprivation does not interact with perceptions of the role of government in the economic crisis when it comes to the more contentious forms.

CONCLUSION

The deep economic crisis suffered by many European countries in recent years has spurred much scholarly writing on the impact of this particular crisis and of economic crises in general (for e.g. see English et al. 2016; Giugni and Grasso 2018c, 2018d; Grasso and Giugni 2016b; Temple et al. 2016; Temple and Grasso 2018). In this chapter, we have explored a number of potential effects on different types of political behaviour, which can all be seen as the political expression of dissatisfaction with the current political and economic situation, using an original dataset stemming from a survey conducted in nine European countries. We were particularly interested in investigating the impact of perceptions of the government's role in the crisis (as measured through satisfaction with the way the government is dealing with unemployment, and blaming the government for the economic situation of the country), as well as their interaction with perceptions about one's own economic conditions in terms of relative deprivation (as measured through the feelings that the economic situation of the household is worse than five years earlier). Moreover, we have looked at the effects of these predictors and their interactions on various forms of political behaviour: an electoral form captured by voting against the incumbent and three non-electoral kinds of participation, namely attending public meetings, participating in demonstrations, and joining strikes.

Our findings suggest that perceptions of the government's role in the crisis are instrumental in pushing people to manifest their disapproval politically. At the same time, however, the impact of these variables is not homogeneous across all forms of political behaviour, as for some—in particular, voting against the incumbent—they matter, while not so for other modes. Most importantly, we found evidence that the perceptions people have of the way in which the government is dealing with the situation, more precisely on the way in which it is dealing with unemployment—a key aspect of the economy in times of crisis—conditions the effect of relative deprivation on political behaviour. This occurs namely with voting against the incumbent and with attending public meetings, that is, the more institutionalised forms of political behaviour, whether electoral or non-electoral.

While we expected such a conditional effect to occur for other forms as well, the variations we observed both in the main effects and in the interaction effects across forms of political behaviour allow us to stress another important point. This is to say that different forms of political behaviour are influenced by different factors. In other words, the economic crisis led people to participate politically, but in different forms and for different reasons pertaining to the way they perceived the crisis and its effects.

Finally, on a more methodological note, our study shows the need to go beyond the traditional distinction between electoral and non-electoral political behaviours and also to consider certain forms of electoral behaviour such as voting against the incumbent as a form of adversarial political action alongside other forms such as attending a meeting, demonstrating, or participating in a strike. We argue that the political context of an action has important repercussions for how we understand it in terms of its contentiousness. As others before us have argued (Heaney and Rojas 2014; Hutter 2014b; Kriesi 2014a; McAdam and Tarrow 2010), electoral politics and protest politics need to be studied together in order to arrive at a better understanding of why and how citizens hold governments to account, both in times of crisis as well as in more 'ordinary' times.

Chapter Eight

Europeans in the Great Recession in Perspective

This book has analysed the effects of the Great Recession on Europeans. This deep and long-lasting economic crisis has had a variety of negative consequences that will likely continue to have an impact for quite some time and particularly amongst more vulnerable social groups and in those countries that were most deeply hit by the crisis, such as Greece, Italy and Spain. Other countries, such as France and the UK, have also paid an important toll. Still others, such as Germany, Sweden and Switzerland, have suffered to a lesser extent, although they have not been entirely spared the negative effects of the crisis. Within this context, we have examined how Europeans have experienced and perceived the crisis and responded to it. More specifically, we have examined individuals' experiences of the economic crisis and the deprivation it may produce and how this depends on individuals' structural location. We also examined capacities for resilience and attitudes towards key politicised themes such as the welfare state and immigration, including support for radical right parties. Moreover, we also examined how the crisis has impacted on political activism and how perceptions of the wider economic and political context may create opportunities for active political engagement for social change, and allowing participants to contribute to developing solutions to current woes.

Our analysis, based on data from an original survey carried out amongst respondents in each of the nine countries included in the study, has pursued three key lines of investigation as sketched in our introduction, each addressed in a pair of chapters. First, we looked at the differential impact of the crisis on different groups in terms of feelings of deprivation, in particular, but also in terms of how citizens have been able to cope with the negative effects of the crisis and to show a capacity for resilience. In particular, we have examined how both feelings of deprivation and resilience vary across social groups. Second, we looked at citizen attitudes with respect to two particularly salient politicised issue fields in the context of the crisis: unemployment and the welfare state, more broadly, and immigration, including support for radical right parties. Third, we examined political activism in the context of the crisis. We examined the extent to which deprivation led to protest activism and how the wider context impacted mobilisation in various forms of political action.

In this concluding chapter we discuss our main findings with respect to these three lines of investigation. Moreover, we examine the issues discussed in the introduction and reassess them in light of our findings. We conclude with a discussion of the economic crisis understood as both constraint and opportunity.

DEPRIVATION AND RESILIENCE AMONGST EUROPEANS

Our first line of investigation has dealt with the effects of the economic crisis on perceptions of deprivation as well as individuals' capacity for resilience. Thus, in chapter 2 we looked at the effects of the economic crisis on Europeans' experiences of deprivation as well as on their perceptions of their economic conditions. Moreover, we asked to what extent such perceptions of economic deprivation depended on individuals' structural positions and in particular on their class locations. As we have seen, the Great Recession has had profound effects on many Europeans. The crisis had produced a deterioration of living standards and the wider economic conditions across Europe, especially in those countries most hard hit by the crisis. The crisis also generated feelings of deprivation. The literature distinguishes between 'egotropic', or pocketbook, and 'sociotropic', or wider economic, evaluations. The former concern one's own situation, whereas the latter refer to the evaluation of the state of the national economy (Kinder and Kiewiet 1981). A second distinction is made between retrospective and prospective evaluations. This is a well-known distinction in the literature on economic voting (Downs 1957; Fiorina 1981) which can be applied to how people view both their own economic situations and that of the countries in which they live. Retrospective evaluations compare the current situation with that of a given previous period in the past—five years in our case—whereas prospective evaluations consist of future outlooks.

We examined retrospective household-level and prospective country-level evaluations. Our analysis showed that both kinds of evaluations are linked to the severity of the economic crisis and that they vary across national contexts.

Generally speaking, economic outlooks tend to be more negative in countries most hard hit by the crisis. Thus, feelings of relative deprivation with respect to one's past situation are connected to how deep the crisis was in a given country. Furthermore, and perhaps more concerning, is the finding that the more severe the crisis, the more hopeless individuals tended to be with respect to believing that the economy of their countries might improve in the future.

Moreover, we have shown how retrospective pocketbook and prospective sociotropic evaluations do not only vary across countries in relation to the severity of the crisis and of the austerity measures implemented by governments, but also depend on individuals' structural positions. Our analysis unveiled the presence of important group-based differences in the ways in which individuals assess their own economic situations with respect to the past and that of their countries from a future-oriented perspective. More specifically, the most vulnerable groups—women, people in the lower social classes, those with lower incomes, and the precariously employed—were more likely to feel deprived or to have a grim outlook about the future of the national economy. Such vulnerabilities, furthermore, were found to be cumulative, with younger and better-off men displaying more positive evaluations than older, working-class women. This rejoins works that have shown how 'social disqualification' is a cumulative process leading to poverty (Paugam 1991). In contrast, individuals in less vulnerable positions and possessing more resources were not only less affected in their personal spheres by the negative effects of the economic crisis but were also more optimistic about the future.

Europeans, however, have not simply suffered passively from the negative consequences of the economic crisis. They have also tried to cope with its effects and have shown resilience in the face of significant challenges. Moreover, we expected that some groups with more resources in particular might have been more resilient than others. This led us to inquire, in chapter 3, to what extent the capacity for resilience varied across countries and across social categories and groups. We did so by drawing on the literature on resilience and, more specifically, social resilience (Batty and Cole 2010; Hall and Lamont 2013). Moreover, we also investigated how resilience was linked to factors such as the social characteristics of people, their economic evaluations and the amount of social capital they could draw on from their social networks and relations. Our analysis suggested that Europeans have often displayed a strong capacity for resilience, allowing them to cope with deprivation and hardship generated by the economic crisis and related austerity measures. More specifically, they have been resilient in two main ways: in terms of being able to proactively face adversity at the individual level and in terms of the communities in which they are embedded.

However, we also observed important variations in people's capacity for resilience across countries and, most importantly, across social groups. On the one hand, proactive resilience is more widespread in countries that have been hardest hit by the economic crisis and austerity measures, whereas community-based resilience plays a greater role in countries that have been less strongly hit. On the other hand, women, older people and upper social classes show a stronger capacity for proactive resilience, while people with lower incomes, those that are unemployed as well as migrants, also display a strong capacity for community-based resilience. Interestingly, the impact of these factors appears to be cumulative. In particular, older women who have professional or managerial occupations and higher levels of education are more resilient than younger men who have manual occupations and lower levels of education.

Thus, our analysis has shown that human capital resources are crucial for individuals when it comes to withstanding the negative consequences of the economic crisis as well as the austerity measures that have accompanied them in many countries. Additionally, social resources, captured through the notion of social capital, are also of fundamental importance. The role of social capital—in terms of social trust, the frequency of meeting with friends or membership in voluntary associations—appears as particularly important both for mitigating the negative effects of the economic crisis measured through perceptions of individual deprivation and evaluations of the future of national economies, but also for enhancing individuals' capacity for resilience to negative effects, particularly with respect to proactive resilience.

ATTITUDES IN TWO POLITICISED FIELDS

Our second line of investigation has focussed on attitudes with respect to unemployment, including precarity and the welfare state more generally, and immigration. These are two key political issues which, in times of crisis, have become more salient and politicised. On the one hand, economic crises very often lead to higher levels of unemployment and, in turn, this gives rise to political debates about causes and, above all, remedies, with some arguing in favour of further austerity measures and others claiming that only investments and economic development can create new jobs and that social protection should be expanded rather than contracted in such hard times. Moreover, economic crises are often accompanied not only by rising unemployment rates but also by increasing precarity around work. This was particularly true in the context of the Great Recession where reforms aimed at reducing unemployment often led to growing precarity and insecurity of labour. On the other hand, far-right populist parties on the rise since the start of the Great Recession or earlier have particularly problematised immigration and its effect on straining culture and resources with migrants often scapegoated for wider social and economic issues. In this book, we examined attitudes to government policy on unemployment as well as towards immigration in the two middle chapters. We aimed, in particular, to examine how such attitudes and policy preferences varied across countries and social groups and how they related to individuals' structural locations, experiences of the economic crisis, and the number of resources which they have at their disposal.

As we saw in chapter 4, unemployment policies and, more generally, welfare policies have become a critical battleground during the Great Recession. The rise of anti-austerity protests and movements presented the political face of a broader skepticism in society towards austerity cuts to public services (Giugni and Grasso 2015a). Looking at popular attitudes towards welfare state policies allowed us to study how Europeans have reacted to the economic crisis. Spending on welfare represents a large share of public spending and attitudes in this respect tell us something quite important about citizen preferences for different types of democracy (Kumlin 2007).

Our analysis of Europeans' views on unemployment focussed on the degree of satisfaction with government action on unemployment, as compared to satisfaction with other policies such as precarious employment, poverty, education, healthcare and the economy, more generally. We saw how satisfaction with these policies is related to the extent to which countries experienced the crisis. Yet, the correlation between the severity of the economic crisis, on the one hand, and dissatisfaction with government policies, on the other, is far from perfect, as in some countries that suffered less from the crisis respondents were still very negative in their policy appraisals. Thus, Europeans' degree of satisfaction with government action on unemployment varies across countries, albeit not linearly depending on the severity of the economic crisis. Also importantly, satisfaction with government policies in this respect also clearly varies between different social groups in the population. Our study thus provides further confirmation of what political sociologists have shown in many respects, namely, that political attitudes, preferences and behaviours are strongly embedded in social structure and will depend to a large extent on people's sociodemographic characteristics, thus leading to heterogeneity in the population. While Europeans are not particularly satisfied with government policy action on the whole, especially when it comes to unemployment and precarious work, certain groups such as, for example, women, people with lower incomes and those in less socially advantaged occupational classes, including those in more precarious employment situations, are more dissatisfied.

The same applies to those who suffer most from the crisis at the individual level, for example those who have been forced to reduce consumption or have experienced deteriorating working conditions. In contrast, satisfaction increases for people who have greater resources, whether in economic terms such as income, or in more social terms, such as social capital and the web of social relations.

As we have seen, the cross-national patterns suggest the severity of the crisis is linked to dissatisfaction with government action, in particular, in the fields of unemployment and precarious work, if to a differential degree in different countries and between different social groups. Moreover, the crisis has also been linked to the rise of anti-immigrant and populist attitudes in the population and concerns over the breakdown of social cohesion and the depletion of scarce resources, at least within certain groups. We turned to this aspect in chapter 5, where we examined xenophobic and populist attitudes in the wake of the Great Recession. These two types of attitudes are linked to the extent that particularly right-wing populist parties tend to be against immigration (Ford and Goodwin 2010). Our analysis here looked to examine the impact of economic hardship and deprivation on xenophobic and populist attitudes in Europe, drawing on the existing literature arguing that both should be influenced by egotropic and sociotropic concerns, though the latter tend to be seen as more important than the former in this regard.

Just as patterns in attitudes with respect to unemployment and precarious work depend in part on the national context of the economic crisis as well as on the structural location of individuals, both xenophobic and populist attitudes are similarly distributed cross-nationally on the basis of the severity of the crisis and also by sociodemographic characteristics. In this respect, we found that more vulnerable groups—what some have understood as those groups that are the 'losers' of processes of globalisation (Kriesi et al. 2006, 2008, 2012)—are more likely to hold negative attitudes towards immigrants and immigration and also to display populist attitudes. This is the electoral reservoir where populist and radical right parties have made their greatest gains in recent years (Ivarsflaten 2008; Lubbers et al. 2002; Ford and Goodwin 2010). Furthermore, we showed how xenophobic and populist attitudes are linked to both sociotropic and pocketbook evaluations of the crisis. Sub jective perceptions were found to be important and evaluations of the role of the government in the crisis also played a key role. At the same time, the likelihood for one to hold xenophobic and populist attitudes depended not only on other political attitudes and values but also on resources, in particular, in terms of social capital. We found this to be the case for xenophobic views but it also applied to populist attitudes. In brief, while certain groups were more likely to hold more negative views of immigrants and immigration and to support populist positions, we also found that cultural, social and political resources were important factors.

Our analysis of attitudes and preferences with regards to unemployment and immigration therefore supports the representation that political scientists have provided of the political space in Europe (Kitschelt 1994) as made up of two main axes: an axis reflecting a left-right opposition on economic or redistributive issues and one representing the opposition in terms of social or cultural values, between libertarian and authoritarian politics. While the latter axis, in particular, can be seen in the contemporary context to have further developed to also include aspects relating to processes of globalisation (Hutter 2014b; Kriesi et al. 2006, 2008, 2012), unemployment and immigration and how to deal with them remain two key issues at stake with respect to the first and second dimensions. Indeed, in many respects it could be argued that the Great Recession has made these two cleavages increasingly politically salient and polarising, both on the supply side with respect to the positioning of parties on these issues, as well as on the demand side, potentially leading to a greater divide within public opinion cross-nationally.

EXPERIENCES OF THE ECONOMIC CRISIS AND POLITICAL ENGAGEMENT

Our third line of investigation examined how the experiences of the economic crisis, including perceived opportunities and government action, have impacted on political engagement. This led us to examine the micro-macro dynamics of political engagement in the aftermath of the crisis. The study of the micro-macro or individual-structural linkages is a long-standing concern in sociology and the social sciences (Alexander et al. 1987; Turner and Markovsky 2007). Students of political behaviour and participation have recently started to pay increasing attention to the interplay between micro- and macro-level factors for activism (Dalton et al. 2010; Grasso and Giugni 2016a; Kern et al. 2015; Quaranta 2015, 2016). In chapter 6 we examined how the experience of the crisis at the individual level impacted protest activism and how the wider macro-level context increased the likelihood that individual-level experience of the crisis led to participation.

Our analysis showed that there is indeed a connection between the impact that the economic crisis has had on people's living conditions and their readiness to engage in politics, more specifically in protest activism. However, contrary to what early grievance theories in the social movement literature have often claimed (see Buechler 2004 for an overview), we found that subjective perceptions of one's own economic situation, or what are known as 'pocketbook' evaluations, were particularly relevant. In other words, individuals who feel that their conditions have deteriorated are more likely to protest, net of their objective economic position in society.

Moreover, we also showed that the effect of individual-level feelings of relative deprivation on protest participation is to a large extent conditioned by certain macro-level contextual factors. In this regard, we have stressed in particular the role of rising unemployment and higher levels of social spending as opening up political opportunities for protest among those who felt a deterioration of living standards during or in the aftermath of the crisis. Both act as political catalysts, providing individuals with cues to understand deteriorating living conditions in a politicised way and to see them as a result of failing policies rather than simply their own, individualised private problems or personal failures. We argue that it is important to study and develop our understanding of micro-macro dynamics given that their interplay is key for making sense of why people who feel economically deprived are more likely to get involved in protest activities. On a theoretical level, this brings together grievance and opportunity theories which have, for a long time, been seen as opposed to each other. In more general terms, this suggests that, while both grievances—conceptualised as subjective feelings of deprivation—and opportunities, help to understand political participation, it is their dynamic interaction which explains different levels of engagement in protest activities. This finding also attests to the importance of making sense of the ways in which opportunities are framed by individuals to become the drivers of political engagement (Gamson and Meyer 1996).

Our analysis of the interaction between individual feelings of hardship and deprivation, on the one hand, and contextual conditions, on the other, suggests that how individuals view and evaluate the government's role in the economic crisis also has an important role in explaining why they engaged in contentious politics during or in the aftermath of the economic crisis. The more dissatisfied people were with how their government dealt with the negative consequences of the crisis—in general, or with regard to specific policies and issues such as unemployment—the more likely they were to engage in protest activities and other forms of contention, including not voting for the incumbent. In this sense, as we also stressed elsewhere (Giugni and Grasso 2018a), our study provides support for Bermeo and Bartels' (2014: 4) argument that 'dramatic political reactions to the Great Recession were associated less with the direct economic repercussions of the crisis than with government initiative to cope with those repercussions''. Therefore, the ways in which individuals evaluate government responses to the crisis—in terms of austerity policies or other aspects such as unemployment—are fundamental.

As we mentioned earlier, our analyses of Europeans' views about government policy action towards unemployment and precarious work, but also that of the rise of anti-immigrant and populist attitudes amongst the citizenry, point in the same direction, showing the important role played by sociotropic evaluations of the role of the government in the crisis.

In chapter 7 we examined how deprivation interacts with individual perceptions of the broader political and economic environment to then impact political behaviour in times of crisis. More specifically, here we examined how perceptions of the government's role in the economic crisis shaped patterns of political action—both electoral and non-electoral—by focussing on the role of blame assignment. Economic voting theory has long stressed the importance of macroeconomic conditions and especially evaluations of how the incumbent has handled the economy as strong predictors of vote choice (Lewis-Beck and Stegmaier 2000, 2007). In this context, blame assignment, or attribution, plays a key role, in particular, to explain the vote against the incumbent. Similarly, students of social movements have also stressed that the way in which people evaluate the role of power holders is instrumental for them to become involved in protest activities, although not necessarily within the framework and notion of blaming. For example, a number of scholars have maintained that the lower the legitimacy granted by individuals to authorities on a given issue, the greater the chances for protest to arise (McAdam 1999; Melucci 1989; Piven and Cloward 1979).

Whether in the electoral or non-electoral sphere, blame assignment impinges upon political participation, among other things, because it politicises political evaluations (Iyengar 1991; Peffley 1984; Sniderman and Brody 1977) and connects personal and social problems to political judgments (Iyengar 1991). As such, a context of deep economic downturn such as the one witnessed by Europeans during the Great Recession is likely to place blame at the heart of evaluations of government responses to the crisis. This is all the more true insofar as the main response in most countries was austerity.

Our analysis here focussed on the impact of perceptions of the role of the government in the crisis in terms of satisfaction with the way the government is dealing with unemployment and more generally blaming the government for the economic situation of the country, as well as on how such perceptions interact with perceptions about own's own economic situation in term of retrospective relative deprivation. We were able to show that political behaviour is linked to the ways in which individuals view the government's role in the crisis. We also saw how this effect varies depending on the specific form of participation at hand. Reflecting expectations and findings in the economic voting research tradition (Lewis-Beck and Stegmaier 2000, 2007) this holds, in particular, for voting against the incumbent. Furthermore, we found that the impact of relative deprivation on political behaviour is conditional upon people's perceptions of how the government is dealing with unemployment, specifically when it comes to voting against the incumbent and attending public meetings, hence the most institutionalised forms. In other words, our analysis suggested that sociotropic and pocketbook concerns interact to an important extent to account for how individuals have reacted to the Great Recession in political terms. It also suggests that the economic crisis has led people to participate politically, but in different ways, depending on how they perceived the crisis and its effects.

THE ECONOMIC CRISIS AS CONSTRAINT AND OPPORTUNITY

Discussions of the Great Recession have mostly stressed the negative consequences of the economic crisis. Europeans have suffered, particularly within certain countries and social groups, from the deep and long-lasting economic crisis that started in 2008 and whose consequences will be felt for many years to come. The crisis and related austerity policies have created or amplified feelings of deprivation in large sectors of society and have deeply affected the lives of many (see Burgard and Kalousova 2015 for a review). Many were forced to reduce consumption due to financial hardship and to suffer deteriorating working conditions, if not the loss of secure employment altogether. Furthermore, in addition to these personal and social effects, the crisis and austerity policies have also had important political consequences and created constraints for the political behaviour of individuals in both the institutional and non-institutional spheres. Those hardest hit by the economic crisis might have been tempted to withdraw from political engagement altogether, as the private sphere takes over from the political sphere (Grasso 2016b). This can also be seen through interrelated diminishing levels of political interest, trust and efficacy, and more general processes of retreat from politics. Thus, the economic crisis could have accelerated a prior trend towards increasing alienation and detachment from politics that many observers had noted (Dalton and Wattenberg 2002; Grasso 2016a; Hay 2007; Mair 2006; Giugni and Grasso 2020).

Yet, just as the economic crisis was more severe in certain countries, its negative effects, as well as those of austerity measures, have been felt more sharply by certain social groups and individuals relative to others. In particular, more vulnerable individuals were more likely to perceive the effects of the crisis in negative terms, both the personal and national level. These groups have been identified as those emerging as 'losers' from processes of globalisation (Kriesi et al. 2006, 2008, 2012): these individuals feel economic and cultural threats more strongly because they are more likely to be affected by the loss of power of the national state and the protection they enjoyed from the latter. In this sense, the Great Recession has thus exacerbated a trend already in motion. These individuals are at the same time those who are most likely to hold xenophobic and populist attitudes and to support radical right populist parties that have tended to scapegoat migrants for wider socioeconomic woes.

Crises, however, do not only pose constraints but they can also be seen as 'critical junctures' which can open up new opportunities. Understood in this sense, crises are turning points, and turning points may open up a variety of potential paths in their aftermath. Seen from this angle, therefore, the Great Recession has not only created deprivation, hardship and constraints for many, but it has also opened up new opportunities for social change, at least to the extent that groups are able to seize such opportunities (Giugni and Grasso 2018b). Opportunities can be seen to open up in both personal and political spheres. One way in which this might have occurred refers to ways in which individuals may have become resilient to the negative consequences of the economic crisis. Such resilience, as we have seen, may take the form of more individual types of proactive resistance to the changing economic and social conditions brought about by the crisis but can also take the form of more collective strategies linked to one's community. In particular, the development of such community-based resources and forms of resilience may prove to be a precious resource in the future.

Concerning the political sphere, while some might withdraw from politics and exhibit lower political engagement, others may have ramped up their political involvement as demonstrated, for example, by the protests against austerity and public spending cuts. Political activism could take the form of voting or of participation in non-electoral activities, such as demonstrations and other forms of protest. As far as the electoral arena is concerned, a typical response during economic downturns can consist in punishing the incumbent—in other words, voting for another party or party coalition than the one that was in place during the crisis, as economic voting theory has suggested (Lewis-Beck and Stegmeier 2000). Scholars have argued that this kind of behaviour becomes more frequent in times of crisis (Hernández and Kriesi 2016), while others have suggested that such patterns of economic voting are not ubiquitous but vary across individuals and contexts (Singer 2011). Irrespective, deep economic crises such as the Great Recession, particularly when accompanied by political crises, are likely to generate opportunities for political involvement, election participation and changes in voting habits. Such shifts in vote choice have led challenger parties to make large electoral gains in recent years: *Syriza* in Greece, the *Movimento 5 Stelle* in Italy, *Podemos* in Spain, to mention only a few well-known examples. These parties, characterised by some as 'movement parties' (della Porta et al. 2017), have capitalised on the economic crisis by using it as a platform for voicing opposition to austerity measures to attract voters to their cause. Similarly, right-wing populist parties, while already on the rise prior to the start of the crisis, have used the crisis for political gains by exploiting the growing economic and cultural insecurity of the 'losers of globalisation'. The so-called 'refugee crisis' of 2015 allowed such political entrepreneurs to further amplify their discourses in this regard. In this way these parties were able to exploit the opportunities that the Great Recession offered. More generally, the latter has contributed to a transformation of the political space of party competition that was already in motion (Kriesi et al. 2006, 2008, 2012) and that, in the crisis context, expanded to include the growing dimension of cultural competition along the lines of either open and cosmopolitan or closed and nativist values in response to processes of globalisation and the demise of the traditional nation state.

The economic crisis has also provided opportunities for social and political engagement outside of the electoral arena. The large anti-austerity protests that spread across Europe are a key example (Giugni and Grasso 2015a). The Great Recession thus created important opportunities for individuals to engage in protest activities. While many were already engaged in such activities before the crisis, others were 'first-timers' who entered contentious politics in this context (Giugni and Grasso 2019b; Verhulst and Walgrave 2009). These types of unconventional political engagement have taken the form of attending demonstrations and other traditional modes of protest participation, or even more novel and creative forms such as, for example, alternative economic practices initiated by citizen groups and networks, or 'alternative forms of resilience' (Kousis 2017). These modes of action include solidarity bartering, trading schemes, local and alternative currencies, ethical banks, local market cooperatives, cooperatives for the supply of social services such as healthcare and education, alternative forms of production, critical consumption, and spontaneous actions of resistance to and reclamation of the reproduction of cultural knowledge via oral and artistic expression (Kousis and Paschou 2017). These types of initiatives and solidary practices—which can be understood as located between political and non-political actions (Giugni and Grasso 2018b)—have emerged from within the crisis (Forno and Graziano 2014). In this respect, the crisis has most certainly accelerated a trend in motion. The development of the capacity for community-based resilience shown by many, as we have stressed earlier, can be seen to have significantly contributed to the development of these alternative practices.

As such, the Great Recession has not only posed constraints for many Europeans but it has also opened up new opportunities, at least for some, at both the personal and political level (Giugni and Grasso 2021). This does not necessarily mean that such opportunities will deterministically lead to positive outcomes, however. Only time will tell whether the opportunities opened up by the crisis will provide avenues for effective social change, addressing current woes through new solutions, or whether further negative consequences will follow. Profound transformations brought on by or accelerated through deep and long-lasting economic downturns, such as the one upon which we have focused, create 'critical junctures', that is, 'situations of uncertainty in which decisions of important actors are causally decisive for the selection of one path of institutional development over other possible paths' (Capoccia 2016). The path that will follow is as yet unclear at this stage, and future outcomes will largely depend on whether Europeans, living through these hard times, can find novel ways to address extant social and political problems, and develop the means to overcome constraints in order to seize potential opportunities for the emergence of progressive social change.

Notes

CHAPTER ONE

1. Eurostat, 'Europe 2020: Main Tables', from the website of the statistical office of the European Union. Last updated 4 March 2021, retrieved on 3 October 2017. http://ec.europa.eu/eurostat/web/europe-2020-indicators/europe-2020-strategy/main-tables.

2. Eurostat, 'Europe 2020'.

3. In strictly economic terms, Poland—together with Slovakia—is the only member of the European Union that has avoided a GDP recession.

4. Data on Switzerland are available only from 2010 onwards. However, looking at national statistics, the unemployment rate in Switzerland has not changed much during the period under consideration.

5. While general government debt-to-GDP ratio is the amount of a country's total gross government debt as a percentage of its GDP (https://data.oecd.org/gga/general-government-debt.htm), general government deficit is defined as the fiscal position of government after accounting for capital expenditures (https://data.oecd.org/gga/general-government-deficit.htm).

6. Grant agreement number 613237.

7. A more detailed description as well as various related documents and outputs are available on the project's website at http://www.livewhat.unige.ch.

8. The initial sample size in each country is the following: 2,027 in France, 2,108 in Germany, 2,048 in Greece, 2,040 in Italy, 2,014 in Poland, 2,035 in Spain, 2,018 in Sweden, 2,046 in Switzerland and 2,022 in the UK.

CHAPTER THREE

1. *Merriam-Webster*, s.v. 'resilience', accessed 6 November 2017, https://www.merriam-webster.com/dictionary/resilience.

2. American Psychological Association (APA), 'Building Your Resilience', accessed on 6 November 2017, http://www.apa.org/helpcenter/road-resilience.aspx.

3. The two items pertaining to community-based resilience were reversed to build this measure, so as to have both types of resilience going in the same direction, namely from the lowest to the highest degree.

4. The third item ('I have a hard time making it through stressful events') behaves similarly to the two community-based items, while the fourth one ('I keep myself active in the community where I live'), while closer two the two proactive items does not strongly correlate with any of the two factors as its content refers to both the proactive and the community-based dimensions. In both cases, we decided to exclude them from subsequent analysis.

5. As always when dealing with cross-sectional data, one must be careful in attributing a direction to the relationships found, let alone speaking of causality. In this case, for example, the capacity of resilience might well be the consequence as much as the cause of the perception of being in a serious crisis, that the state of the economy has gotten worse, and of being satisfied with the way in which the government is dealing with the crisis. This also applies to other relationships, especially those involving attitudes on both sides of the equation.

6. In technical terms, the two new variables in the model act as 'suppressor' variables since their inclusion strengthens the effect of another independent variable on the dependent variable. (Conger 1974).

7. Question wording: 'Generally speaking, would you say that most people can be trusted, or that you can't be too careful in dealing with people?'

CHAPTER FIVE

1. This overview of works on attitudes towards immigrants and immigration draws extensively from the excellent reviews by Ceobanu and Escandell (2010) and Hainmueller and Hopkins (2014). We invite readers to refer directly to these reviews for further details and references.

2. Explanations in the two disciplines are sometimes described in slightly different ways. Thus, for example, Ceobanu and Escandell (2010) mention three prominent micro-sociological perspectives highlighting the role of socioeconomic correlates and self-interest, identities and values, and contact with outgroup members respectively, whereas, from a political science perspective, Hainmueller and Hopkins (2014) refer to two broad research traditions: the political economy and sociopsychological traditions. In both cases, however, the main distinction is between theories and explanations that stress group competition and self-interest and those that emphasise sociopsychological dynamics and symbolic interests.

3. Our analysis of populist attitudes owes much to the one conducted by Rico and Anduiza (2017), which originates in the very same research project and data on which the present book rests.

4. It should be noted, however, that this characterisation of the linkages between the weakening of the parties' representative function and the rise of populism applies for Western Europe. When considering Central and Eastern Europe, one should keep in mind that party systems there are less institutionalised and therefore it is not a matter of parties no longer fulfilling their representative function, but rather of them not yet adequately representing their constituencies (Kriesi 2014b).

5. In this chapter we use xenophobic and anti-immigrant attitudes or views interchangeably, although the former often has a broader meaning than the latter.

6. We refer to these indices as xenophobic and populist attitudes respectively, as we are mostly interested in the 'negative' side of such attitudes. However, it should be clear that the degree of xenophobia or populism depends on how people rank on both scales. Obviously, those who display lower scores on the xenophobic attitudes scale and respectively higher scores on the populism attitudes scale might be qualified as xenophobic or populist, whereas those who show higher, respectively lower scores might not. In other words, both indexes merely place individuals on a continuum from pro-migrant to anti-migrant, respectively from weakly populist to strongly populist attitudes.

7. We distinguish between subjective and objective evaluations although both are based on perceptions. However, while the former consists in a subjective assessment of one's country or one's own economic situation as compared to a reference point (hence measuring relative deprivation), the latter refers to objective facts or events.

8. These groups of variables are similar to those used in the regression models in chapters 2 and 3 but with two major changes: firstly, we grouped the variable pertaining to the degree of satisfaction with the way in which the government is dealing with the economy along with blame assignment (hence also moving it after the variables concerning perceptions of how the crisis has impacted one's personal life, in the stepwise procedure); and secondly, we include a number of variables referring to the respondents' political attitudes and values.

9. It should be noted that a statistically significant effect of both gender and income appears once we control for political attitudes and values (gender, see model 6), respectively pocketbook relative deprivation (income, see model 2). These variables therefore act as 'suppressor' variables.

10. In this model we also include xenophobic attitudes among the political variables to investigate the relationship between xenophobia and populism. As we can see, their effect is statistically significant.

CHAPTER SIX

1. This chapter is an adapted version of a previously published article: Grasso, Maria T. and Marco Giugni. 2016. 'Protest Participation and Economic Crisis: The Conditioning Role of Political Opportunities'. *European Journal of Political Research* 55 (4): 663–80. The original text was minimally adapted, mainly concerning style, for the purpose of the present book.

CHAPTER SEVEN

1. This chapter is an adapted version of a previously published article: Giugni, Marco, and Grasso, Maria T. 2017. 'Blame and Contention: How Perceptions of the Government's Role in the Economic Crisis Shape Patterns of Political Pction''. *Acta Politica*. https://doi.org/10.1057/s41269-017-0073-x. The original text was minimally adapted, mainly concerning style, for the purpose of the present book.

References

Agger, Robert E., Marshall N. Goldstein and Stanley A. Pearl. 1961. 'Political Cynicism: Measurement and Meaning'. *Journal of Politics* 23 (3): 477–506.

Akkerman, Agnes, Cas Mudde and Andrej Zaslove. 2014. 'How Populist Are the People? Measuring Populist Attitudes in Voters'. *Comparative Political Studies* 47 (9): 1324–53.

Aldrich, Daniel. 2010. 'Fixing Recovery: Social Capital in Post-Crisis Resilience'. *Journal of Homeland Security* 6: 1–10.

Alexander, Jeffrey C., Bernhard Giesen, Richard Munch and Neil J. Smelser (eds.). 1987. *The Micro-Macro Link*. Berkeley: University of California Press.

Allberg, Toril. 2003. *Achieving Justice: Comparative Public Opinion on Income Distribution*. Leiden: Brill.

Almeida, Paul D. 2007. 'Defensive Mobilization: Popular Movements Against Economic Adjustment Policies in Latin America'. *Latin American Perspectives* 34 (3): 123–39.

Alvarez, R. Michael, and Jonathan Nagler. 1995. 'Economics, Issues and the Perot Candidacy: Voter Choice in the 1992 Presidential Election'. *American Journal of Political Science* 39 (3): 714–44.

Andersen, Kristi. 1999. 'The Gender Gap and Experiences with the Welfare State'. *PS: Political Science & Politics* 32 (1): 17–19.

Ansolabehere, Stephen, Marc Meredith, and Erik Snowberg. 2014. 'Mecro-Economic Voting: Local Information as and Micro-Perceptions of the Macro-Economy'. *Economics & Politics* 26 (3): 380–410.

Atkinson, Anthony B. 2015. *Inequality: What can be done*? Cambridge, MA: Harvard University Press.

Aysa-Lastra, Maria, and Lorenzo Cachón (eds.). 2015. *Immigrant Vulnerability and Resilience: Comparative Perspectives on Latin American Immigrants During the Great Recession*. Cham: Springer.

Baglioni, Simone, Britta Baumgarten, Didier Chabanet and Christian Lahusen. 2008. 'Transcending Marginalization: The Mobilization of the Unemployed in France, Germany, and Italy in a Comparative Perspective'. *Mobilization* 13 (3): 323–35.

Bartels, Larry. 2005. 'Homer Gets aTax Cut: Inequality and Public Policy in the American Mind'. *Perspectives on Politics* 3 (1): 15–31.

Batty, Elaine, and Ian Cole. 2010. 'Resilience and the Recession in Six Deprived Communities: Preparing for the Worse to Come?'. JRF Programme Paper, Poverty and Place Programme. York: Joseph Rowntree Foundation.

Beck, Vanessa, Debbie Wagener and Jonathan Grix. 2005. 'Resilience and Unemployment: A Case Study of East German Women'. *German Politics* 14 (1): 1–13.

Becker, Gary S. 1993 (1964). *Human Capital: A Theoretical and Empirical Analysis, with Special Reference to Education*, third edition. Chicago: University of Chicago Press.

Bell, Daniel. 1976. *The Coming of Post-Industrial Society: A Venture in Social Forecasting*. New York: Basic Books.

Bennett, W. Lance. 2012. 'The Personalization of Politics: Political Identity, Social Media and Changing Patterns of Participation'. *Annals of the American Academy of Political and Social Science* 644: 20–39.

Berclaz, Julie, and Marco Giugni. 2005. 'Specifying the Concept of Political Opportunity Structures'. 15–32, in Maria Kousis and Charles Tilly (eds.), *Economic and Political Contention in Comparative Perspective*. Boulder, CO: Paradigm Publishers.

Berclaz, Michel, Katharina Fuglister and Marco Giugni. 2004. 'Etats-providence, opportunites politiques et mobilisation des chomeurs: Une approche neo-institutionaliste'. *Revue Suisse de Sociologie* 30 (3): 421–40.

Berinsky, Adam J., and Gabriel S. Lenz. 2011. 'Education and Political Participation: Exploring the Causal Link'. *Political Behavior* 33 (3): 357–73.

Bermeo, Nancy, and Larry M. Bartels. 2014. 'Mass Politics in Tough Times'. 1–39, in Nancy Bermeo and Larry M. Bartels (eds.), *Mass Politics in Tough Times: Opinions, Votes and Protest in the Great Recession*. Oxford: Oxford University Press.

Bernburg, Jón Gunnar. 2015. 'Economic Crisis and Popular Protest in Iceland, January 2009: The Role of Perceived Economic Loss and Political Attitudes in Protest Participation and Support'. *Mobilization* 20 (2): 231–52.

Bessant, Judith, Rys Farthing and Rob Watts. 2017. *The Precarious Generation: A Political Economy of Young People*. London: Routledge.

Blekesaune, Morten, and Jill Quadagno. 2003. 'Public Attitudes toward Welfare State Policies: A Comparative Analysis of 24 Nations'. *European Sociological Review* 19 (5): 415–27.

Blumer, Herbert. 1958. 'Race Prejudice as a Sense of Group Position'. *Pacific Sociological Review* 1 (1): 3–7.

Bonoli, Giuliano. 2003. 'Social Policy through Labor Markets: Understanding National Differences in the Provision of Economic Security to Wage Earners'. *Comparative Political Studies* 36 (9): 1007–30.

Bornschier, Simon. 2017. 'Populist Mobilization Across Time and Space: An Introduction'. *Swiss Political Science Review* 24 (4): 301–12.

Borre, Ole, and Elinor Scarbrough (eds.). 1995. *The Scope of Government*. Oxford: Oxford University Press.

Bourdieu, Pierre. 1985. 'The Forms of Capital'. 241–58, in John G. Richardson (ed.), *Handbook of Theory and Research for the Sociology of Education*. New York: Greenwood.

Bowen, Gary L. Jack M. Richman and Natasha K. Bowen. 2000. 'Families in the Context of Community Across Time'. 117–28, in Sharon J. Price, Patrick C. McKenry and Megan J. Murphy (eds.), *Families Across Time: A Life Course Perspective*. Los Angeles: Roxbury.

Bradshaw, Jonathan, and Naomi Finch. 2003. 'Overlaps in Dimensions of Poverty'. *Journal of Social Policy* 32 (4): 513–25.

Brady, David, and Thomas Biegert. 2017. 'The Rise of Precarious Employment in Germany'. 245–71, in Arne L. Kalleberg and Steven P. Vallas (eds.), *Research in Sociology of Work: Precarious Employment*. New Milford, CT: Emerald Books.

Brady, Henry E. 1999. 'Political Participation'. 737–801, in John P. Robinson, Phillip R. Shaver and Laurence S. Wrightsman (eds.), *Measures of Political Attitudes*. San Diego, CA: Academic Press.

Brady, Henry E. Sidney Verba and Kay Lehman Scholzman. 1995. 'Beyond SES? A Resource Model of Political Participation'. *American Political Science Review* 89 (2): 271–94.

Brody, Richard A., and Paul M. Sniderman. 1977. 'From Life Space to Polling Place: The Relevance of Personal Concerns for Voting Behavior'. *British Journal of Political Science* 7 (3): 337–60.

Broman, Clifford L., V. Lee Hamilton and William S. Hoffman. 2001. *Stress and Distress Among the Unemployed: Hard Times and Vulnerable People*. New York: Springer.

Buechler, Steven M. 2004. 'The Strange Career of Strain and Breakdown Theories of Collection Action'. 47–66, in David A. Snow, Sarah A. Soule and Hanspeter Kriesi (eds.), *The Blackwell Companion to Social Movements*. Oxford: Blackwell.

Burchartdt, Tania, Julian Le Grand and David Piachaud. 2002. 'Degrees of Exclusion: Developing a Dynamic, Multidimensional Measure'. 30–43, in John Hills, Julian Le Grand and David Piachaud (eds.), *Understanding Social Exclusion*. Oxford: Oxford University Press.

Burgard, Sarah A., and Lucie Kalousova. 2015. 'Effects of the Great Recession: Health and Well-Being'. *Annual Review of Sociology* 41: 181–201.

Burns, Peter, and James G. Gimpel. 2000. 'Economic Insecurity, Prejudicial Stereotypes, and Public Opinion on Immigration Policy'. *Political Science Quarterly* 115 (2): 201–25.

Burton-Jones, Alan, and J.-C. Spender (eds.). 2011. *The Oxford Handbook of Human Capital*. Oxford: Oxford University Press.

Bynner, John, and Samantha Parsons. 1997. *It Doesn't Get Any Better: The Impact of Poor Basic Skill Attainment on the Lives of 27-Year-olds*. London: The Basic Skills Agency.

Callan, Tim, Brian Nolan and Christopher T. Whelan. 1993. 'Resources, Deprivation and the Measurement of Poverty'. *Journal of Social Policy* 22 (2): 141–72.

Campbell, Andrea Louise, Cara Wong, and Jack Citrin. 2006. 'Racial Threat, Partisan Climate, and Direct Democracy: Contextual Effects in Three California Initiatives'. Political Behavior 28 (2): 129–50.

Campbell, Angus, Philip E. Converse, Warren E. Miller and David E. Stokes. 1960. *The American Voter*. New York: Wiley.

Capoccia, Giovanni. 2016. 'Critical Junctures'. In *The Oxford Handbook of Historical Institutionalism*. Oxford: Oxford University Press. Retrieved 20 June 2018, from http://www.oxfordhandbooks.com/view/10.1093/oxfordhb/9780199662814.001.0001/oxfordhb-9780199662814-e-5.

Card David, Christian Dustmann and Ian Preston. 2012. 'Immigration, Wages, and Compositional Amenities'. *Journal of the European Economic Association* 10 (1): 78–119.

Caren, Neal, Sarah Gaby and Catherine Herrold. 2017. 'Economic Breakdown and Collective Action'. *Social Problems* 64 (1): 133–55.

Carver, Charles S., and Jennifer Connor-Smith. 2010. 'Personality and Coping'. *Annual Review of Psychology* 61: 679–704.

Ceobanu, Alin M., and Xavier Escandell. 2010. 'Comparative Analyses of Public Attitudes Toward Immigrants and Immigration Using Multinational Survey Data: A Review of Theories and Research'. *Annual Review of Sociology* 36: 309–28.

Chabanet, Didier, and Jean Faniel. 2012. 'Introduction: The Mobilization of the Unemployed in a Comparative Perspective'. 1–27, in Didier Chabanet and Jean Faniel (eds.), *The Mobilization of the Unemployed in Europe: From Acquiescence to Protest*? Basingstoke: Palgrave Macmillan.

Chabanet, Didier, and Marco Giugni. 2008. 'Citizenship, Welfare, and the Opportunities for Political Mobilization: Migrants and Unemployed Compared'. 127–47, in William Maloney and Jan W. van Deth (eds.), *From National toward International Linkages: Civil Society and Multi-level Governance*. Cheltenham: Edward Elgar.

Chandler, Charles R., and Yung-mei Tsai. 2001. 'Social Factors Influencing Immigration Attitudes: An Analysis of Data from the General Social Survey'. *Social Science Journal* 38 (2): 177–88.

Chauvel, Louis. 2006. 'Social Generations, Life Chances and Welfare Regime Sustainability'. 341–52, in Pepper D. Culpepper, Peter A. Hall and Bruno Palier (eds.), *Changing France: The Politics that Markets Make*. Basingstoke: Palgrave Macmillan.

Cinalli, Manlio, and Marco Giugni. 2010. 'Welfare States, Political Opportunities, and Claim Making in the Field of Unemployment Politics'. 19–42, in Marco Giugni (ed.), *The Contentious Politics of Unemployment in Europe: Welfare States and Political Opportunities*. New York: Palgrave MacMillan.

———. 2013. 'New Challenges for the Welfare State: The Emergence of Youth Unemployment Regimes in Europe?' *International Journal of Social Welfare* 22 (3): 290–99.

Citrin, Jack, Donald P. Green, Christopher Muste and Cara Wong. 1997. 'Public Opinion Toward Immigration Reform: The Role of Economic Motivations'. *Journal of Politics* 59 (3): 858–81.

Clarke, Tom, and Anthony Heath. 2014. *Hard Times: The Divisive Toll of the Economic Slump*. New Haven, CT: Yale University Press.

Clegg, Daniel, and Jochen Clasen. 2011. 'The Transformation of Unemployment Protection in Europe'. 333–45, in Jochen Clasen and Daniel Clegg (eds.), *Regulating the Risk of Unemployment: National Adaptations to Post-Industrial Labour Markets in Europe*. Oxford: Oxford University Press.

Coenders, Marcel, and Peer Scheepers. 2003. 'The Effect of Education on Nationalism and Ethnic Exclusionism: An International Comparison'. *Political Psychology* 24 (2): 313–43.

Coleman, James S. 1988. 'Social Capital in the Creation of Human Capital'. *American Journal of Sociology* 94 (Supplement: Organizations and Institutions: Sociological and Economic Approaches to the Analysis of Social Structure): 95–120.

———. 1990. *Foundations of Social Theory*. Cambridge, MA: Harvard University Press.

Conger, Anthony J. 1974. 'A Revised Definition for Suppressor Variables: A Guide to Their Identification and Interpretation'. *Educational and Psychological Measurement* 34 (1): 35–46.

Conger, Rand D., Martha A. Rueter and Glen H. Elder. 1999. 'Couple Resilience to Economic Pressure'. *Journal of Personality and Social Psychology* 76 (1): 54–71.

Conger, Rand D., Xiaojia Ge and Frederick O. Lorenz. 1994. 'Economic Stress and Marital Relations'. 187–203, in Rand D. Conger and Glen H. Elder (eds.), *Families in Troubled Times: Adapting to Change in Rural America*. New York: Aldine de Gruyter.

Cooper, Ryan. 2017. 'The Great Recession Never Ended'. The Week, 27 July 2017. http://theweek.com/articles/714423/great-recession-never-ended.

Coser, Lewis. 1956. *The Functions of Social Conflict*. Glencoe, IL: Free Press.

Coughlin, Richard. 1980. *Ideology, Public Opinion and Welfare Policy: Attitudes Towards Taxes and Spending in Industrialized Societies*. Berkeley: Institute of International Studies, University of California.

Crompton, Rosemary. 1987. 'Gender, Status and Professionalism'. *Sociology* 21 (3): 413–28.

Crouch, Colin. 2004. *Post-Democracy*. Cambridge: Polity.

Dalton, Russell, Alix Van Sickle and Steven Weldon. 2010. 'The Individual-Institutional Nexus of Protest Behaviour'. *British Journal of Political Science* 40 (1): 51–73.

Dalton, Russell J., and Martin P. Wattenberg. 2002. *Parties Without Partisans: Political Change in Advanced Industrial Democracies*. Oxford: Oxford University Press.

Danziger, Sheldon, and Peter Gottschalk. 1995. *American Unequal*. New York: Russell Sage Foundation.

Davidov, Eldad, Bart Meuleman, Jaak Billiet and Peter Schmidt. 2008. 'Values and Support for Immigration: A Cross-Country Comparison'. *European Sociological Review* 24 (5): 583–99.

Davies, James C. 1962. 'Towards a Theory of Revolution'. *American Sociological Review* 27 (1): 5–19.

De Grauwe, Paul, and Yuemei, Ji. 2013. 'From Panic-Driven Austerity to Symmetric Macroeconomic Policies in the Eurozone'. *Journal of Common Market Studies* 51 (S1): 31–41.

della Porta, Donatella. 2015. *Social Movements in Times of Austerity: Bringing Capitalism Back into Protest Analysis*. Cambridge: Polity Press.

della Porta, Donatella, and Alice Mattoni. 2014. *Spreading Protests in Social Movements of the Crisis*. Colchester: ECPR Press.

della Porta, Donatella, Joseba Fernández, Hara Kouki and Lorenzo Mosca. 2017. *Movement Parties against Austerity*. Cambridge: Polity Press.

Devine, Fiona, and Mike Savage. 2000. 'Conclusion: Renewing Class Analysis'. 184–199, in Rosemary Crompton, Fiona Devine, and Mike Savage (eds.), *Renewing Class Analysis*. Oxford: Blackwell Publishers.

Dodson, Kyle. 2015. 'Economic Threat and Protest Behavior in Comparative Perspective'. *Sociological Perspectives*. https://doi.org/10.1177/0731121415608508.

Dorling, Danny. 2014. *Inequality and the 1%*. London: Verso.

Downs, Anthony. 1957. *An Economic Theory of Democracy*. New York: Harper and Row.

Duch, Raymond M. 2007. 'Comparative Studies of the Economy and the Vote'. 805–844, in Carles Boix and Susan C. Stokes (eds.), *The Oxford Handbook of Comparative Politics*. Oxford: Oxford University Press.

Duch, Raymond M., Harvey D. Palmer and Christopher J. Anderson. 2000. 'Heterogeneity in Perceptions of National Economic Conditions'. *American Journal of Political Science* 44 (4): 635–52.

Duch, Raymond M., and Iñaki Sagarzazu. 2014. 'Crisis Perceptions and Economic Voting Amogn the Rich and the Poor: The United Kingdom and Germany'. 224–65, in Nancy Bermeo and Larry M. Bartels *Mass Politics in Tough Times: Opinions, Votes and Protest in the Great Recession*. Oxford: Oxford University Press.

Duch, Raymond M., and Randy T. Stevenson. 2011. 'Context and Economic Expectations: When Do Voters Get It Right?' *British Journal of Political Science* 41 (1): 1–31.

Dunleavy, Patrick. 1979. 'The Urban Basis of Political Alignment: Social Class, Domestic Property Ownership, and State Intervention in Consumption Processes'. *British Journal of Political Science* 9 (4): 409–43.

Dunn, Andrew, Maria T. Grasso and Clare Saunders. 2014. 'Unemployment and Attitudes to Work: Asking the 'Right' Question'. *Work, Employment and Society* 28 (6): 904–25.

Dustmann, Christian, and Ian Preston. 2007. 'Racial and Economic Factors in Attitudes to Immigration'. *B. E. Journal of Economic Analysis & Policy* 7 (1): Article 62.

DWP (Department for Work and Pensions). 2003. *Measuring Child Poverty*. London: Department for Work and Pensions.

Edlund, Jonas. 2006. 'Trust in the Capability of the Welfare State and General Welfare State Support: Sweden 1997–2002'. *Acta Sociologica* 49 (4): 395–417.

Eisinger, Peter K. 1973. 'The Conditions of Protest Behavior in American Cities'. *American Political Science Review* 67 (1): 11–28.

English, Patrick, Maria T. Grasso, Barbara Buraczynska, Sotirios Karampampas and Luke Temple. 2016. 'Convergence on Crisis? Comparing Labour and Conservative Party Framing of the Economic Crisis in Britain, 2008–2014'. *Politics & Policy* 44 (3): 577–603.

Erikson, Robert, John H. Goldthorpe and Lucienne Portocarero. 1979. 'Intergenerational Class Mobility in Three Western European Countries: England, France and Sweden'. *British Journal of Sociology* 30 (4): 415–51.

Esping-Andersen, Gøsta. 1990. *The Three Worlds of Welfare Capitalism*. Princeton, NJ: Princeton University Press.

——— (ed.). 1996. *Welfare States in Transition: National Adaptation in Gloibal Economies*. London: Sage.

Esses, Victoria M., John F. Dovidio, Lynne M. Jackson and Tamara L. Armstrong. 2001. 'The immigration Dilemma: The Role of Perceived Group Competition, Ethnic Prejudice, and National Identity'. *Journal of Social Issues* 57 (3): 389–412.

Feldman, Stanley. 1982. 'Economic Self-Interest and Political Behavior'. *American Journal of Political Science* 26 (3): 446–66.

Fetzer, Joel S. 2000. *Public Attitudes Toward Immigration in the United States, France, and Germany*. New York and Cambridge: Cambridge University Press.

Fiorina, Morris P. 1981. *Retrospective Voting in American National Elections*. New Haven, CT: Yale University Press.

Fischer, Claude, Martin Sanchez-Jankowski, Samuel Lucas, Ann Swidler and Kim Voss. 1996. *Inequality by Design: Cracking the Bell Curve Myth*. Princeton, NJ: Princeton University Press.

Folkman, Susan, and Judith Tedlie Moskowitz. 2004. 'Coping: Pitfalls and Promise'. *Annual Review of Psychology* 55: 745–74.

Ford, Robert, and Matthew J. Goodwin. 2010. 'Angry White Men: Individual and Contextual Predictors of Support for the British National Party'. *Political Studies* 58 (1): 1–25.

Forno, Francesca, and Paolo R. Graziano. 2014. 'Sustainable Community Movement Organisations'. *Journal of Consumer Culture* 14 (2): 139–57.

Foster, Mindi D., and Kimberly Matheson. 1995. 'Double Relative Deprivation: Combining the Personal and Political'. *Personality and Social Psychology Bulletin* 21 (11): 1167–77.

Galais, Carole, and Jasmine Lorenzini. 2017. 'Half a Loaf Is (Not) Better Than None: How Austerity-Related Grievances and Emotions Triggered Protest in Spain'. *Mobilization* 22 (1): 77–95.

Gallie, Duncan, and Serge Paugam. 2000. 'The Experience of Unemployment in Europe: The Debate'. 1–22, in Duncan Gallie and Serge Paugam (eds.), *Welfare Regimes and the Experience of Unemployment in Europe*. Oxford: Oxford University Press.

Gamson, William A., and David S. Meyer. 1996. 'Framing Political Opportunity'. 275–90, in Doug McAdam, John D. McCarthy and Meyer N. Zald (eds.), *Comparative Perspectives on Social Movements: Political Opportunities, Mobilizing Structures, and Cultural Framings*. Cambridge: Cambridge University Press.

Gardiner, Laura. 2016. *Stagnation Generation: The Case for Renewing the Intergenerational Contract*. London: The Intergenerational Commission/Resolution Foundation.

Garmezy, Norman. 1991. 'Resilience and Vulnerability to Adverse Developmental Outcomes Associated with Poverty'. *American Behavioral Scientist* 34 (3): 416–30.

Genschel, Philipp, and Peter Schwarz. 2013. 'Tax Competition and Fiscal Democracy'. 59–93, in Armin Schäfer and Wolfgang Streeck (eds.), *Politics in the Age of Austerity*. Cambridge: Polity.

Geschwender, James A. 1968. 'Explorations in the Theory of Social Movements and Revolutions'. *Social Forces* 47 (2): 127–35.

Giugni, Marco. 2008. 'Welfare States, Political Opportunities and the Mobilization of the Unemployed: A Cross-National Analysis'. *Mobilization* 13 (3): 297–310.

——— (ed.). 2010. *The Contentious Politics of Unemployment in Europe: Welfare States and Political Opportunities*. Houndmills: Palgrave.

Giugni, Marco, and Florence Passy. 2004. 'Migrant Mobilization Between Political Institutions and Citizenship Regimes: A Comparison of France and Switzerland'. European Journal of Political Research 43 (1): 51–82.

Giugni, Marco, and Jasmine Lorenzini. 2014. 'Living in Hard Times: Thirty Hypotheses on Citizens' Reactions to Economic Crises'. ECPR General Conference, Section on 'Citizens' Resilience in Times of Crisis'. Glasgow (United Kindgom), September 3–6.

———. 2017. Jobless Citizens: Political Engagement of Unemployed Youth. Houndmills: Palgrave.

———. 2020. 'The Politics of Economic Crisis: From Voter Retreat to the Rise of New Populisms'. 715–737 in Thomas Janoski, Cedric de Leon, Joya Misra and Isaac William Martin (eds.), *The New Handbook of Political Sociology: States, Parties, Movements, Citizenship and Globalization*. Cambridge: Cambridge University Press.

Giugni, Marco, and Maria T. Grasso (eds.). 2015a. *Austerity and Protest: Popular Contention in Times of Economic Crisis*. London: Routledge.

———. 2015b. 'Environmental Movements in Advanced Industrial Democracies: Heterogeneity, Transformation, and Institutionalization'. *Annual Review of Environment and Resources* 40: 337–61.

———. 2016. 'How Civil Society Actors Responded to the Economic Crisis: The Interaction of Material Deprivation and Perceptions of Political Opportunity Structures'. *Politics & Policy* 44 (3): 447–72.

———. 2017. "Blame and contention: how perceptions of the government's role in the economic crisis shape patterns of political action." *Acta Polit* 54, 346–370. https://doi.org/10.1057/s41269-017-0073-x

——— (eds.). 2018a. *Citizens and the Crisis: Perceptions, Experiences, and Responses to the Great Recession in Europe*. Houndmills: Palgrave Macmillan.

———. 2018b. 'Alternative Action Organizations: Social Solidarity or Political Advocacy?' *American Behavioral Scientist* 62 (6): 778–95.

———. 2018c. 'Citizens and the Crisis: Perceptions, Experiences, and Responses to the Great Recession in Nine Democracies'. 1–25, in Marco Giugni and Maria T. Grasso (eds.), *Citizens and the Crisis: Perceptions, Experiences, and Responses to the Great Recession in Europe*. Houndmills: Palgrave Macmillan.

———. 2018d. 'Citizens and the Crisis: The Great Recession as Constraint and Opportunity'. 261–78, in Marco Giugni and Maria T. Grasso (eds.), *Citizens and the Crisis: Perceptions, Experiences, and Responses to the Great Recession in Europe*. Houndmills: Palgrave Macmillan.

———. 2019a. 'Economic Outcomes of Social Movements'. 466–481 in David A. Snow, Sarah A. Soule, Hanspeter Kriesi and Holly McCammon (eds.), *The Wiley-Blackwell Companion to Social Movements*. Oxford: Blackwell.

———. 2019b. *Street Citizens: Protest Politics and Social Movement Activism in the Age of Globalization*. Cambridge: Cambridge University Press.

———. 2019c. "Mechanisms of Responsiveness: What MPs Think of Interest Organizations and How They Deal with Them." *Political Studies*. 67(3):557-575. doi:10.1177/0032321718784156

———. 2019d. "Do Unto Others? Individual-Level Mechanisms of Political Altruism." *American Behavioral Scientist*. 63(4):430-443. doi:10.1177/0002764218823851

———. 2020a. "Trust, Identity, Skills, or Recruitment?: Assessing Four Explanations of the Relationship between Associational Involvement and the Political Participation of Migrants." *International Migration Review*. 54(2):585-610. doi:10.1177/0197918319856362

———. 2020b. "Talking About Youth: The Depoliticization of Young People in the Public Domain." *American Behavioral Scientist*. 64(5):591-607. doi:10.1177/0002764219885429

———. 2021. "Party membership and social movement activism: A macro–micro analysis." *Party Politics*. 27(1):92-102. doi:10.1177/1354068818823446

Giugni, Marco, Michel Berclaz, and Katharina Fuglister. 2009. 'Welfare States, Labour Markets and the Political Opportunities for Collective Action in the Field of Unemployment: A Theoretical Framework'. 133–49, in Marco Giugni (ed.), The Politics of Unemployment in Europe: State and Civil Society Responses. Marco Giugni. Burlington, VT: Ashgate.

Goldstone, Jack A. 1986. 'Introduction: The Comparative and Historical Study of Revolutions'. 1–17, in Jack A. Goldstone (ed.), *Revolutions: Theoretical, comparative and historical studies*. San Diego, CA: Harcourt Brace Jovanovich.

———. 1991a. 'An Analytical Framework'. 37–51, in Jack A. Goldstone, Ted Robert Gurr and Farrokh Moshiri (eds.), *Revolutions of the Late Twentieth Century*. Boulder, CO: Westview Press.

———. 1991b. *Revolution and Rebellion in the Early Modern World*. Berkeley, CA: University of California Press.

Goldthorpe, John H. 2000. 'Rent, Class Conflict, and Class Structure: A Commentary on Sørenson'. *American Journal of Sociology* 105 (6): 1572–1582.

Goldthorpe, John H., David Lockwood, Frank Bechoffer and Jennifer Platt. 1967. 'The Affluent Worker and the Thesis of Embourgeoisement: Some Preliminary Research Findings'. *Sociology* 1 (1): 11–31.

Gordon, David, Ruth Levitas, Christina Pantazis, Demi Patsios, Sarah Payne and Peter Townsend. 2000. *Poverty and Social Exclusion in Britain*. York: Joseph Roundtree Foundation.

Gore, Susan. 1978. 'The Effect of Social Support in Moderating the Health Consequences of Unemployment'. *Journal of Health and Social Behavior* 19 (2): 157–65.

Grasso, Maria T. 2011. *Political Participation in Western Europe*. D.Phil. Thesis, Nuffield College, University of Oxford.

———. 2013. 'The Differential Impact of Education on Young People's Political Activism: Comparing Italy and the United Kingdom'. *Comparative Sociology* 12 (1): 1–30.

———. 2014. 'Age-Period-Cohort Analysis in a Comparative Context: Political Generations and Political Participation Repertoires'. *Electoral Studies* 33: 63–76.

———. 2016a. *Generations, Political Participation and Social Change in Western Europe*. London: Routledge.

———. 2016b. 'Political Participation'. 143–58, in Richard Heffernan, Colin Hay, Meg Russell, and Philip Cowley (eds.), *Developments in British Politics 10*. Basingstoke: Palgrave Macmillan.

———. 2018. 'Young People's Political Participation in Times of Crisis'. 179–196, in Sarah Pickard and Judith Bessant (eds.), *Young People Regenerating Politics in Times of Crisis*. London: Palgrave Macmillan.

Grasso, Maria T., and Marco Giugni. 2013. 'Anti-austerity Movements: Old Wine in New Vessels?' Paper presented at the XXVII Meeting of the Italian Political Science Association (SISP), Florence, 12–14 September.

———. 2016a. 'Do Issues Matter? Anti-Austerity Protests' Composition, Values, and Action Repertoires Compared'. *Research in Social Movements, Conflicts and Change* 39: 31–58.

———. 2016b. 'Protest Participation and Economic Crisis: The Conditioning Role of Political Opportunities'. *European Journal of Political Research* 55 (4): 663–80.

Grasso, Maria T., Stephen Farrall, Emily Gray, Colin Hay and Will Jennings. 2017. 'Thatcher's Children, Blair's Babies, Political Socialisation and Trickle-Down Value-Change: An Age, Period and Cohort Analysis'. *British Journal of Political Science*. https://doi.org/10.1017/S0007123416000375.

Grasso, Maria T., Sotirios Karampampas, Luke Temple & Barbara Yoxon (née Buraczynska). 2017. 'Relative deprivation and inequalities in social and political activism' *Acta Politica* (Open Access) https://link.springer.com/article/10.1057%2Fs41269-017-0072-y

Grasso, Maria, Sotirios Karampampas, Luke Temple & Barbara Yoxon. 2019. 'Deprivation, class and crisis in Europe: a comparative analysis.' *European Societies*, 21:2, 190-213, DOI: 10.1080/14616696.2019.1584324

Grimm, Sabine, and Klaus Robbeberger. 2007. 'An Invisible History of Work: Interview with Sergio Bologna'. *Springerin* 1/2007. https://springerin.at/en/2007/1/eine-unsichtbare-geschichte-der-arbeit/.

Gurr, Ted Robert. 1970. *Why Men Rebel*. Princeton, NJ: Princeton University Press.

Hainmueller, Jens, and Daniel J. Hopkins. 2014. 'Public Attitudes Toward Immigration'. Annual Review of Political Science 17: 225–49.

Hainmueller, Jens, and Michael J. Hiscox. 2007. 'Educated Preferences: Explaining Attitudes Toward Immigration in Europe'. *International Organization* 61 (2): 399–442.

———. 2010. 'Attitudes toward Highly Skilled and Low-skilled Immigration: Evidence from a Survey Experiment'. *American Political Science Review* 104 (1): 61–84.

Hainmueller Jens, Michael J. Hiscox and Yotam M. Margalit. 2011. 'Do Concerns about Labour Market Competition Shape Attitudes Toward Immigration? New Evidence'. MIT Political Science Department Research Paper, 2011–20.

Hall, Peter A., and Michèle Lamont (eds.). 2013. *Social Resilience in the Neoliberal Age*. Cambridge: Cambridge University Press.

Hay, Colin. 2007. *Why We Hate Politics*. Cambridge: Polity.

Heaney, Michael T., and Fabio Rojas. 2014. *Party in the Street: The Antiwar Movement and the Democratic Party After 9/11*. Cambridge: Cambridge University Press.

Heath, Anthony. 1981. *Social Mobility*. London: Fontana.

Hello, Evelyn, Peer Scheepers and Mérove Gijsberts. 2002. 'Education and Ethnic Prejudice in Europe: Explanations for Crossnational Variances in the Educational Effect on Ethnic Prejudice'. *Scandinavian Journal of Educational Research* 46 (1): 5–24.

Hellwig, Timothy. 2010. 'Elections and the Economy'. 184–201, in Lawrence LeDuc, Richard G. Niemi and Pippa Norris (eds.), *Comparing Democracies 3: Elections and Voting in the 21st Century*, third edition. Thousand Oaks, CA: Sage.

Hemerijck, Anton. 2012. *Changing Welfare States*. Oxford: Oxford University Press.

Hernández, Enrique, and Hanspeter Kriesi. 2016. 'The Electoral Consequences of the Financial and Economic Crisis in Europe'. *European Journal of Political Research* 55 (2): 203–24.

Hetherington, Marc. 1996. 'The Media's Role in Forming Voters' Retrospective Economic Evaluations in 1992'. *American Journal of Political Science* 40 (2): 372–95.

Hirschman, Albert O. 1970. *Exit, Voice, and Loyalty: Responses to Decline in Firms, Organizations, and States*. Cambridge, MA: Harvard University Press.

Huffman, Ann H., Satoris S. Culbertson, Heidi A. Waymenta and Louis H. Irving. 2015. 'Resource Replacement and Psychological Well-being During Unemployment: The Role of Family Support'. *Journal of Vocational Behavior* 89: 74–82.

Huntington, Samuel P. 1996. *The Clash of Civilizations and the Remaking of the World Order*. New York: Simon & Schuster.

Huseby, Beate. 2000. *Government Performance and Political Support: A Study of How Evaluations of Economic Performance, Social Policy and Environmental Protection Influence the Popular Assessments of the Political System*. Norges teknisk-naturvitenskapelige universitet.

Hutter, Swen. 2014a. 'Protest Event Analysis and Its Offspring'. 335–67, in Donatella della Porta (ed.), *Methodological Practices in Social Movement Research*. Oxford: Oxford University Press.

———. 2014b. *Protesting Culture and Economics in Western Europe: New Cleavages in Left and Right Politics*. Minneapolis: University of Minnesota Press.

Ivarsflaten, Elisabeth. 2005. 'Threatened by Diversity: Why Restrictive Asylum and Immigration Policies Appeal to Western Europeans'. *Journal of Elections, Public Opinion and Parties* 15 (1): 21–45.

———. 2008. 'What Unites Right-Wing Populists in Western Europe?' *Comparative Political Studies* 41 (1): 3–23.

Iyengar, Shanto. 1991. *Is Anyone Responsible? How Television Frames Political Issues*. Chicago: University of Chicago Press.

Jackson, James S., Kendrick T. Brown, Tony N. Brown and Bryant Marks. 2001. 'Contemporary Immigration Policy Orientations Among Dominant-Group Members in Western Europe'. *Journal of Social Issues* 57 (3): 431–56.

Jahoda, Marie., Paul F. Lazarsfeld, and Herbert Zeisel. 1971 [1933]. *Marienthal: The Sociography of an Unemployed Community.* New York: Aldine-Atherton.

Johnston, Hank, and Paul Almeida (eds.). 2006. *Latin American Social Movements: Globalization, Democratization, and Transnational Networks*. Lanham, MD: Rowman & Littlefield.

Judis, John B. 2016. *The Populist Explosion: How the Great Recession Transformed American and European Politics*. New York: Columbia Global Reports.

Kaase, Max, and Alan Marsh. 1979. 'Political Action: A Theoretical Perspective'. 27–56, inSamuel Barnes, Max Kaase et al. (eds.), *Political Action: Mass Participation in Five Western Democracies*. Beverly Hills, CA: Sage.

Kaase, Max, and Kenneth Newton. 1995. *Beliefs in Government*. Oxford: Oxford University Press.

Katz, Richard S., and Peter Mair. 1995. 'Changing Models of Party Organization and Party Democracy: The Emergence of the Cartel Party'. *Party Politics* 1 (1): 5–28.

———. 2009. 'The Cartel Party Thesis: A Restatement'. *Perspectives on Politics* 7 (4): 753–66.

Kern, Anna, Sofie Marien and Marc Hooghe. 2015. 'Economic Crisis and Levels of Political Participation in Europe (2002–2010): The Role of Resources and Grievances'. *West European Politics* 38 (3): 465–90.

Kieselbach, Thomas. 2003. 'Long-Term Unemployment Among Young People: The Risk of Social Exclusion'. *American Journal of Community Psychology* 32 (1): 69–76.

Kiewiet, D. R. 1983. *Macroeconomics and Micropolitics: The Electoral Effects of Economic Issues*. Chicago: University of Chicago Press.

Kinder, Donald R., and D. Roderick Kiewiet. 1979. 'Economic Discontent and Political Behavior: The Role of Personal Grievances and Collective Economic Judgments in Congressional Voting'. *American Journal of Political Science* 23 (3): 495–527.

———. 1981. 'Sociotropic Politics: The American Case'. *British Journal of Political Science* 11 (2): 129–61.

Kitschelt, Herbert. 1986. 'Political Opportunity Structures and Political Protest: Anti-Nuclear Movements in Four Democracies'. *British Journal of Political Science* 16 (1): 57–85.

———. 1994. *The Transformation of European Social Democracy*. Cambridge: Cambridge University Press.

——— (in collaboration with Anthony J. McGann). 1995. *The Radical Right in Western Europe: A Comparative Analysis*. Ann Arbor: University of Michigan Press.

Klandermans, Bert, Jojanneke van der Toorn and Jacquelien van Stekelenburg. 2008. 'Embeddedness and Identity: How Immigrants Turn Grievances into Action'. *American Sociological Review* 73 (6): 992–1012.

Koopmans, Ruud, Paul Statham, Marco Giugni and Florence Passy. 2005. *Contested Citizenship: Immigration and Cultural Diversity in Europe*. Minneapolis: University of Minnesota Press.

Kornhauser, William. 1959. *The Politics of Mass Society*. New York: Free Press.

Korpi, Walter. 1983. *The Democratic Class Struggle*. London: Routledge.

Kousis, Maria. 2014. 'The Transnational Dimension of the Greek Protest Campaign Against Troika Memoranda and Austerity Policies 2010–2012'. 137–69, in Donatella della Porta and Alice Mattoni (eds.), *Spreading Protest: Social Movements in Times of Crisis*. Colchester: ECPR Press.

———. 2017. 'Alternative Forms of Resilience Confronting Hard Economic Times: A South European Perspective'. *Partecipazione e Conflitto* 10 (1): 119–35.

Kousis, Maria, and Maria Paschou. 2017. 'Alternative Forms of Resilience: A Typology of Approaches for the Study of Citizen Collective Responses in Hard Economic Times'. *Partecipazione e Conflitto* 10 (1): 136–68.

Kriesi, Hanspeter. 2004. 'Political Context and Opportunity'. 67–90, in David A. Snow, Sarah A. Soule, and Hanspeter Kriesi (eds.), *The Blackwell Companion to Social Movements*. Malden, MA: Blackwell.

———. 2014a. 'The Political Consequences of the Economic Crises in Europe: Electoral Punishment and Popular Protest'. 297–333, in Nancy Bermeo and Larry M. Bartels (eds.), *Mass Politics in Tough Times: Opinions, Votes and Protest in the Great Recession.* Oxford: Oxford University Press.

———. 2014b. 'The Populist Challenge'. *West European Politics* 37 (2): 361–78.

Kriesi, Hanspeter, Edgar Grande, Martin Dolezal, Marc Helbling, Dominic Höglinger, Swen Hutter and Bruno Wüest. 2012. *Political Conflict in Western Europe.* Cambridge: Cambridge University Press.

Kriesi, Hanspeter, Edgar Grande, Romain Lachat, Martin Dolezal, Simon Bornschier and Timotheos Frey. 2006. 'Globalisation and the Transformation of the National Political Space: Six European Countries Compared'. *European Journal of Political Research* 45 (6): 921–56.

———. 2008. *West European Politics in the Age of Globalisation.* Cambridge: Cambridge University Press.

Kriesi, Hanspeter, Ruud Koopmans, Jan Willem Duyvendak and Marco Giugni. 1995. *New Social Movements in Western Europe: A Comparative Analysis*. Minneapolis: University of Minnesota Press.

Kriesi, Hanspeter, and Takis S. Pappas (eds.). 2015. *European Populism in the Shadow of the Great Recession*. Colchester: ECPR Press.

Krugman, Paul. 2012. *End this Depression Now!* New York: W. W. Norton & Company.

Kumlin, Staffan. 2004a. 'Blaming Europe: Why Welfare State Dissatisfaction Breeds Euroscepticism'. Paper presented at the Annual Meeting of the American Political Science Association, Chicago, 2 September 2004.

———. 2004b. *The Personal and the Political: How Personal Welfare State Experiences Affect Political Trust and Ideology*. New York: Palgrave Macmillan.

———. 2007. 'The Welfare State: Values, Policy Preferences, and Performance Evaluations'. 362–82, in Russell J. Dalton and Hahs-Dieter Klingemann (eds.), *The Oxford Handbook of Political Behaviour*. Oxford: Oxford University Press.

Kumlin, Staffan, and Bo Rothstein. 2005. 'Making and Breaking Social Capital: The Impact of Welfare State Institutions'. *Comparative Political Studies* 38 (4): 339–65.

Lahav, Gallya. 2004. 'Public Opinion Toward Immigration in the European Union: Does it Matter?' *Comparative Political Studies* 37 (10): 1151–83.

Laurence, James, and Chaeyoon Lim. 2012. 'The Long-Term and Deepening Scars of Job Displacement on Civic Participation Over the Life-course: A Cross-National Comparative Study Between the UK and the US'. Paper presented at the American Sociological Association Meeting, Denver, CO.

Laville, Jean-Louis. 2010. 'Solidarity Economy'. 225–35, in Keith Hart, Jean-Louis Laville and Antonio David Cattani (eds.), *The Human Economy*. Cambridge: Polity Press.

Levin, Ines, J. Andrew Sinclair and R. Michael Alvarez. 2015. 'Participation in the Wake of Adversity: Blame Attribution and Policy-Oriented Evaluations'. *Political Behavior*. https://doi.org/10.1007/s111109-015-9316-6.

Levitsky, Steven, and Kenneth M. Roberts. 2011. 'Latin America's "Left Turn": A Framework for Analysis'. 1–28, in Steven Levitsky and Kenneth M. Roberts (eds.), *The Resurgence of the Latin American Left*. Baltimore, MD: Johns Hopkins University Press.

Lewis-Beck, Michael S. 1988. *Economics and Elections: The Major Western Democracies*. Ann Arbor: University of Michigan Press.

Lewis-Beck, Michael S., and Martin Paldam. 2000. 'Economic Voting: An Introduction'. *Electoral Studies* 19 (2–3): 113–21.

Lewis-Beck, Michael S., and Mary Stegmaier. 2000. 'Economic Determinants of Electoral Outcomes'. *Annual Review of Political Science* 3 (1): 183–219.

———. 2007. 'Economic Models of Voting'. 518–37, in Russell J. Dalton and Hans-Dieter Klingemann (eds.), *The Oxford Handbook of Political Behavior*. Oxford: Oxford University Press.

Lim, Chaeyoon and James Laurence. 2015. 'Doing Good When Times Are Bad: Volunteering Behaviour in Economic Hard Times'. *British Journal of Sociology* 66 (2): 319–44.

Lin, Nan. 2001. *Social Capital: A Theory of Social Structure and Action*. Cambridge: Cambridge University Press.

Lohmann, Susanne. 1994. 'The Dynamics of Informational Cascades: The Monday Demonstrations in Leipzig, East Germany, 1989–1991'. *World Politics* 47 (1): 42–101.

Lorenzini, Jasmine, and Marco Giugni. 2011. 'Youth Coping with Unemployment: The Role of Social Support'. *Revue Suisse de Travail Social* 11: 80–99.

Lubbers, Marcel, Mérove Gijsberts and Peer Scheepers. 2002. 'Extreme Right-Wing Voting in Western Europe'. *European Journal of Political Research* 41 (3): 345–78.

Luthar, Sunyia S., Dante Cicchetti and Bronwyn Becker. 2000. 'The Construct of Resilience: A Critical Evaluation and Guidelines for Future Work'. *Child Development* 71 (3): 543–62.

Mack, Joanna, and Stewart Lansley. 1985. *Poor Britain*. London: Allen and Unwin.

Mair, Peter. 2002. 'Populist Democracy vs Party Democracy'. 81–98, in Yves Mény and Yves Surel (eds.), *Democracies and the Populist Challenge*. Basingstoke: Palgrave.

———. 2006. 'Ruling the Void? The Hollowing of Western Democracy'. *New Left Review* 42: 25–51.

———. 2013. 'Smaghi versus the Parties: Representative Government and Institutional Constraints'. 143–68, in Armin Schäfer and Wolfgang Streeck (eds.), *Politics in the Age of Austerity*. Cambridge: Polity.

Malhotra, Neil, and Yotam Margalit. 2010. 'Short-Term Communication Effects or Longstanding Dispositions? The Public's Response to the Financial Crisis of 2008'. *Journal of Politics* 72 (3): 852–67.

Manza, Jeff, and Clem Brooks. 1998. 'The Gender Gap in US Presidential Elections: When? Why? Implications?' *American Journal of Sociology* 103 (5): 1235–66.

Margalit, Yotam. 2013. 'Explaining Social Policy Preferences: Evidence from the Great Recession'. *American Political Science Review* 107 (1): 80–103.

Marsh, Micheal, and James Tilley. 2010. 'The Attribution of Credit and Blame to Governments and Its Impact on Vote Choice'. *British Journal of Political Science* 40 (1): 115–34.

Marttila, Anneli, Margaret Whitehead, Krysia Canvin, and Bo Burström. 2010. 'Controlled and Dependent: Experiences of Living on Social Assistance in Sweden'. *International Journal of Social Welfare* 19 (2): 142–51.

Massey, Douglas. 1996. 'The Age of Extremes: Concentrated Affluence and Poverty in the Twenty-First Century'. *Demography* 33 (4): 395–412.

Mayda, Anna Maria. 2006. 'Who Is Against Immigration? A Cross-Country Investigation of Individual Attitudes Toward Immigrants'. *Review of Economics and Statistics* 88 (3): 510–30.

McAdam, Doug. 1982. *Political Process and the Development of Black Insurgency*. Chicago: University of Chicago Press.

———. 1996. 'Conceptual Origins, Current Problems, Future Directions'. 23–40, in Doug McAdam, John D. McCarthy and Meyer N. Zald (eds.), *Comparative Perspectives on Social Movements: Political Opportunities, Mobilising Structures and Cultural Framings*. Cambridge: Cambridge University Press.

———. 1999 (1982). *Political Process and the Development of Black Insurgency, 1930–1970*, second edition. Chicago: University of Chicago Press.

McAdam, Doug, and Sidney Tarrow. 2010. 'Ballots and Barricades: On the Reciprocal Relationship Between Elections and Social Movements'. *Perspectives on Politics* 8 (2): 529–42.

McAdam, Doug, Sidney Tarrow and Charles Tilly. 2001. *Dynamics of Contention*. Cambridge: Cambridge University Press.

McCarthy, John D., and Mayer N. Zald. 1973. *The Trend of Social Movements in America: Professionalization and Resource Mobilization*. New York: General Learning Press.

———. 1977. 'Resource Mobilization and Social Movements: A Partial Theory'. *American Journal of Sociology* 82 (6): 1212–41.

McLaren, Lauren M. 2003. 'Anti-Immigrant Prejudice in Europe: Contact, Threat Perception and Preferences for the Exclusion of Migrants'. *Social Forces* 81 (3): 909–36.

McVeigh, Rory. 2009. *The Rise of the Ku Klux Klan: Right-Wing Movements and National Politics*. Minneapolis: University of Minnesota Press.

Melucci, Alberto. 1989. *Nomads of the Present: Social Movements and Individual Needs in Contemporary Society*. London: Hutchinson Radius.

Mény, Yves, and Yves Surel (eds.). 2002. *Democracy and the Populist Challenge*. Baskingstoke, UK: Palgrave.

Meyer, David S. 2004. 'Protest and Political Opportunities'. *Annual Review of Sociology* 30: 125–45.

Mincer, Jacob. 1958. 'Investment in Human Capital and Personal Income Distribution'. *Journal of Political Economy* 66 (4): 281–302.

Morales, Laura, and Marco Giugni (eds.). 2011. *Social Capital, Political Participation and Migration in Europe: Making Multicultural Democracy Work?* London: Palgrave Macmillan.

Morel, Nathalie, Bruno Palier and Joakim Palme. 2011. *Towards A Social Investment Welfare State? Ideas, Policies and Challenges*. Bristol: Policy Press.

Mudde, Cas. 2004. 'The Populist Zeitgeist'. *Government and Opposition* 39 (4): 541–63.

———. 2007. *Populist Radical Right Parties in Europe*. Cambridge: Cambridge University Press.

———. 2013. 'Three Decades of Populist Radical Right Parties in Western Europe: So What?' *European Journal of Political Research* 52 (1): 1–19.

Mudde, Cas, and Cristóbal Rovira Kaltwasser. 2013. 'Populism'. 493–512, in Michael Freeden, Lyman Tower Sargent and Marc Stears (eds.), *The Oxford Handbook of Political Ideologies*. Oxford: Oxford University Press.

———. 2017. *Populism: A Very Short Introduction*. Oxford and New York: Oxford University Press.

Musterd, Sako, and Wim Ostendorf (eds.). 2013. *Urban Segregation and the Welfare State: Inequality and Exclusion in Western Cities*. London: Routledge.

NBER (National Bureau of Economic Research). 2010. 'Business Cycle Dating Committee Announcement September 20, 2010'. Published online 20 September 2010. http://www.nber.org/cycles/sept2010.html.NBER 2010.

Nolan, Brian, and Christopher T. Whelan. 1996. *Resources, Deprivation and Poverty*. Oxford: Clarendon Press.

———. 2007. 'On the Multidimensionality of Poverty and Social Exclusion'. 146–65, in Stephen O. Jenkins and John Micklewright (eds.), *Inequality and Poverty Reexamined*. Oxford: Oxford University Press.

———. 2011. *Poverty and Deprivation in Europe*. Oxford: Oxford University Press.

Oberschall, Anthony. 1973. *Social Conflict and Social Movements*. Englewood Cliffs, NJ: Prentice-Hall.

Obinger, Herbert. 2012. 'Die Finanzkrise und die Zukunft des Wohlfahrtsstaates'. *Leviathan* 40 (3): 441–61.

O'Conner, James R. 1973. *The Fiscal Crisis of the State*. New York: St. Martin's Press.

OECD (Organisation for Economic Co-operation and Development). 2011. 'Divided We Stand: Why Inequality Keeps Rising'. Paris: OECD.

Olzak, Susan. 1992. *The Dynamic of Ethnic Competition and Conflict*. Stanford, CA: Stanford University Press.

Opp, Karl-Dieter. 1988. 'Grievances and Participation in Social Movements'. *American Sociological Review* 53 (6): 853–64.

———. 2009. *Political Protest and Social Movements: A Multidisciplinary Introduction, Critique and Synthesis*. London: Routledge.

Pantazis, Christina, David Gordon and Ruth Levitas (eds.). 2006. *Poverty and Social Exclusion in Britain: The Millenium Survey*. Bristol: Policy Press.

Pattie, Charles, Patrick Seyd and Paul Whiteley. 2004. *Citizenship in Britain: Values, Participation and Democracy*. Cambridge: Cambridge University Press.

Paugam, Serge. 1991. *La disqualification sociale: Essai sur la nouvelle pauvreté*. Paris: PUF.

Pauwels, Teun. 2014. *Populism in Western Europe: Comparing Belgium, Germany and The Netherlands*. London: Routledge.

Peffley, Mark. 1984. 'The Voter as Juror: Attributing Responsibility for Economic Conditions'. *Political Behavior* 6 (3): 285–94.

Pettigrew, Thomas F. 2000. 'Systematizing the Predictors of Prejudice'. 280–301, in David O. Sears, James Sidanius and Lawrence Bobo (eds.), *Racialized Politics: The Debate About Racism in America*. Chicago and London: University of Chicago Press.

Pew Research Center. 2015. 'The American Middle Class Is Losing Ground: No Longer the Majority and Falling behind Financially'. Washington, DC, December.

Pickerill, Jenny, and John Krinsky. 2012. 'Why Does Occupy Matter?' *Social Movement Studies* 11 (3–4): 279–87.

Pierson, Paul (ed.). 2001a. *The New Politics of the Welfare State*. Oxford: Oxford University Press.

———. 2001b. 'From Expansion to Austerity: The New Politics of Taxing and Spending'. 54–80, in Martin A. Levin, Marc K. Landy and Martin Shapiro (eds.), *Seeking the Center: Politics and Policymaking at the New Century*. Washington, DC: Georgetown University Press.

———. 2001c. 'Coping with Permanent Austerity: Welfare State Retructuring in Affluent Democracies'. 410–56, in Paul Pierson (ed.), *The New Politics of the Welfare State*. Oxford: Oxford University Press.

Piketty, Thomas. 2014. *Capital in the Twenty-First Century*. Cambridge, MA: Belknap Press of Harvard University Press.

Piven, Frances Fox, and Richard A. Cloward. 1977. *Poor People's Movements: Why They Succeed, How They Fail*. New York: Pantheon Books.

Pontusson, Jonas, and David Rueda. 2010. 'Politics of Inequality: Voter Mobilization and Left Parties in Advanced Industrial States'. *Comparative Political Studies* 43 (6): 675–705.

Pontusson, Jonas, and Noam Lupu. 2011. 'The Structure of Inequality and the Politics of Redistribution'. *American Political Science Review* 105 (2): 316–36.

Popp, Elizabeth, and Thomas J. Rudolph. 2011. 'A Tale of Two Ideologies: Explaining Public Support for Economic Interventions'. *Journal of Politics* 73 (3): 808–20.

Portes, Alejandro. 1998. 'Social Capital: Its Origins and Applications in Modern Sociology'. *Annual Review of Sociology* 22: 1–24.

Putnam, Robert D. 1993. *Making Democracy Work: Civic Traditions in Modern Italy*. Princeton, NJ: Princeton University Press.

———. 2000. *Bowling Alone: The Collapse and Revival of American Community*. New York: Simon & Schuster.

Quaranta, Mario. 2015. *Political Protest in Western Europe: Exploring the Role of Context in Political Action*. Heidelberg and New York: Springer.

———. 2016. 'Protesting in "Hard Times": Evidence from a Comparative Analysis of Europe, 2000–2014. *Current Sociology* 64 (5): 736–56.

Quillian Lincoln. 1995. 'Prejudice as a Response to Perceived Threat: Population Composition and Anti-Immigrant and Racial Prejudice in Europe'. *American Sociological Review* 60 (4): 586–611.

Reinhart, Carmen M., and Kenneth S. Rogoff. 2009. *This Time Is Different: Eight Centuries of Financial Folly*. Princeton, NJ: Princeton University Press.

Rico, Guillem, and Eva Anduiza. 2017. 'Economic Correlates of Populist Attitudes: An Analysis of Nine European Countries in the Aftermath of the Great Recession'. *Acta Politica*. https://doi.org/10.1057/s41269-017-0073-x.

Ringen, Stein. 1987. *The Possibility of Politics: A Study in the Political Economy of the Welfare State*. Oxford: Clarendon Press.

———. 1988. 'Direct and Indirect Measures of Poverty'. *Journal of Social Policy* 17 (3): 351–65.

Rooduijn, Matthijs. 2014. 'The Nucleus of Populism: In Search of the Lowest Common Denominator'. *Government and Opposition* 49 (4): 573–99.

Rüdig, Wolfgang, and Georgios Karyotis. 2013a. 'Beyond the Usual Suspects? New Participants in Anti-Austerity Protests in Greece'. *Mobilization* 18 (3): 313–30.

———. 2013b. 'Who Protests in Greece? Mass Opposition to Austerity'. *British Journal of Political Science*. https://doi.org/10.1017/S0007123413000112.

———. 2014. 'Who Protests in Greece? Mass Opposition to Austerity'. *British Journal of Political Science* 44 (3): 487–513.

Sakellaropoulos, Spyros. 2012. 'On the Causes and Significance of the December 2008 Social Explosion in Greece'. *Science & Society* 76 (3): 340–64.

Salverda, Wiemer, and Ken Mayhew. 2009. 'Capitalist Economic and Wage Inequality'. *Oxford Review of Economic Policy* 25 (1): 126–54.

Saunders, Clare, Marie T. Grasso, Cristiana Olcese, Emily Rainsford, and Christopher Rootes. 2012. 'Explaining Differential Protest Participation: Novices, Returners, Repeaters and Stalwarts'. *Mobilization* 17 (3): 263–80.

Savage, M, and K Williams. 2008. *Remembering Elites*. Oxford: Blackwell Publishing.
Schäfer, Armin. 2013. 'Liberalization, Inequality and Democracy's Discontent'. 169–95, in Armin Schäfer and Wolfgang Streeck (eds.), in *Politics in the Age of Austerity*. Cambridge: Polity.
Schäfer, Armin, and Wolfgang Streeck. 2013. 'Introduction: Politics in the Age of Austerity'. 1–25, in Armin Schäfer and Wolfgang Streeck (eds.), *Politics in the Age of Austerity*. Cambridge: Polity.
Scharpf, Fritz. 1970. *Demokratietheorie zwischen Utopie und Anpassung*. Konstanz: Universitätsverlag.
———. 2000. 'Interdependence and Democratic Legitimation'. 101–20 in Susanne J. Pharr and Robert D. Putnam (eds.), *Disaffected Democracies: What's Troubling the Trilateral Countries?* Princeton, NJ: Princeton University Press.
Scheepers, Peer, Mérove Gijsberts and Marcel Coenders. 2002. 'Ethnic Exclusionism in European Countries: Public Opposition to Civil Rights for Legal Migrants as a Response to Perceived Group Threat'. *European Sociological Review* 18 (1): 17–34.
Scheve, Kenneth F., and Matthew J. Slaughter. 2001. 'Labor Market Competition and Individual Preferences over Immigration Policy'. *Review of Economics and Statistics* 83 (1): 133–45.
Schneider, Silke. 2008. 'Anti-Immigrant Attitudes in Europe: Outgroup Size and Perceived Ethnic Threat'. *European Sociological Review* 24 (1): 53–67.
Schultz, Theodore W. 1961. 'Investment in Human Capital'. *American Economic Review* 51 (1): 1–17.
Scott, J. C. 1976. *The Moral Economy of the Peasant: Rebellion and Subsistence in Southeast Asia*. New Haven, CT: Yale University Press.
Seccombe, Karen. 2002. ''Beating the Odds' Versus "Changing the Odds": Poverty, Resilience, and Family Policy'. *Journal of Marriage and Family* 64 (2): 384–94.
Seery, Mark D. 2011. 'Resilience: A Silver Lining to Experiencing Adverse Life Events?' *Current Directions in Psychological Science* 20 (6): 390–394.
Semyonov Moshe, Rebeca Raijman and Anastasia Gorodzeisky. 2006. 'The Rise of Anti-foreigner Sentiment in European Societies, 1988–2000'. *American Sociological Review* 71 (3): 426–49.
———. 2008. 'Foreigners' Impact on European Societies: Public Views and Perceptions in a Cross-National Comparative Perspective'. *International Journal of Comparative Sociology* 49 (1): 5–29.
Shapiro, Robert Y., and John T. Young. 1989. 'Public Opinion and the Welfare State: The United States in Comparative Perspective'. *Political Science Quarterly* 104 (1): 59–89.
Sides, John, and Jack Citrin. 2007. 'European Opinion About Immigration: The Role of Identities, Interests and Information'. *British Journal of Political Science* 37 (3): 477–504.
Simonian, Haig. 2010. 'Adecco Rejects Slowdown Fears'. *Financial Times*, 12 August 2010.
Singer, Matthew M. 2011. 'Who Says 'It's the Economy'? Cross-National and Cross-Individual Variation in the Salience of Economic Performance'. *Comparative Political Studies* 44 (3): 284–312.

Skeggs, Beverly. 2004. *Class, Self, Culture*. London: Routledge.

Skocpol, Theda, and Vanessa Williamson. 2013. *The Tea Party and the Remaking of Republican Conservatism*. New York: Oxford University Press.

Smelser, Neil J. 1962. *Theory of Collective Behavior*. New York: Free Press.

Sniderman, Paul M., and Louk Hagendoorn. 2007. When Ways of Life Collide: Multiculturalism and Its Discontents in the Netherlands. Princeton, NJ: Princeton University Press.

Sniderman, Paul M., Louk Hagendoorn and Markus Prior. 2004. 'Predisposing Factors and Situational Triggers: Exclusionary Reactions to Immigrant Minorities'. *American Political Science Review* 98 (1): 35–49.

Sniderman, Paul M., and Richard A. Brody. 1977. 'Coping: The Ethic of Self-Reliance'. *American Journal of Political Science* 21 (3): 501–21.

Snijders, Ton A. B., and Roel J. Bosker. 1999. *Multilevel Analysis: An Introduction to Basic and Advanced Multilevel Modelling*. London: Sage.

Snow, David A., Daniel M. Cress, Liam Downey and Andrew W. Jones. 1998. 'Disrupting the "Quotidian": Reconceptualizing the Relationship Between Breakdown and the Emergence of Collective Action'. *Mobilization* 3 (1): 1–22.

Snow, David A., and Sarah A. Soule, S. 2009. A Primer on Social Movements. New York: W.W. Norton.

Snow, David A, Sarah A. Soule and Daniel M. Cress. 2005. 'Identifying the Precipitants of Homeless Protest across 17 US Cities, 1980 to 1990'. *Social Forces* 83 (3): 1183–1210.

Sparkes, Jo, and Howard Glennerster. 2002. 'Preventing Social Exclusion: Education's Contribution'. 178–201, in John Hills, Julian Le Grand and David Piachaud (eds.), *Understanding Social Exclusion*. Oxford: Oxford University Press.

Stacey, Margaret. 1981. 'The Division of Labour Revisited or Overcoming the Two Adams'. 172–190, in Philip Abrams, Rosemary Deem, Janet Finch and Paul Rock (eds.), *Practice and Progress: British Sociology 1950–1980*. London: Allen & Unwin.

Standing, Guy. 2011. *The Precariat: The New Dangerous Class*. London: Bloomsbury.

Steinmo, Sven. 2013. 'Governing as an Engineering Problem: The Political Economy of Swedish Success'. 84–107, in Armin Schäfer and Wolfgang Streeck (eds.), *Politics in the Age of Austerity*. Cambridge: Polity.

Stiglitz, Joseph E.. 2012. *The Price of Inequality*. New York: W. W. Norton & Company.

Stokes, Bruce. 2015. 'Who are Europe's Millennials?' *Pew Research Center*.

Stokes, Donald E. 1963. 'Spatial Models of Party Competition'. *American Political Science Review* 57 (2): 368–77.

Stolle, Dietlind. 2007. 'Social Capital'. 655–74, in Russell J. Dalton and Hans-Dieter Klingemann (eds.), *The Oxford Handbook of Political Behavior*. Stanford: Oxford University Press.

Streeck, Wolfgang, and Daniel Mertens. 2013. 'Public Finance and the Decline of State Capacity in Democratic Capitalism'. 26–58, in Armin Schäfer and Wolfgang Streeck (eds.), *Politics in the Age of Austerity*. Cambridge: Polity.

Svallfors, Stefan. 1996. *Valfardsstatens moraliska ekonomi: Valfardsopinionen i 90-talets Sverige*. Umea: Borea.

Svallfors, Stefan. 2006. *The Moral Economy of Class: Class and Attitudes in Comparative Perspective*. Sanford, CA : Stanford University Press.

Taggart, Paul. 2004. 'Populism and Representative Politics in Contemporary Europe'. *Journal of Political Ideologies* 9 (3): 269–88.

Tarrow, Sidney. 1989. *Democracy and Disorder: Protest and Politics in Italy, 1965–1975*. Oxford: Oxford University Press

———. 1994. *Power in Movement: Social Movements, Collective Action and Politics*. Cambridge: Cambridge University Press.

———. 1996. 'States and Opportunities: The Political Structuring of Social Movements'. 41–61, in Doug McAdam, John D. McCarthy and Meyer N. Zald (eds.), *Comparative Perspectives on Social Movements: Political Opportunities, Mobilising Structures and Cultural Framings*. Cambridge: Cambridge University Press.

Taylor-Gooby, Peter. 1985. *Public Opinion, Ideology and State Welfare*. London: Routledge.

Temple, Luke, and Maria T. Grasso. 2018. 'Austerity, Politics, and Partisanship in the UK'. 29–60, in Marco Giugni and Maria T. Grasso (eds.), *Citizens and the Crisis: Perceptions, Experiences and Responses to the Great Recession in Europe*. London: Palgrave Macmillan.

Temple, Luke, Maria T. Grasso, Barbara Buraczynska, Sotirios Karampampas and Patrick English. 2016. 'Neoliberal Narrative in Times of Economic Crisis: A Political Claims Analysis of the UK Press, 2007–2014'. *Politics & Policy* 44 (3): 553–76.

Theiss, Maria, and Anna Kurowska. 2018. 'Unfinished Transformation or Neoliberal Economy? Exploring the Legitimization Divide in Poland'. 83–112, in Marco Giugni and Maria T. Grasso (eds.), *Citizens and the Crisis: Perceptions, Experiences and Responses to the Great Recession in Europe*. Basingstoke, UK: Palgrave.

Thoits, Peggy A. 1995. 'Stress, Coping, and Social Support Processes: Where Are We? What Next?' *Journal of Health and Social Behavior* 35: 53–79.

Thomassen, Jacques J. A. 1989. 'Economic Crisis, Dissatisfaction, and Protest'. 103–34, in M. Kent Jennings, Jan W. van Deth, Samuel H. Barnes, Dieter Fuchs, F. J. Heunks, Ronald Inglehart, Max Kaase, Hans-Dieter Klingemann and Jacques J. A. Thomassen (eds.), *Continuities in Political Action: A Longitudinal Study of Political Orientations in Three Western Democracies*. New York: de Gruyter.

Thompson, E. P. 1971. 'The Moral Economy of the English Crowd in the Eighteenth Century'. *Past and Present* 50: 76–136.

Tilly, Charles. 1978. *From Mobilization to Revolution*. Reading, MA: Addison-Wesley.

———. 1998. *Durable Inequality*. Berkeley: University of California Press.

Tilly, Charles, Louise Tilly and Richard Tilly. 1975. *The Rebellious Century, 1830–1930*. Cambridge, MA: Harvard University Press.

Togeby, Lise. 1994. 'Political Implications of Increasing Numbers of Women in the Labor Force'. *Comparative Political Studies* 27 (2): 211–40.

Touraine, A. 1981. *The Voice and the Eye: An Analysis of Social Movements*. Cambridge: Cambridge University Press.

Townsend, Peter. 1979. *Poverty in the United Kingdom*. London: Penguin.

Traugott, Mark (ed.). 1995. *Repertoires and Cycles of Collective Action*. Durham, NC: Duke University Press.

Turner, Jonathan, and Barry Markovsky. 2007. 'Micro-Macro Links'. 2997–3007, in George Ritzer (ed.), *The Blackwell Encyclopedia of Sociology*. Malden, MA: Blackwell.

Useem, Bert. 1980. 'Solidarity Model, Breakdown Model and the Boston Anti-Busing Movement'. *American Sociological Review* 45 (3): 357–69.

———. 1998. 'Breakdown Theories of Collective Action. *Annual Review of Sociology* 24: 215–38.

Van Dyke, Nella, and Sarah A. Soule. 2002. 'Structural Social Change and the Mobilizing Effect of Threat: Explaining Levels of Patriot and Militia Organizing in the United States'. *Social Problems* 49 (4): 497–520.

Van Hauwaert, Steven M., and Stijn van Kessel. 2018. 'Beyond Protest and Discontent: A Cross-National Analysis of the Effect of Populist Attitudes and Issue Positions on Populist Party Support'. *European Journal of Political Research* 57 (1): 68–92.

van Kessel, Stijn. 2013. 'A Matter of Supply and Demand: The Electoral Performance of Populist Parties in Three European Countries'. *Government and Opposition* 48 (2): 175–99.

———. 2015. *Populist Parties in Europe: Agents of Discontent?* New York: Palgrave Macmillan.

van Oorschot, Wim. 2006. 'Making the Difference in Social Europe: Dervingness Perceptions Among Citizens of European Welfare States'. *Journal of European Public Policy* 16 (1): 23–42.

Verba, Sidney, Kay Lehman Schlozman and Henry E. Brady. 1995. *Voice and Equality: Civic Voluntarism in American Politics*. Cambridge, MA: Harvard University Press.

Verhulst, Joris, and Stefaan Walgrave. 2009. 'The First Time is the Hardest? A Cross-National and Cross-Issue Comparison of First-Time Protest Participants'. *Political Behavior* 31 (3): 455–84.

Vincent, Carol, Nicola Rollock, Stephen Ball and David Gillborn. 2012. 'Raising Middle-class Black Children: Parenting Priorities, Actions and Strategies'. *Sociology* 47 (3): 427–42.

Visser, Jelle. 2006. 'Union Membership Statistics in 24 Countries'. *Monthly Labor Review* 129 (1): 38–49.

Vráblíková, Kateřina. 2014. 'How Context Matters? Mobilization, Political Opportunity Structures, and Nonelectoral Political Participation in Old and New Democracies'. *Comparative Political Studies* 47 (2): 203–29.

Wagner, Markus. 2013. 'Fear and Anger in Great Britain: Blame Assignment and Emotional Reactions to the Financial Crisis'. *Political Behavior* 36 (3): 683–703.

Wagner, Ulrich, and Andreas Zick. 1995. 'The Relationship of Formal Education to Ethnic Prejudice: Its Reliability, Validity and Explanation'. *European Journal of Social Psychology* 25 (1): 41–56.

Wallace, Claire. 1993. 'Reflections on the Concept of 'Strategy.'. 94–117, in David Morgan and Liz Stanley (eds.), *Debates in Sociology*. Manchester and New York: Manchester University Press.

Weitz, Rose. 2001. *The Sociology of Health, Illness, and Health Care: A Critical Approach*. Belmont, CA: Wadsworth.

Welzel, Christian, and Franziska Deutsch. 2012. 'Emancipative Values and Nonviolent Protest: The Importance of "Ecological" Effects'. *British Journal of Political Science* 42 (2): 465–79.

Weyland, Kurt. 2001. 'Clarifying a Contested Concept: Populism in the Study of Latin American Politics'. *Comparative Politics* 34 (1): 1–22.

Whelan, Christopher T., Helen Russell, and Bertrand Maître. 2016. 'Economic Stress and the Great Recession in Ireland: Polarization, Individualization or "Middle Class Squeeze"'? *Social Indicators Research* 126: 503–526.

Whitty, Geoff, Sally Power, Eva Gamarnikow, Peter Aggleton, Paul Tyrer and Paula Youdell. 1999. 'Health, Housing and Education: Tackling Multiple Disadvantage'. 67–79, in Annette Hayton (ed.), *Tackling Disaffection and Social Exclusion: Education Perspectives and Policies*. London: Koogan Page.

Wilkes, Rima, Neil Guppy and Lily Farris. 2008. '"No Thanks, We're Full": Individual Characteristics, National Context, and Changing Attitudes Toward Immigration'. *International Migration Review* 42 (2): 302–29.

Wilson, William Julius. 1996. *When Work Disappears: The World of the New Urban Poor*. New York: Knopf.

Wolfinger, Raymond E., and Steven J. Rosenstone. 1980. *Who Votes?* New Haven, CT: Yale University Press.

Women's Budget Group. 2015. 'The Impact on Women of July Budget 2015: A Budget that Undermines Women's Security'. http://wbg.org.uk/wp-content/uploads/2015/04/Julybudget-briefing-2015-WBG.pdf.

Index

About the Authors

Marco Giugni is Professor in the Department of Political Science and International Relations and Director of the Institute of Citizenship Studies (InCite) at the University of Geneva. His research focuses on social movements and political participation. He is European Editor of *Mobilization.*

Maria Grasso is Professor of Political Science and Political Sociology at the School of Politics and International Relations, Queen Mary University of London, UK. She is European Editor of *Mobilization* and the author of *Generations, Political Participation and Social Change in Western Europe* and co-author of *Street Citizens: Protest Politics and Social Movement Activism in the Age of Globalization* and *Living with Hard Times: Europeans in the Great Recession.*

www.ingramcontent.com/pod-product-compliance
Lightning Source LLC
LaVergne TN
LVHW101501200926
848483LV00001B/191
9781538151150